Attachment and Emotional Development in the Classroom

by the same author

Promoting Emotional Education
Engaging Children and Young People with Social, Emotional and Behavioural Difficulties
Edited by Carmel Cefai and Paul Cooper
ISBN 978 1 84310 996 9
eISBN 978 0 85700 188 7
Part of the Innovative Learning for All series

Nurture Groups in School and at Home
Connecting with Children with Social, Emotional and Behavioural Difficulties
Paul Cooper and Yonca Tiknaz
ISBN 978 1 84310 528 2
ISBN 978 1 84985 751 2 (Large Print)
eISBN 978 1 84642 600 1
Part of the Innovative Learning for All series

Understanding and Supporting Children with Emotional and Behavioural Difficulties
Edited by Paul Cooper
ISBN 978 1 85302 666 9
ISBN 978 1 84985 566 2 (Large Print)
eISBN 978 1 84642 897 5

of related interest

Observing Adolescents with Attachment Difficulties in Educational Settings
A Tool for Identifying and Supporting Emotional and Social Difficulties in Young People Aged 11-16
Kim S. Golding, Mary T. Turner, Helen Worrall, Jennifer Roberts and Ann E. Cadman
ISBN 978 1 84905 617 5
eISBN 978 1 78450 174 7

The Teacher's Introduction to Attachment
Practical Essentials for Teachers, Carers and School Support Staff
Nicola Marshall
ISBN 978 1 84905 550 5
eISBN 978 0 85700 973 9

A Short Introduction to Attachment and Attachment Disorder, Second Edition
Colby Pearce
ISBN 978 1 78592 058 5
eISBN 978 1 78450 315 4

The Simple Guide to Child Trauma
What It Is and How to Help
Betsy de Thierry
Foreword by David Shemmings
Illustrated by Emma Reeves
ISBN 978 1 78592 136 0
eISBN 978 1 78450 401 4
Part of the Simple Guides series

Educating Children and Young People in Care
Learning Placements and Caring Schools
Claire Cameron, Graham Connelly and Sonia Jackson
ISBN 978 1 84905 365 5
eISBN 978 0 85700 719 3

Attachment and Emotional Development in the Classroom

THEORY AND PRACTICE

Edited by David Colley
and Paul Cooper

Foreword by Barry Carpenter

Jessica Kingsley *Publishers*
London and Philadelphia

Figure 4.1 on page 67 © Richard Parker, Janet Rose and Louise Gilbert 2016, is used with kind permission of Springer Nature.

First published in 2017
by Jessica Kingsley Publishers
73 Collier Street
London N1 9BE, UK
and
400 Market Street, Suite 400
Philadelphia, PA 19106, USA

www.*jkp*.com

Library of Congress Cataloging in Publication Data
Names: Colley, David, editor. | Cooper, Paul, 1955- editor.
Title: Emotional development and attachment in the classroom : theory and practice / edited by David Colley and Paul Cooper.
Description: London ; Philadelphia : Jessica Kingsley Publishers, [2017] | Includes bibliographical references.
Identifiers: LCCN 2017006579 | ISBN 9781785921346
Subjects: LCSH: Emotions and cognition. | Attachment behavior. | Emotions in children. | Learning, Psychology of. | Teacher student relationships--Psychological aspects.
Classification: LCC LB1073 .E458 2017 | DDC 370.15/34--dc23
LC record available at https://lccn.loc.gov/2017006579

British Library Cataloguing in Publication Data
A CIP catalogue record for this book is available from the British Library

ISBN 978 1 78592 134 6
eISBN 978 1 78450 399 4

Printed and bound in Great Britain

Contents

Foreword

For too many children, childhood is a promise society does not keep. Trauma, anxiety and depression can rob them of the joy, happiness and freedom normally associated with those years. In this book informed and knowledgeable contributions are gathered that give us insights into the emotional development of children, and what life must be like for them. The book offers not only high-quality exposition, but also practical suggestions as to how we may shape opportunities and style interventions to support and nurture these children towards a more fulfilling life.

A major feature of this book is its timely focus on attachment, a concept that has been in vogue and out of vogue as each post-Bowlby decade has passed. Of one thing I am sure – now is very much the time to focus on attachment and its influences on how children learn. The teaching profession does not have a secure knowledge base in this area, and this book begins to effectively fill that gap.

From my own research with the 'new generation' of children with complex learning difficulties and disabilities (CLDD) (Carpenter *et al.* 2015), we have seen how attachment significantly influences children who are born prematurely and those with foetal alcohol spectrum disorders (FASDs) in particular. Attachment and relationships are extremely important in forming who we are; they have a major impact on how we see ourselves, and how we develop, maintain and negotiate relationships throughout our lives. Through successful attachments and healthy relationships we maintain our emotional regulation and wellbeing.

So, for the child born into this world very prematurely (e.g. before 31 weeks' gestation), they will find their emotional wiring hugely disrupted, and opportunities for secure and nurturing attachments significantly reduced. You cannot hold, stroke, touch, coo or rock your prematurely born infant as you can a full-term infant. However, if secure and nurturing attachments are not made and maintained within the early years of life, children will demonstrate insecure patterns of attachment as they grow through childhood.

Infants are born biologically predisposed to form relationships from which they can experience security and comfort (Golding 2008). Although some aspects of the emotional brain are already functioning at birth – for example, the amygdala or the part of the brain that experiences fear – the development of emotional regulation is very dependent on the infant experiencing a relationship built on social interaction with an adult. Infants attune to the voices of the mother and other primary caregivers, and seek comfort in these.

For the child who experiences a premature birth, with long periods of time in the incubator, considerable stress is placed on their attachment system. Wolke (2011) discovered in his research that by the age of 11, 10 per cent of surviving prematurely born children (which, in the UK, is now around 72,000 per year) had received a diagnosis of autistic spectrum disorder (see www.bliss.org.uk). When investigated further, the profile of these children's autism mirrored that observed in Romanian orphanage children who had been deprived of human interaction in their early childhoods and denied the fundamental social reciprocity so vital to brain growth and development. Hence, we have an emerging phenomenon of attachment-based autism.

Children born with FASD are the largest group of children entering the fostering and adoption system in the UK (Carpenter, Blackburn and Egerton 2013). Emotional dysregulation due to the multiple environments children may find themselves in becomes a feature of their behaviour very early in life. Not feeding well or poor sleep patterns may continue as the child grows, and accumulates other behaviours of concern – fleeting attention, hyperactivity, lack of concentration and focus. Observations of children with FASD in classroom settings reported children as 'disengaged' in learning, challenged by the demands of social interaction and emotionally unable to process the demands of peer interaction. As a consequence, friendships with peers – so vital to emotional wellbeing – were difficult for these children to sustain (Carpenter et al. 2013).

Often children with FASD who enter the care system find that their emotional development is severely interrupted. Case studies of these children have shown that they may suffer physical abuse and neglect from both biological parents, who will still be dependent on the alcohol that has caused significant damage to the infant in utero.

Once in a foster placement, siblings may be allocated to different homes, and the child's emotional responses may be perceived as immature and erratic, a kind of 'emotional incontinence'.

These early formative years are the child's foundation for their journey through life. Yet the evidence through to adulthood for children with FASD is bleak. They are more likely to end up homeless, resort to drug and alcohol misuse, have mental health issues and lower educational attainment.

It is on this issue of education that we need better training for teachers, particularly in how we can build emotional resilience in children with FASD, social and emotional difficulties – and special educational needs and difficulties (SEND) in general. Education can provide these children with a greater sense of emotional wellbeing as armour to protect themselves against some of the inevitable battles they will have in their lives.

The recent legislation from the *Special Educational Needs and Disability (SEND) Code of Practice* (DfE 2015) has at long last given status to the area of social, emotional and mental health (SEMH). So, emotional development, alongside its natural bedfellows of social and mental health, has a clear leadership role in a school. Indeed, if the recommendations of the Rochford Review (STA 2016) are accepted, then SEMH will become one of four learning domains against which the curriculum framework for children with SEND will be set.

What is particularly exciting in the new *SEND Code of Practice* is that in the definition of SEMH, attachment is listed. At long last it has found a home within education, giving teachers 'permission' to create meaningful pathways to effective learning for children with emotional needs, and thus to reduce the pedagogical vulnerability experienced by so many of them.

What we see in this new generation of children with complex learning needs is vulnerability, particularly in their emotional development. Vulnerable children are fragile learners, and our quest as educators has to be 'how do we make our children emotionally strong?' This book is a treasure trove of rich thought and helpful ideas that will enable teachers to do that, and then enable children to thrive.

I commend this book to you as an essential source of information as you journey onwards for, and with, the children.

Professor Barry Carpenter, CBE, OBE, PhD
January 2017

Bibliography

Carpenter, B., Blackburn, C. and Egerton, J. (2013) *Fetal Alcohol Spectrum Disorder: Interdisciplinary Perspectives*. Abingdon: Routledge.

Carpenter, B., Egerton, J., Cockbill, B., Bloom, T., Fotheringham, J. and Rawson, H. (2015) *Engaging Learners with Complex Learning Difficulties and Disabilities*. Abingdon: Routledge.

DfE (Department for Education) (2015) *Special Educational Needs and Disability Code of Practice: 0–25 Years*. London: DfE.

Golding, K. (2008) *Nurturing Attachments: Supporting Children Who Are Fostered or Adopted*. London: Jessica Kingsley Publishers.

STA (Standards and Testing Agency) (2016) *The Rochford Review: Final Report. Review of Assessment for Pupils Working Below the Standard of National Curriculum Tests*. London: STA.

Wolke, D. (2011) 'Preterm and Low Birth Weight Babies.' In P.A. Howlin, T. Charman and M. Ghaziuddin (eds) *The Sage Handbook of Developmental Disorders* (pp.497–528). London: Sage.

Introduction

DAVID COLLEY AND PAUL COOPER

The UK government's recent interest in mental health issues among children and young people in schools is to be welcomed because it marks a genuine step forward in the long-standing quest for an education system that focuses on educating the whole person. That said, the scale of the challenge posed by this belated awakening is daunting. Evidence from a range of sources suggests that at least 10 per cent of children and young people aged 5–16 have a diagnosable mental health problem (The Children's Society 2008; Mental Health Foundation 2015; YoungMinds 2017), while one in fifteen children may be actively self-harming (AYPH 2013). The communication of an underlying social, emotional or mental health (SEMH) difficulty – through persistent, disruptive behaviour in the classroom – remains the most common reason for permanent and fixed term exclusions from school (DfE 2016).

Significant UK organisations such as the Social, Emotional and Behavioural Difficulties Association (SEBDA), the Consortium for Emotional Well-being in Schools, and more recently, the Children and Young People's Mental Health Coalition, have been urging governments of the day to respond to the messages that children are communicating to us clearly through their behaviour.

Given the apparent crisis in the SEMH of our children, there is now a growing demand that teachers, trainee teachers, teaching assistants and all staff employed in schools should develop their knowledge and skills around the emotional development of children in order that the children are better understood and supported. This is now recognised by the Department for Education's (DfE) *A Framework of Core Content for Initial Teacher Training (ITT)* (2016a), which states that all Initial Teacher Training (ITT) providers should:

> …emphasise the importance of emotional development (such as attachment issues and mental health) on pupils' performance, supporting trainees to recognise typical child and adolescent

> development, and to respond to atypical development. (DfE 2016a, Part 1, Teaching, p.5)

This book has been devised to be a core text for ITT programmes across the UK, and will explore key issues around emotional development and attachment in the classroom. In the chapters that follow, internationally renowned authors explore the concepts associated with attachment theory, the trauma continuum and the promotion of resilience in the classroom. The neuroscience of emotion is considered along with the specific needs of children in care and those children presenting with disorganised attachment. In addition, successful classroom management approaches are critically reviewed along with practical interventions such as nurture groups, Emotion Coaching projects and Therapeutic Mentoring Rooms.

Beginning teachers are encouraged to understand that all learning is emotion-based, and that where emotional development is appropriately supported, high-quality learning can take place.

Of equal importance is the prevention of mental health difficulties, disaffection and behavioural problems arising from the unmet emotional needs of children in the classroom. By enhancing the knowledge, understanding and skills of beginning teachers in relation to emotional development and attachment, providers of ITT will be contributing to the prevention of mental health difficulties in our schools and communities.

This book sets out to illustrate how the commitment to fostering positive and supportive teacher–pupil relationships (characterised by trust, humour, play, acceptance and empathy) can contribute to the positive emotional growth of children in the classroom. It is these high-quality relationships that then nurture the expression of curiosity and educational engagement on which all effective learning depends. This process applies to all children and young people in schools, but is particularly important for those who are both troubled in their own beings, and who are often troubling to others (Hughes 2006).

It is our belief that, one shared by the contributors of this book, an understanding of emotional development and attachment in the classroom provides the basis from which effective intervention might proceed. We contend that these understandings provide the foundations for drawing these children back from conflict and the edge of suspension and exclusion.

In *Chapter 1*, David Colley and Paul Cooper explore the very nature of emotions and how emotional development proceeds in interaction with the physical, cognitive and social development of every child. Aspects of emotional self-awareness and self-management are explored, and six key models for understanding social-emotional development are introduced: psychodynamic approaches, behaviourism, cognitive behaviourism, humanism, systemic approaches and the biopsychosocial framework. These theoretical approaches then pervade the rest of the book.

Heather Geddes is the author of the seminal book on attachment theory in schools, *Attachment in the Classroom* (2006). In *Chapter 2*, Heather sets out the key principles of attachment theory as identified by Bowlby (1969, 1973, 1980), with a specific focus on attachment behaviour and patterns of relating. Here, the styles of secure and insecure attachment (i.e. avoidant, ambivalent and disorganised) are introduced and critically analysed. Interventions for the classroom are reviewed in relation to each of the distinctive attachment styles.

A basic understanding of the brain is essential if we are to understand the actions and emotions of children and young people in the classroom. In *Chapter 3*, Maisie Satchwell-Hirst explores the basic information that we have about brain development in an accessible way, and introduces the key anatomical areas that link to emotion regulation, decision-making and survival responses. As a team member of the University of Oxford's Research into Emotional Development and Disorders (REDD) laboratory, Maisie alerts the beginning teacher to the ways in which adverse early life experiences can affect both brain development and stress hormone levels in the developing child. There is an emphasis on the 'plasticity' of the brain and its ability to recover from abuse, neglect and traumatic experiences, with the confirmation that new neural pathways can be forged as a result of supportive, positive experiences.

In *Chapters 4 and 5*, Janet Rose, Louise Gilbert, Licette Gus and Felicia Wood explore the Attachment Aware Schools (AAS) project and the Emotion Coaching intervention that is a central feature of AAS. The AAS project aims to promote nurturing relationships in school that support the social-emotional development, learning and behaviour of all children. It is a whole-school approach that raises teachers' awareness of attachment, attunement and trauma-informed practice. Emotion Coaching (Gottman *et al.* 1996) is an evidence-based strategy that helps children to become more aware of their emotions and to manage their own feelings, particularly during instances of heightened emotions that invariably lead to misbehaviour. Emotion Coaching is integral to the AAS approach and is based on the principle that emotionally supportive and nurturing relationships provide optimal contexts for the promotion of resilience in children.

For Dr Mike Solomon, the promotion of resilience in the classroom is central to *Chapter 6*. Defining resilience as the ability 'to cope with life's challenges, especially when life is hard', Mike suggests that the components of resilience will include: feeling good enough about ourselves; having the ability to 'bounce back' from setbacks; and having good relationships both with the self and with others. Promoting these skills in children can be undertaken in a very practical way, and this chapter outlines a specific training programme that is a brief systemic approach, based on empirical understanding and knowledge from research.

In *Chapter 7*, David Colley introduces nurture group practice as a structured, social-emotional intervention with a robust research evidence base (see Cooper and Whitebread 2007; Ofsted 2011; Pyle and Rae 2015). Informed by the psychological theory of Bowlby (1969, 1973, 1980) and Maslow (1954), nurture groups represent a well-established and effective means of supporting the emotional development of children who have 'missed early learning experiences', which are then communicated through behaviour that troubles and concerns us. Assessment through the Boxall Profile allows individual gaps in social-emotional learning to be identified and bespoke programmes of learning to be delivered. After a time-limited period (and where targets have been met), children then return to full-time mainstream placements armed with the new social-emotional skills developed in the nurture group environment.

Betsy de Thierry is a qualified teacher and psychotherapist who founded the Trauma Recovery Centre (TRC) in 2011 (see www.trc-uk.org). In *Chapter 8*, Betsy describes trauma as being 'an experience that causes powerlessness and terror', and urges school staff to understand the impact of trauma on children in the classroom. The trauma continuum is described in detail and the impact trauma can have on emotional development is explored. Betsy contends that trauma can change how we perceive ourselves and the world around us, how we process information – and how we behave in response to our environment (Cozolino 2006). Throughout the chapter, the work of Therapeutic Mentoring Rooms and the TRC is explained and analysed.

Chapters 9, 10 and 11 have in common a particular psychological perspective that informs our understanding of human interaction and emotional responses. Psychodynamic approaches refer to all models of mind that are primarily concerned with unconscious processes (Howard 2006). Taking a psychodynamic approach offers us a way of understanding human relationships, emotions and behaviour in the context of our inner feelings, memories, beliefs and fantasies (Jacobs 1998). This perspective places particular emphasis on how the learning experience in the classroom can be strongly influenced by a range of emotional tensions and conflicts that reside within the teacher–student relationship. Many of these are irrational and unconscious and can have a disturbing effect on how learning takes place. By taking cognisance of these unconscious drives, beginning teachers might be better placed to understand why certain children behave in the ways that they do. In *Chapter 9*, Peter Wilson explores the understandings (and misunderstandings) that feature in an everyday classroom as a teacher interacts with her students, imploring teachers to reflect carefully on their own emotional dispositions as a way of best supporting and managing the emotions of their students. In *Chapter 10*, Biddy Youell reflects on the importance of change and transition in education from the psychoanalytical perspective. Here, key transitions that include the experience of being born, of starting school and then transitioning from primary to secondary school are all considered in the kind of detail that brings these oft-overlooked, formative experiences into sharp relief. In *Chapter 11*, Kathy Evans and Erica Pavord continue with a psychodynamic understanding of the skills required for effective multi-agency team working. Current policy and guidance relating to multi-agency working in education is provided, including an overview of some of the services available to teachers, children and families. Theoretical models of multi-agency working are introduced while the potential strengths and barriers to effective multi-agency working are also critically discussed. The chapter then illustrates the value of a psychodynamic understanding of multi-agency working to enhance the professional skills of beginning teachers and experienced staff alike.

In *Chapters 12, 13 and 14* the emotional needs of children in care (or looked-after children) are reflected on and highlighted. The role of the virtual headteacher, the virtual school and the designated teacher for children in care are all explained in detail by Tony Clifford and Anne-Marie McBlain in *Chapter 12*. Using a number of carefully crafted case studies, the chapter raises awareness of the unmet attachment needs that are particular to children in care. The trauma of being placed in care – and the instability of care placements that can often follow – places extreme emotional pressure on these children and young people. As a beginning teacher, you cannot impact on how placements are maintained, but you do have a role to play in understanding how the children might be feeling as they join you and your class for the first time. This theme is then extended by Emma Black, Michael Bettencourt and Claire Cameron in *Chapter 13* who argue that, for children to thrive and flourish, the integration of care and education in daily life is key. They believe that this is particularly pertinent to those children and young people who have experienced difficult childhoods and who have consequently been placed in care. 'Social pedagogy' in the classroom is presented as a springboard to recovery for those children who have experienced trauma, while also providing a context for establishing and maintaining the synergy between care and education for all children and young people in the classroom. Social pedagogy has a focus on the 'head, heart and hands' of practice, providing teachers with a practical approach to supporting the children in their care who are also 'in care'. Maggie Swarbrick leads the Treatment Foster Care Oxfordshire (TFCO) programme, an intensive intervention for traumatised children in care based on attachment and social learning approaches. In *Chapter 14*, Maggie highlights the features of a programme that supports children with disorganised attachment styles within the mainstream classroom. Given that disorganised attachment often involves the communication of a child's negative, hostile and frightening emotions, the practical support offered to staff through this chapter is invaluable.

Managing and supporting children and young people with complex emotional needs can be hugely rewarding, but it can also be challenging and draining. The profession needs people with the passion and commitment to stick by these children, but it also has a duty of care to support and protect the staff who are engaging with these children every day. Professional supervision has been the accepted practice in health, social care and therapy settings for decades, but education has been slow to see the benefits in terms of staff resilience, retention, health and wellbeing. In *Chapter 15*, Dave Roberts of the Mulberry Bush School, Oxfordshire, explains the benefits of schools engaging in formal, professional supervision procedures as a means of supporting staff and improving learning outcomes.

In *Chapter 16*, Jon Reid challenges the recommendations made by the DfE regarding classroom management, behaviour and discipline in schools (e.g. DfE 2016b, 2016c), arguing that the emotional needs of a significant minority of students will reject the behaviourist approaches employed (rewards, sanctions, detentions) – and that they will keep rejecting them until they are permanently excluded. To stay connected with this vulnerable group of learners and to help them fulfil their potential, a different approach to classroom management must be sought. In this chapter, Jon explores a range of alternative approaches that fix on understanding, empathy and compassion.

In *Chapter 17*, Poppy Nash returns to the core themes around attachment theory and asks whether teachers are misinterpreting disruptive behaviour in the classroom. Based on her own primary research, Poppy questions whether certain students are in a position to 'choose' the actions they undertake, and appeals for the introduction of a 'Collaborative and Proactive Solutions' (CPS) model to be employed in schools with those who disrupt and subvert. Poppy argues that challenging students may be '…challenging because they're lacking the skills to not be challenging' (Greene 2016, p.5). In other words, their challenging behaviour reflects a developmental delay in skill acquisition and they do not yet possess the skills to manage their emotions and regulate their behaviour. Put simply, 'if the kid *could* do well – he *would* do well. And if he's not doing well, he must be lacking the skills to do well' (Greene 2016, p.5).

John Visser is a much-published authority on social, emotional and behavioural difficulties and distils his years of experience into recording the eight *eternal verities* of effective classroom practice in *Chapter 18*. Extolling beginning teachers to 'find what works for you', John also recognises that there are some features of effective practice that span time and context. Whether the children in your care are securely attached or struggling with a range of emotional issues, his sagely advice will help guide you towards success in the classroom.

The Pendlebury Centre in Stockport is a Pupil Referral Unit that has just received its fifth consecutive 'Outstanding' award from Ofsted (2017). In *Chapter 19*, headteacher Janice Cahill shares some of the values and approaches that have shaped its provision for young people with SEMH needs. The young people themselves were asked to provide some advice for beginning teachers on what they feel are the qualities needed to be a good teacher. Their responses provide the framework for this chapter alongside a review of the '5 PCs' on which the outstanding practice at the Pendlebury Centre is based.

In *Chapter 20*, the co-editors draw together the threads of the book, and emphasise that while we cannot second-guess the reasons why a learner is presenting with social, emotional and attachment difficulties (as these are many and varied), we can prepare to meet those needs. This chapter begins with an acknowledgement that fear drives many of the behaviours that trouble us in school, and that a range of interventions is available to promote relationship building and security in the classroom.

The final key message for the beginning teacher is to enjoy your teaching and enjoy the children. You are there to support their learning at every turn and, given that emotions and learning are inextricably linked, a sound knowledge of emotional development and attachment in the classroom can only enhance the learning opportunities that you will provide.

Bibliography

AYPH (Association for Young People's Health) (2013) 'Key data on adolescence 2013.' Available at www.ayph.org.uk/publications/457_AYPH_KeyData2013_WebVersion. pdf, accessed on 20 March 2017.

Bowlby, J. (1969) *Attachment and Loss. Volume 1: Attachment.* London: Hogarth Press and The Institute of Psychoanalysis.

Bowlby, J. (1973) *Attachment and Loss. Volume 2: Separation: Anxiety and Anger.* London: Hogarth Press and The Institute of Psychoanalysis.

Bowlby, J. (1980) *Attachment and Loss. Volume 3: Loss: Sadness and Depression.* London: Hogarth Press and The Institute of Psychoanalysis.

Children's Society, The (2008) *Well-being.* Available at www.childrenssociety.org.uk/wellbeing.

Cooper, P. and Whitebread, D. (2007) 'The effectiveness of nurture groups on student progress: Evidence from a national research study.' *Emotional and Behavioural Difficulties 12*, 3, 171–190.

Cozolino, L. (2006) *The Neuroscience of Human Relationships. Attachment and the Social Brain.* New York: Norton Publishers.

DfE (Department for Education) (2016) 'Permanent and fixed period exclusions in England 2014 to 2015.' Available at www.gov.uk/government/uploads/system/uploads/attachment_data/file/539704/SFR_26_2016_text.pdf, accessed on 20 March 2017.

DfE (2016a) *A Framework of Core Content for Initial Teacher Training (ITT)*. London: DfE. Available at www.gov.uk/government/uploads/system/uploads/attachment_data/file/536890/ Framework_Report_11_July_2016_Final.pdf, accessed on 20 March 2017.

DfE (2016b) *Behaviour and Discipline in Schools: Advice for Headteachers and School Staff*. Reference DFE-00023-201. London: DfE.

DfE (2016c) *Mental Health and Behaviour in Schools*. Reference DFE-00435-2014. London: DfE.

Geddes, H. (2006) *Attachment in the Classroom: The Links Between Children's Early Experience, Emotional Well-being and Performance in School: A Practical Guide for Schools*. Belper: Worth Publishing Ltd.

Gottman, J.M., Katz, L.F. and Hooven, C. (1996) 'Parental meta-emotion philosophy and the emotional life of families: Theoretical models and preliminary data.' *Journal of Family Psychology 10*, 3, 243–268.

Greene, R.W. (2016) *Lost and Found: Helping Behaviorally Challenging Students (And, While You're At It, All the Others)*. San Francisco, CA: Jossey-Bass.

Howard, S. (2006) *Psychodynamic Counselling in a Nutshell*. London: Sage.

Hughes, D. (2006) *Building the Bonds of Attachment. Awakening Love in Deeply Troubled Children*. Oxford: Aronson.

Jacobs, M. (1998) *The Presenting Past* (2nd edn). Maidenhead: Open University Press.

Maslow, A.H. (1954) *Motivation and Personality*. New York: Harper & Row.

Mental Health Foundation (2015) 'Fundamental facts about mental health 2015.' Available at www.mentalhealth.org.uk/publications/fundamental-facts-about-mental-health-2015, accessed on 20 March 2017.

Ofsted (2011) *Supporting Children with Challenging Behaviour Through a Nurture Group Approach*. Available at www.ofsted.gov.uk/resources/supporting-children-challenging-behaviour-through-nurture-group-approach, accessed on 23 March 2017.

Ofstead (2017) The Pendlebury Centre. Available at https://reports.ofsted.gov.uk/inspection.reports/findinspection.report/provider/ELS/106022, accessed on 2 July 2017.

Pyle, A. and Rae, T. (2015) 'Nurture groups and parent–child relationships.' *The International Journal of Nurture in Education 1*, 1.

YoungMinds (2017) 'What's the problem?' Available at www.youngminds.org.uk/about/whats_the_problem, accessed 15 December 2016.

1

Models of Emotional Development

DAVID COLLEY AND PAUL COOPER

Emotions are central to the human experience of life and living where feelings of joy, sadness, pride, indignation and their variants permeate our lives on a daily basis. There can be no action without an affective response and emotions represent our most basic motivational system. In many ways, emotions define what it is to be human (Izard 1991).

The way in which we respond to the experiences of everyday life are complex, combining our genetic predispositions and temperaments with cultural norms, specific environments and relationships. In addition, our ability to reason and self-regulate emotions will affect the way that we respond and behave.

Consider your own skills in this area. Perhaps you know your own emotions well and can pre-empt inappropriate emotional displays through the reading of subtle changes in your own physical state? Perhaps you will remove yourself physically from an emotionally charged situation or talk yourself down, employing meta-emotional thinking? Or perhaps you are an individual who can self-regulate well in the workplace but collapse into an emotional Catherine wheel once across the threshold of your own home? For some adults, the self-management of emotions is precarious in all settings and this has a profound impact on their professional performance, their personal relationships and their personal happiness.

But how did the quality of your own emotional self-regulation develop, and what can this tell us about the children and young people that you are preparing to teach and support?

Let us first consider the nature of emotions – what they are and why we have them.

To be precise, an emotion is the automatic body change that prompts us to act (Carter 2006). The consequence of the action undertaken is then reinforced by pleasant or unpleasant conscious states that we understand as feelings. Feelings, then, are the mental representation of the automatic body reaction or emotion (Carter 2006). For example, when faced with an uncaged jaguar the automatic body reaction (or emotion) is to run, while the conscious state (or feeling) is fear.

Emotions, then, are essentially survival mechanisms that contribute to our ability to act intelligently and form 'the cement that binds human society together' (Evans 2001, p.21). The feelings that follow our emotional response will help inform and organise both our thoughts and actions effectively. As humans, we are exceptionally social creatures, and if our survival depends on successful interactions, then it is our emotions that ensure communication can take place and that social bonding can occur (Izard 1991). This begins with the infant–adult bond and infants are born with a range of skills and powerful instincts around social interaction. For example, infants attune to faces and can recognise voices; they can imitate models and read the basic emotions of anger, joy and fear (Music 2011). This initial infant–adult bond then extends to wider family, peer and partner bonding over time. At its heart, successful social bonding is achieved with others in a range of settings when emotions are managed and communication is thoughtful, sensitive, warm and connected.

How emotions develop

Emotional development is inextricably linked to the development and maturation of a child's thinking, language, motor skills and social skills. These developments are made symbiotically over time through daily interactions with the environment. However, research suggests that there are six basic emotions that are universal to our species and which are observable in infants within their first six months (Ekman 1972; Ekman and Friesen 1971; Izard 1979). These primary emotions are said to be fear, joy, sadness, surprise, anger and disgust. Claxton (2015) argues that these emotions must have an evolutionary component – otherwise they would not exist – and cross-cultural similarities suggest that these primary emotions are, indeed, the product of our biology (Ekman 1972). In this section, the emotional development of happy, healthy and securely attached children will be considered so that the impact of abuse, trauma and neglect on emotional development can be critically considered.

As a child develops, the six primary emotions that have been named become blended and overlaid into a rich array of nuanced feelings and moods. For most children, emotional development progresses in an orderly fashion and passes through a number of observable stages from infancy into the early years, school years and adolescence. Table 1.1 indicates the general stages of emotional development associated with childhood and adolescence (Doherty and Hughes 2009).

The references made to Erik Erikson (1964) in Table 1.1 refer to the eight stages that he proposed around the psychosocial development of children. The references made to John Bowlby (1969) link to the proposed features of attachment theory that will be discussed in Chapter 2.

Table 1.1: The general stages of emotional development associated with childhood and adolescence

Stage of emotional development	Age	Communication and understanding of emotions
1	Birth–1 year	Appearance of six primary emotions via facial expressions Brain stem and limbic systems dominant (survival systems) Instinctive behaviours that elicit care-giving and bonding Cries to signal physical need Copies facial expression of others Discriminates expressions Increasingly expressive responses (including stranger anxiety) Emotional development of trust or mistrust (Erikson 1964) Are my needs being met consistently and reliably? (Bowlby 1969)
2	1–2 years	Now conscious of own emotional responses (self-conscious) Shame, pride, coyness now extend the primary emotions Verbal expressions of emotion Early signs of empathy now evident Egocentric and demands attention (very dependent still) Irritated by constraints Emotional outbursts, tantrums, impulsivity Single emotions communicated and understood Emotional development of pride or shame (Erikson 1964) Is a safe base established with an attuned carer? (Bowlby 1969)

Stage of emotional development	Age	Communication and understanding of emotions
3	3–6 years	Can verbalise emotions Causes and consequences of emotions can be articulated Agency and action (pretend play, teasing, 'false' expressions can mislead others) Self-awareness emerging (personal moods) Regulation emerging (can respond to reason) Empathy emerging (following self-awareness) Multiple emotions communicated and understood Reliance on parent/carer to resolve emotional challenges Emotional development of 'I can' or 'I can't' (Erikson 1964) Is emotional co-regulation taking place with the 'significant other'? What are the unconscious internal working models of myself and others that I carry with me into school? (Bowlby 1969)
4	7–10 years	Multiple feelings and close friendships emerge Complex range of relationships and emotions Relationship management skills developing Increasing self-awareness and emotional self-regulation Emotional self-efficacy – taking responsibility for problem-solving emotional challenges In control Decision-making on emotions and responses to others In contact with social scripts (what you are meant to say in a given situation) In contact with social roles (how you are meant to act in a given situation) Emotional development of competency or inferiority (Erikson 1964) What are the internal working models of myself and others that I now carry? Am I loved? Am I loveable? If I am not, why am I not? (Bowlby 1969, 1973, 1980)
5	10–13 years	Understanding that thoughts can control emotions Internalised strategies for self-regulation Increased empathy for strangers Awareness that expressed emotion may be 'fake' (in self and others) Discern between genuine emotion and managed displays (in self and others) Internalising social scripts (what you are meant to say in a given situation) Internalising social roles (how you are meant to act in a given situation) Emotions around identity, values and beliefs Emotional development of role identity: adaptation or confusion (Erikson 1964) How emotionally attuned am I? Can I attune to others? Can I maintain relationships? Can I predict emotional temperatures accurately and adapt? (Gottman and Declaire 1997)

6	13+ years	Secure attachments to peers and to other adults (teachers, teaching assistants), to romantic partners, to institutions (school, clubs, workplaces) and the web of relationships associated with these institutions A consolidation and refinement of the five key areas of emotional competency (see CASEL 2017; Goleman 1996; SEAL 2005): 1. Self-awareness 2. Self-regulation 3. Social awareness (empathy) 4. Relationship management 5. Responsible decision-making Emotional development around sharing, commitment, intimacy, giving back and contemplation (Erikson 1964)

Table 1.1 alludes to five key areas of emotional competence that have been linked to the successful emotional development of children by a range of practitioners and authors (e.g. CASEL 2017; Goleman 1996; SEAL 2005). At the risk of being pedantic, it has been suggested in Table 1.1 that positive emotional development might comprise five key competencies, namely:

1. Emotional self-awareness

2. Emotional self-management (or self-regulation)

3. Social awareness (or empathy)

4. Relationship management

5. Responsible decision-making

But what do these competencies look like for a child who is making good emotional progress that is both positive and healthy?

Emotional self-awareness refers to the way in which children learn, over time, to accurately recognise and understand their own personal moods, emotions and drives. They can name their emotions and monitor the impact that the emotions are having on their own behaviour. Where this skill is successfully developed, children can realistically self-assess their own limits or strengths, and a sense of optimism and confidence pervades their interactions.

When *emotional self-management (or self-regulation)* is achieved, emotional impulses are controlled effectively and judgement can be suspended until all the relevant information has been gathered. Responses are appropriate and sensitive to the immediate context. There is a self-discipline and organisation that links to both motivation and goal setting.

It is important to note that the development of *social awareness (or empathy)* is predicated upon the child's own self-awareness and emotional self-regulation. Where a child has not developed through the phases of self-awareness (as a result, perhaps, of insecure attachment, abuse, trauma or neglect), their ability to empathise and understand the emotional reactions of others will be severely compromised. The social awareness aspect of emotional development is complex and requires an emotional 'attunement' with another person plus a degree of perspective taking and the ability to feel how another is feeling. Respect for others and an appreciation of diversity are also closely related to this component of a child's emotional development.

In *relationship management* children develop skills, over time, in the areas of communication, active listening, rapport building and conflict management. The advantages of cooperation become apparent along with the use of humour to bond healthy, rewarding relationships. Where help is needed, they seek it – and where help is requested, they provide it. Children, young people (and adults) with these emotional skills can negotiate conflict and resist pressure to act in a way that contravenes their personal preferences. These individuals have learned to lead their peers and to communicate persuasively.

For the Collaborative Academic, Social and Emotional Learning project (CASEL 2017), *responsible decision-making* represents the final key area of emotional competency. With these skills, children are able to identify problems, analyse situations and solve the problems that present themselves. They can reflect on the ethical issues and discern 'right or wrong' choices in a given situation. They can also evaluate the consequences of their actions and behave accordingly.

Mastering all five aspects of emotional competency is an uneven developmental process for children and will inevitably take time – but evidence suggests that secure attachment relationships, emotional 'attunement' and emotional co-regulation with a significant other will be central to the healthy negotiation of this process (Perry 1998, 2006; Schore 2000; Sroufe 1985, 1988). For most children, progress towards a healthy emotional disposition will be almost effortless and will emerge as naturally as the physical and cognitive aspects of their development. The incremental growth of self-awareness, self-management and self-regulation will require little conscious attention and will combine with increased empathic understandings. Indeed, as a trainee teacher, you may recognise this process of almost effortless emotional development during childhood, as it may reflect your own experience. If this is the case, you may already have a range of personal qualities around self-management, empathy and relationship-making – and these will offer you a great advantage in the complex social hub of the school.

However, you may need to reflect with extra intensity on those in your classroom who are struggling with issues around emotional self-awareness and emotional self-management. For a variety of reasons associated with insecure attachment, neglect, trauma or abuse, these children may be struggling to navigate a successful course and may not yet have the raw materials required to forge successful relationships based on empathy and social understanding. The will may be there, the desire may be there – but as yet, the skills required are not.

For a significant minority of children in your classroom the inability to recognise their own emotional states or regulate their own impulses will be undermining both their learning and their relationships in school. Locked in stages of emotional development that are now out of step with their chronological age, these children will be battling to manage emotions and feelings that might include mistrust, aggression, disdain, anxiety and shame. As teachers and leaders in the classroom, our responses to these emotional cues will serve to either calm the feelings the children are having – or compound them.

Our role as professionals in schools is to understand that all behaviour is a form of communication, and that the emotional expression of hostile, negative and inappropriate behaviour is, in fact, a communication of an unmet need. These children require us to set firm boundaries for them and to offer structures and routines. But they also require us to understand the gaps in their emotional learning and to provide opportunities for the 'missed early experiences' associated with emotional competency to be revisited.

Six theoretical models of social-emotional development and functioning

In the course of this book, several theoretical models of child development will be referred to. Historically, there are six fundamental approaches that are highly relevant to our understanding of social-emotional development and functioning. The first five are essentially psychological in nature and the sixth locates psychological factors within a broader framework. An overview of all six might be helpful, by way of introduction.

1. *Psychodynamic approaches* (which include the psychoanalytic perspectives) focus on the ways in which early interpersonal relationships influence personality development and social-emotional engagement with others (e.g. Bowlby 1969; Erikson 1964; Shaver and Mikulincer 2002). This approach provides important insights into the ways in which emotional health can be promoted through the development of key relationships, and attachment theory has been greatly influenced by psychodynamic understandings. For the classroom, this means a focus on the development of high-quality relationships and an understanding that the child's past experiences will have helped create a model of the world within the child. These formative and influential experiences that create this 'internal working model' will give the child a sense of who they are – and who you will be, as a new adult (and teacher) in their lives.

2. *Behaviourist approaches* are based on the ways in which behaviour can be understood in terms of involuntary responses to external stimuli (e.g. Pavlov 1960; Skinner 1938; Watson 1913). Behaviourist interventions exploit this theory by encouraging desired behaviours and extinguishing undesired behaviours. This is undertaken through the manipulation of the stimuli that precede target behaviours and the consequences that then follow from target behaviours. In short, behaviourist approaches in the classroom involve the use of positive reinforcement (i.e. praise, rewards, token economies), negative reinforcement (i.e. no praise or rewards) and aversives (i.e. punishment, sanctions, detentions, suspensions).

3. *Cognitive and cognitive-behavioural* approaches are concerned with the ways in which the relationship between external stimuli and target behaviours can sometimes be mediated and moderated by thought processes. Social learning theory (e.g. Bandura 1977) builds on the traditional behaviourist model by introducing social and cognitive elements that emphasise the ways in which human beings learn behaviours through imitating and modelling the behaviours of significant others, such as parents and other role models. The aim of cognitive behavioural therapy (CBT) (e.g. Meichenbaum 1977) is to encourage the development of functional ways of behaving by challenging and changing the ways that a child may be thinking (or interpreting a situation), that then gives rise to their 'dysfunctional' behaviour. A key principle here is that entrenched patterns of thinking, although difficult to change, can be made open to change and control by the individual with the right kind of support from an informed and supportive companion, such as a therapist or teacher. In the classroom, this means that the child's past experiences (that may be formative and influential) are not, in fact, dwelt on. The focus is on the here and now. What is the thinking (or interpretation) that leads to the negative feeling that then leads to the negative behaviour? CBT is intended to change the thinking that then changes the feeling and behaviour that follows. Techniques designed to aid this process include strategies such as role-play and simulation in which individuals follow exercises designed to identify dysfunctional thinking and alternative ways of responding.

4. *Humanistic approaches* focus on ways in which self-concept is influenced by social and interpersonal relationships. Interventions based on this approach, such as Rogers' (1951) person-centred approach, emphasise the value of affirming relationships characterised by unconditional positive regard, empathy and honesty. In the classroom, these approaches might allude to Maslow's hierarchy of needs (1954) and include school counselling, active listening, non-judgemental support and the importance of the child's own agency and motivation. More recently, the rise of 'social pedagogy' (see Chapter 13) is firmly located within the dynamic humanistic tradition.

5. *Systemic approaches* focus on the ways in which a child's behaviour can be understood as a function of the social systems in which they are embedded (Bronfenbrenner 1979). From an educational perspective, systemic theory would argue that an apparent problem associated with an individual pupil may best be understood in the context of what is happening around the pupil (e.g. in the home, in the classroom, in the peer group, in relation to the teacher or the wider school community) rather than seeing the problem residing within the individual pupil. In the classroom, this means that problematic, emotional behaviour is understood to be the responsibility of all parties and not just the child in question. Everyone is playing a part in maintaining this failing situation – and everyone can play an active part in finding the solution. This approach has given rise to interventions that focus less on the individual pupil and more on these external 'sub-systems' (Molnar and Lindquist 1989).

6. *The biopsychosocial (BPS) framework* (Engel 1977) is not a psychological approach *per se* but it provides a further model of social-emotional functioning that must also be considered. As the term implies, this framework is concerned with the ways in which biological (including genetic and neurological), social and psychological factors interact and influence mental processes and behaviour. A key insight from the BPS framework is that biological predispositions that may exist at the genetic level and are therefore inherited (or that spring from pre or early post-natal influences) do not determine life outcomes in a simplistic manner. For example, beginning teachers are likely to be familiar with a range of developmental disorders such as autistic spectrum conditions (ASC) and attention deficit hyperactivity disorder (ADHD). A BPS perspective can help educators to understand that the ways in which the limitations associated with these disorders are sometimes assumed to impact on the learning capacity and educational performance of individuals are by no means fixed; far from it. The more we understand about the nature of such disorders, the more we can do to ameliorate their impact on the learning experiences of diagnosed individuals. This approach to understanding is also important because it helps us to avoid often overly

simplistic causal explanations for problems that can lead to inappropriate interventions. For example, if we take the view that ADHD is caused by biological factors alone, then we run the risk of seeing ADHD as a medical problem outside the province of education professionals. On the other hand, if we understand ADHD from a BPS perspective, we can begin to see how particular social and educational interventions can play a significant role in influencing social, emotional and educational outcomes associated with ADHD. The vast body of cognitive neuroscientific research that is now available on ADHD can also be helpful to educational professionals in identifying those pedagogical and support strategies that are least likely to exploit cognitive deficits associated with ADHD and most likely to play to the considerable strengths that often accompany ADHD (e.g. Cooper and Bilton 2002; Hughes and Cooper 2007).

It is important to acknowledge that some commentators might choose to highlight points of conflict between some of the theoretical approaches outlined above. And it is true to say that theoretical conflict is part of the history of the development of these approaches, with one perspective emerging to challenge or reject the dominance of another. Behaviourism, in particular, has come in for strong criticism for giving rise to controlling and manipulative forms of intervention in schools (Porter 2006), though it should be acknowledged that behaviourism can be seen as an attempt to bring scientific rigour in the form of systematic observation to the study of behaviour. In this way behaviourism can be seen as a part reaction to the psychodynamic approach. Such 'paradigm wars' are common in the history of science. For we practically minded educators, however, not only is there no need for theoretical purity in our thinking about practice, there is also much to be gained from theoretical eclecticism.

We would argue that each of the perspectives outlined above has something to offer to the beginning teacher seeking to understand the complexities of social, emotional and mental health difficulties. So, for example, we would caution against what might be termed radical behaviourist approaches in schools that focus entirely on the manipulation of surface behaviours, and yet we strongly support the use of behavioural techniques for identifying behavioural patterns and possible relationships between behaviours and their antecedents and consequences. The judicious use of rewards and sanctions in the school and classroom can be extremely powerful in helping to create a setting that is conducive to positive educational engagement. We also argue, however, that behaviourist approaches alone have their limitations, and that relational approaches influenced by humanistic and psychodynamic understandings are vital to the creation of emotionally supportive interpersonal relationships. It is relationships that are, in the end, the essential components of emotional-social growth and effective deep learning. Psychodynamic and systemic insights can also help us to understand the ways in which our own emotional responses and functioning can affect our students. In addition a cognitive-behavioural perspective can help us to understand that self-management, social behaviour and emotional self-regulation are all skills that can be actively taught.

Final thoughts

The review of the key approaches to understanding and intervening with SEMH difficulties indicates (and we hope, convincingly) that there is a sophisticated theoretical toolkit available to beginning teachers that will enable deep understandings of how and why SEMH difficulties develop and how they can be ameliorated. One thing that we hope is clear from this brief exploration of theories is that behaviour and emotions do not form spontaneously out of nothing. Just as they can be influenced by positive intervention, so it is always the case that the SEMH difficulties that we encounter in our schools and classrooms are themselves the product of various influences. Genetic influences and family environments play crucial and often interactional roles in shaping aspects of our development, as do temperamental differences. There are also broader societal influences that might be experienced as social and economic inequalities and the relentless pressure from social media to conform to unrealistic ideals and consume at levels beyond that which we can afford. Schooling is, of course, an integral part of the society in which a child develops. The school is the place in which most children first come into close contact with adults who are not their relatives or neighbours. These contacts can in themselves be problematic for many children who find it difficult (at first, at least) to relate to unfamiliar adults in the challenging context of the school where they also have to contend with new peers, not to mention the formal curriculum.

For some children their adjustment to the school environment is aided by the growing sense of familiarity that they experience as they recognise that, actually, these new adults are not too dissimilar from those in their own families and neighbourhoods. Similarly, they may also find reassurance in the similarities they share with their new peers. They may even find that they recognise the formal learning experiences that are on offer and the ways that they are expected to engage with them.

For other children, however, the new experience of schooling is one of alienation and threat. They do not recognise the adults as being like those with whom they are familiar. They do not share a frame of reference with these people, or readily understand what is expected of them in terms of behaviour and engagement. They may even find their habitual ways of behaving and responding to these adults to be misunderstood and a source of conflict. Added to this, some children will find the very experience of being thrown together with their same age peers in large numbers unsettling and frightening.

This book has a great deal to say about what schools and teachers can do to help support those children who have such aversive reactions to school. However, it is important to recognise that schools are rarely neutral in their influence. There are, in fact, many features of schools that are (like the wider society in which they are embedded) potentially damaging to the emotional security and wellbeing of children in general and are particularly 'toxic' to the most vulnerable children. Schools across the phases are under intense pressure to raise levels of academic achievement for all students in the face of serious financial constraints. The punitive use of crude 'market forces' thinking at the policy level pits school against school, teacher against teacher, and ultimately pupil against pupil. 'Failing' schools are lambasted, staff are criticised and pupils are made only too aware of where they sit within the academic hierarchy of their school and where their school fits within the league table hierarchy so beloved of government ministers and journalists. It seems reasonable to ask questions about how the current (and very welcome) spotlight on mental health in schools can be anything more than tokenistic in a climate that seems best characterised by words such as 'stress', 'anxiety' and 'fear of failure'. Should it come as a surprise to anyone that SEMH difficulties are a source of growing concern in such an environment?

But this chapter is not intended to contribute to a counsel of despair; far from it. It is important, however, to be honest and realistic about issues of SEMH difficulties and the ways in which schools may be part of the problem as well as the solution. Perhaps the most important point to be made here is that we must avoid the temptation to deny that these negative pressures exist, and to take the easy way out of blaming the children and young people who suffer under these pressures. We must face up to the fact that sometimes these pressures lead students into patterns of withdrawal, disaffection and/or hostile reactions towards their teachers that may, in fact, be an entirely reasonable and rational response to an educational environment that is socially and emotionally toxic.

With this in mind, the rest of this book shows that the first step in dealing with these kinds of negative reactions is to try to find out where these reactions come from and to try to empathise with the individual. If we can achieve empathy, then we have a basis for dialogue and the opportunity to seek a practical solution. We cannot create perfect schools in an imperfect society, but we can do our best to promote harmonious, caring relationships with our students that, in turn, help us all to find ways of making the best of the situations in which we find ourselves and avoiding the temptation to give in to negativity and despair.

There are no simple answers to these problems, other than to say that we should always try to keep them in mind. In the immediate sense this brings to mind a key feature of the systemic approach (#5, above) which gives rise to the eternal question: to what extent should we be trying to enable the individual to adapt to the environment, or be trying to make the environment capable of accommodating the individual? Often there is a need for both. The key is to maintain a reflexive stance whereby we, the professionals, constantly monitor and evaluate the professional decisions we make against our beliefs about what is best for our students and what the student is telling us about what is going on from their point of view.

As a beginning teacher, these are questions that must be acknowledged as you consider the social-emotional development and wellbeing of the learners in your care. One thing is certain: as a teacher you will have a significant impact on the social-emotional climate of your classroom. The decisions you make will determine whether or not you are seriously trying to have a positive influence on the wellbeing of all the children in your care. As in any endeavour, there will be times when what you undertake works better on one day than it does on another. There will be times at the end of a long day when you feel defeated and frustrated because your best efforts seem to have produced nothing positive. And yet at other times you will have a sense of elation because you feel you have made a positive difference.

This book is intended to help you to understand the influences on learners' wellbeing in schools and the vital role that you have to play in this. We hope that this will help you to be resilient when you have one of those bad days. We also hope that it will help you to deepen your insights into how you might have more and more of those good days!

REFLECTION POINTS

Take a moment to consider how schools would be structured if the mental health and wellbeing of children were to be the absolute priority – *above all else*.

1. If we could create a system from inception with this in mind, what would the school system look like?

2. What would children be taught, and how would they be taught?

3. How would relationships be fostered, and how would power dynamics in schools be affected?

4. To what degree does the focus on standards and academic achievement act as a protective factor for some students who thrive on the routines and boundaries set by school life?

Bibliography

Bandura, A. (1977) *Social Learning Theory*. Englewood Cliffs, NJ: Prentice Hall.

Bowlby, J. (1969) *Attachment and Loss. Volume 1: Attachment*. London: Hogarth Press and The Institute of Psychoanalysis.

Bowlby, J. (1973) *Attachment and Loss. Volume 2: Separation: Anxiety and Anger*. London: Hogarth Press and The Institute of Psychoanalysis.

Bowlby, J. (1980) *Attachment and Loss. Volume 3: Loss: Sadness and Depression*. London: Hogarth Press and The Institute of Psychoanalysis.

Bronfenbrenner, U. (1979) *The Ecology of Human Development: Experiments by Nature and Design*. Cambridge, MA: Harvard University Press.

Carter, R. (2006) *The Human Brain Book*. New York: DK Publishing.

Claxton, G. (2015) *Intelligence in the Flesh*. Padstow: Yale University Press.

CASEL (Collaborative Academic, Social and Emotional Learning). Available at www.casel.org, accessed on 17 January 2017.

Cooper, P. and Bilton, K.M. (2002) *Attention Deficit/Hyperactivity Disorder: A Practical Guide for Teachers.* London: Routledge.

DfES (2005) *Excellence and Enjoyment: Social and Emotional Aspects of Learning Guidance.* London: Crown Copyright: Ref: DfES 1378–2005.

Doherty, J. and Hughes, M. (2009) *Child Development.* Harlow: Pearson Education.

Ekman, P. (1972) 'Universals and Cultural Differences in Facial Expressions of Emotions.' In J. Cole (ed.) *Nebraska Symposium of Motivation* (pp.207–282). Lincoln, NB: University of Nebraska Press.

Ekman, P. and Friesen, W. (1971) 'Constants across cultures in the face and emotion.' *Journal of Personality and Social Psychology 17*, 2, 124–129.

Engel, G.L. (1977) 'The need for a new medical model: A challenge for biomedicine.' *Science 196*, 129–136.

Evans, D. (2001) *Emotion: The Science of Sentiment.* Oxford: Oxford University Press.

Erikson, E.H. (1964) *Childhood and Society.* New York: Norton.

Erikson, E.H., Paul, I.H., Heider, F. and Gardner, R.W. (1959) *Psychological Issues (Volume 1).* New York: International Universities Press.

Goleman, D. (1996) *Emotional Intelligence.* London: Bloomsbury.

Gottman, J. and Declaire, J. (1997) *Raising an Emotionally Intelligent Child. The Heart of Parenting.* New York: Simon & Schuster.

Hughes, L. and Cooper, P. (2007) *Understanding and Supporting Children with ADHD.* London: Sage.

Izard, C.E. (1979) *Emotions in Personality and Psychopathology.* New York: Plenum Press.

Izard, C.E. (1991) *The Psychology of Emotions.* New York: Plenum Press.

Maslow, A.H. (1954) *Motivation and Personality.* New York: Harper & Row.

Meichenbaum, D. (1977) *Cognitive-behavior Modification: An Integrative Approach.* New York: Plenum Press.

Molnar, A. and Lindquist, B. (1989) *Changing Problem Behavior in Schools.* San Francisco, CA: Jossey-Bass.

Music, G. (2011) *Nurturing Natures: Attachment and Children's Emotional, Sociocultural, and Brain Development.* Hove: Psychology Press.

Pavlov, I.P. (1960) *Conditioned Reflexes: An Investigation of the Physiological Activity of the Cerebral Cortex.* New York: Dover Publications.

Perry, B.D. (1998) 'Homeostasis, stress, trauma and adaptation: A neurodevelopmental view of childhood trauma.' *Child and Adolescent Psychiatric Clinics of North America 7*, 1, 33–51.

Perry, B.D. (2006) 'Applying Principles of Neurodevelopment to Clinical Work with Maltreated and Traumatized Children.' In N. Boyd Webb (ed.) *Working with Traumatized Youth in Child Welfare* (pp.27–52). New York: The Guilford Press.

Porter, L. (2006) *Behaviour in Schools: Theory and Practice for Teachers* (2nd edn). Maidenhead: Open University Press.

Rogers, C.R. (1951) *Client-centered Therapy: Its Current Practice, Implications, and Theory.* Boston, MA: Houghton Mifflin Co.

Schore, A.N. (2000) 'Attachment and the regulation of the right brain.' *Attachment and Human Development 2*, 1, 23–47.

Shaver, P.R. and Mikulincer, M. (2002) 'Attachment-related psychodynamics.' *Attachment and Human Development 4*, 133–161.

Skinner, B.F. (1938) *The Behavior of Organisms: An Experimental Analysis.* New York: Appleton-Century.

Sroufe, L.A. (1985) 'Attachment classification from the perspective of infant–caregiver relationships and infant temperament.' *Child Development 56*, 1–14.

Sroufe, L.A. (1988) 'The Role of Infant–Caregiver Attachment in Adult Development.' In J. Belsky and T. Nezworski (eds) *Clinical Implications of Attachment* (pp.18–38). Hillsdale, NJ: Erlbaum.

Watson, J.B. (1913) 'Psychology as the behaviorist views it.' *Psychological Review 20*, 158–178.

2

Attachment Behaviour and Learning

HEATHER GEDDES

Teachers are at the front line of all the social issues that affect our society. Each day, children bring with them to school their social and emotional experiences, their expectations of relationships, their differing religious and ethnic expectations, their varied experiences of listening and understanding and their capacities to articulate experience and process information. Most children flourish in the classroom and enjoy the experience of learning in the social environment of the classroom with the support of a committed and reliable adult staff. However, there is a significant minority of children who do not flourish in school and these children can create challenges for the teacher, whether newly qualified or experienced.

This chapter sets out to offer an understanding of the factors affecting a child's emotional, social and cognitive development before he or she arrives in your classroom. The theoretical framework of attachment theory – a well-researched theoretical paradigm concerning all children's social and emotional development – is outlined here and linked to behaviour and learning.

Attachment theory

Attachment theory was developed by John Bowlby who first began to make links between early childhood experience and later behaviours when working in a school for delinquent boys. He wrote the paper 'Forty-four juvenile thieves' (1944) in which he linked their difficulties to their disrupted and disturbing childhoods. He went on to work with the World Health Organization (WHO) to investigate the mental health problems of refugee children following the Second World War, and concluded that separation from the carer in the early years had profound negative implications for a child's emotional and intellectual development, leading to 'cycles of disadvantage' whereby today's neglected children become tomorrow's 'neglectful' parents – or intergenerational re-enactment. Bowlby recognised the significance of the infant–mother relationship and formulated a new theoretical paradigm – attachment theory (1951, 1953).

Attachment theory describes the significant experiences of the infant from birth in the context of a relationship with a significant other. Bowlby identified the primary experiences of early development as *attachment, separation and loss* (1969, 1973, 1980).

The human infant is vulnerable and requires support for a considerable amount of time to protect and nurture his or her survival and development. This is provided primarily by the mother, who is regarded as the primary carer, but it is also acknowledged that others can fulfil this role. The father, family members and others are significant in the support and nurture provided by the infant's environment. Indeed, there is considerable evidence that the engagement of fathers contributes to better outcomes in terms of future relationships and engagement in learning and work (NSPCC 2001). This, in turn, raises the issue of the importance of a male presence in schools.

Bowlby suggests that a significant affectional bond develops between infant and carer known as *attachment*. This reflects the experience of the presence and reliability of the carer – *the secure base* – which is crucial to the infant's early sense of safety and reliability. The secure base represents a 'safe haven' to turn to when strong feelings are aroused whether following a loud noise, feeling hunger, feeling cold, or passing waste – all of which are startling to a new infant! The human infant is highly responsive to the human face. In the face-to-face relationship between infant and carer, the 'sensitive enough' mother reads the infant's needs and distress with appropriate responses. This attentive care communicates an understanding of the infant's needs and so imparts reassurance that the fundamental safety needs (that we are all born with) will be met.

During the infant's first year, the experience of being held, noticed, understood and reassured when afraid are critical to a child's emotional development. These early experiences will affect the development of trust in others, self-awareness, managing uncertainty and developing the capacity to think and communicate when challenged or afraid. All of these factors help to forge the young child's capacity to be resilient.

Gradually, as movement develops, the infant can feel safe to explore, knowing he or she can return to the secure base whenever uncertainty is aroused. As the primary carer becomes embedded in the infant's experience, the child can be assured that the carer will return, even when the carer is not actually in the room. The child can hold the carer 'in mind' until contact with them is restored. The reunion is always significant and imbued with relief, but also perhaps some anger at the separation. In summary, the emotions generated by separation and absence become tolerable when the carer can be relied upon to return.

Within the bonding associated with a close and consistent environment of care, the infant develops a sense of attachment to a primary carer and a sense of him or herself in relation to others. Strong feelings are co-regulated within the attachment relationship and, in the words of Kate Barrows (1984, p.15), '…the first gift from another person is the maternal gift of taking in his feelings, absorbing them, thinking about them and giving them back to him in a way he can accept'.

Over time, the natural developmental process allows the child to experience his or her own self as *separate* and autonomous and begin to make sense of his or her own feelings and emotions using words and thoughts. The origins of self-awareness and of empathy with others begin with these early life experiences and, in many ways, we know ourselves because someone else knew us first.

A further significant outcome related to the experience of early attachment is the child's perception of him or herself and others. This emerging sense of the self and 'who others are' is known as the 'internal working model' and represents a key concept in attachment theory. The child who experiences 'secure enough' attachment, in Bowlby's terms, is likely to 'possess a representational model of the attachment figure(s) as being available, responsive and helpful' and a working model of him or herself as 'a potentially lovable and valuable person' (Bowlby 1980, p.242). The child who has developed this kind of internal working model based on his or her early life experiences is likely to 'approach the world with confidence' and will 'tackle potentially alarming situations effectively – or will seek help in doing so' (Bowlby 1973, p.208). In contrast, where the internal working model is based on early life experiences of fear, neglect and worthlessness, this will inevitably impact on the child's confidence, learning and expectations of the teacher in the classroom.

Attachment behaviour

The carer's characteristics naturally shape the interactions with the infant and, between them, they negotiate a way of relating that meets both their needs. This becomes a pattern of relating which can be recognised and known as *attachment behaviour*. Considerable research was carried out into attachment behaviour by Ainsworth and Wittig (1969), and known as the 'strange situation procedure'. This was a series of recorded interactions between many carer–infant dyads. Analysis of the observations revealed recognisable patterns of relating that they described as either secure or insecure (anxious) attachment. The insecure (anxious) patterns were ultimately broken down into three insecure types, namely, avoidant, ambivalent and disorganised. These 'secure enough' or insecure attachment patterns were found to be consistent by the age of one year and to vary in intensity across a wide continuum. Research found that these attachment patterns were the template for the child's expectations of other relationships – including the relationships developed with adults and peers when beginning school. The characteristics of these patterns, or attachment behaviours in the classroom, will now be reviewed.

Secure attachment in the classroom

Learning demands certain capabilities. Children initially have to experience separation in order to attend the classroom, and rely on other adults to understand them, support them and respond to any distress they might feel. Learning is therefore a challenge for all children and requires a variety of skills, including:

- tolerating not knowing

- being able to ask for help when needed

- tolerating the challenge of making mistakes/being wrong

- accepting that others can do things that they cannot yet do

- persisting when the task gets difficult.

Engaging with what the child does not understand – that is, the task – and trusting the teacher to help and support the child through the process represent the two core characteristics of successful engagement in learning. There is convincing evidence that links 'secure enough' attachment experience to a capacity to adapt to school and to respond to the demands of academic learning in the social setting of the classroom (Sroufe 1983, 1986). Indeed, Main and Solomon found that 'children who are judged secure with mother in infancy are found to be more co-operative, more empathetic, more socially competent, more invested in learning and exploration and more self-confident than children who were judged insecure with mother in infancy' (Main and Solomon 1982, p.101).

The majority of children in your classroom are likely to be securely enough attached to cope with the challenges of learning and to trust in the support that you will offer in pursuit of learning. Their expectations of you will be that you can be trusted, that you care, that you are interested in them and that you will offer a 'safe base' when they are afraid, confused or distressed.

Challenging life events occur for all children, but the securely attached child will be able to articulate experiences in thoughts and words in a way that resolves the emotional trauma of, for example, a death in the family or parental conflict or sibling issues. In this way, learning may be interrupted by distress, but the interruption to learning is not long term or critical to learning outcomes. For example, in a Year 2 class, the teacher was leading circle time knowing that a boy in her class had recently experienced the death of his mother. She read *Badger's Parting Gifts* (Varley 2013) describing how the population of animals had dealt with the death of an old and faithful friend. The boy opened up to the class and told of his mother's death, and others also told of their experiences of lost grandparents, siblings and pets. In this way, sympathy and harmony was shared by the class through trust and communication, and the boy in question was more able to restore his interest in learning and re-engage with the class.

'Secure enough' attachment experience enables children to articulate and process their distress more effectively and reduces the impact on learning and school disengagement.

Insecure attachment in the classroom

Bowlby (1969), Ainsworth and Wittig (1969) and Main and Solomon (1982) argue that insecure attachment behaviours develop in children due to the quality of the nurturing care that they receive as infants. Where secure attachment patterns emerge from care that is attentive, reliable and consistent, the three types of insecure attachment are generated by care experiences that are inconsistent, insufficient or, in some cases, frightening for the child.

As a beginning teacher, you will find that insecure early attachment experiences have real implications for learning and teaching, not least because the 'behaviour' of these children will draw your attention. This behaviour might include severe disruption to your teaching or withdrawal and non-participation in tasks. This reluctance to engage may lead to long-term absences and exclusions. Children with insecure attachment behaviours draw attention to themselves in a wide variety of ways that cause the adult to notice them. In the absence of a capacity to communicate distress in words, it is behaviour through which vulnerable children communicate their distress, for behaviour is a form of communication, be it mild or severe.

Insecure avoidant – the pupil who avoids relating to the teacher

Attachment theory suggests that insecure avoidant patterns emerge when the child experiences a lack of availability to care and safety when strong feelings have been aroused, resulting in a feeling of rejection. Caught in an emotional trap, Main suggests that 'the infant cannot approach because of the parent's rejection and cannot withdraw because of its attachment needs' (Main 1986, cited in Hopkins 1987, p.145). This perceived rejection heightens the infant's alarm and increases the need for attachment. Bowlby described this as the experience of being an 'unwanted child, likely to feel not only unwanted by his parents but to believe he is essentially unwantable' (Bowlby 1973, p.204).

In the classroom this can be represented by the pupil who avoids the relationship with the teacher, avoids asking for help and copes by being *self-reliant*. The insecure avoidant pattern of attachment behaviours may reflect the carer's response to the child's emotional needs, and may reflect the pupil's difficulties in acknowledging and responding to feelings.

At the mild end of the continuum this can be the pupil who is admired for his or her independence but at the extreme end, the pupil who avoids any collaboration will not accept help, 'sits at the back' and underachieves because he or she is unable to accept the support of the teacher without also feeling anger at the original attachment figure. Any sense of 'need' is then accompanied by anger. The teacher can take the brunt of this anger and rejection that can be disheartening and stressful. What you will find, however, is that the pupil will focus on the task as a way of avoiding the pain associated with relationships.

Intervention can be led by acknowledging that this self-reliance is a coping mechanism. Initially the task needs to be do-able with all necessary information and tools available so that the pupil can approach the task with confidence. When the task is achieved, acknowledging the achievement is a way of communicating that he or she has been noticed. The child can then experience a respect for his or her approach to learning and an experience of being thought about and understood. This can gradually move on to sharing a mutual interest in the task but avoiding face-to-face encounters. With the task as mediator, the pupil can begin to tolerate the teacher's presence and interest and to experience a sense of being 'understood emotionally'. The development of language, perhaps through stories, around rejection and anger can develop the language needed for the pupil to reflect on his or her own feelings and express anger in words rather than action. For example, *Where the Wild Things Are* (Sendak 1963) is an excellent example of the experience of avoidant children and, in one case, a Year 7 boy chose this book to review and to present in assembly. He also liked to play board games with the teacher (Friday afternoon awaiting transport home) when he could defeat her and safely express his rage by 'wiping her off the board'. Over time this boy made significant progress in his engagement with the teacher, but always mediated by the task.

Insecure ambivalent – the 'attention-seeking' pupil

The classroom behaviour associated with this pattern of relating is 'attention seeking'. The teacher can feel distracted and overwhelmed by the incessant demand to be noticed. Lessons can be disrupted and the full-time attention of the classroom assistant is often the only apparent solution. However, attachment theory argues that this behaviour is driven by the pupil's early experience of a carer whose own emotional needs take precedence over the needs of the child. In order to be noticed the child develops the skills of responding to the carer with incessant engagement. Separation in this relationship is very challenging as the child's presence is, in fact, meeting the adult's needs and the carer is unable to 'cope' alone. School attendance then becomes vulnerable and this attachment pattern is often associated with high rates of apparent sickness and absence.

Such children can become very skilled at achieving adult attention in the classroom – initiating conversations that interest the adult, persistent talking and activity that is difficult to ignore. Or they may ignore the task that is set, as this distracts from engagement with the adult. These children will often seek to take charge, as if assuming the role of the adult, and will try to 'merge' with the teacher rather than accept that they are separate and autonomous.

Reframing this behaviour as attention needing rather than attention seeking can help to shift the experience from a nuisance to a need, for these children need to be reassured that they are not forgotten. Frequently such pupils are allocated a classroom assistant to provide continuous support so that the teacher can address the needs of the whole class, but this may collude with their difficulty in separation.

Interventions here are aimed at enabling some experience of separation and autonomy. Break the task down into small steps that require minimal 'attention absences'. An egg timer can be employed to measure small amounts of time after which the adult will return and support the child. Further interventions include holding a special object that can help to reassure the child he or she is not alone – much like the transitional object that small children take to bed with them. Allocating appropriate class responsibilities can help the child to feel noticed and valued and satisfy his or her need to feel identified with the adult – but in a more appropriate way. The skills that these children have invariably developed to catch and hold attention can be exploited through reading tasks and story writing. Separations at the end of the day, week and term are critical times and can be used to explore feelings of separation and absence. Structuring these events with planning, calendars and reassurances about meeting again can help to relieve the anxiety that will inevitably build up. In addition, you might also build up a vocabulary and awareness that separations are not the same as abandonments, and that children can be 'held in mind' in the absences. Reassurances that 'I'll be thinking about you' can reduce the anxiety that these children might feel when they are away from you. With this principle in mind, end of term assemblies can be particularly significant moments.

Insecure disorganised (or disoriented) – the unpredictable, anxious and behaviourally challenging pupil

The disorganised attachment style is presented by the most challenging children in our classrooms. They will test all of our educational resources, and these children are frequently excluded and referred to off-site units from the age of five onwards. Disorganised attachment behaviour lowers the threshold of vulnerability and has been linked to later mental health disorders. It is the only form of attachment difficulty that can be given a formal, clinical diagnosis, and the only form of attachment insecurity that can be referred to as an attachment 'disorder' (see 'reactive attachment disorder' in the *Diagnostic and Statistical Manual of Mental Disorders, 5th edition,* DSM-5).

The extreme behaviours of aggression, disruption and hypervigilance that are associated with disorganised attachment represent a very insecure early experience of neglect and often frightening abuse. Research suggests that brain development is profoundly affected by these early experiences and that the brain becomes organised by fear and uncertainty with a hypersensitivity towards danger and to any sudden event (Perry 1998, 2006). These children have experienced profound difficulties and their behaviour reflects this: anger can dominate their behaviour, with Kohut (1972) arguing that a child 'calls forth rage to protect the self from feelings of infantile vulnerability' (cited in Fonagy 2001, p.220).

In the classroom these children are likely to reflect:

- a heightened state of anxiety

- high vigilance and reactivity

- little trust of adults

- defiance of the teacher

- unable to tolerate 'not knowing'

- insensitivity to others

- may bully others who remind them of their own vulnerability

- may be extremely sensitive to criticism and failure and mock others who make mistakes

- aggressive behaviour in unsupervised areas such as the playground

- omnipotence as protection against chronic uncertainty

- emotional dysregulation (mood swings that are poorly self-managed).

For these children, learning in the social context of the classroom presents a significant challenge.

Interventions need to be consistent and led by the fundamental need for these children to feel safe. For many such children, school is their first experience of feeling safe and accepted and, for this reason, they can be 'persistent attenders'!

As a beginning teacher, safety is maintained by firm and consistent boundaries and predictable routines and activities. Consistency of staff and relationships is crucial so that reliability and trust can begin to be experienced. The curriculum needs to be adjusted to help to develop a sense of time and geography often disrupted by total inconsistency and unreliability in early childhood.

Dates and calendars help to reassure that events can be anticipated and planned. At times of outbursts and reactivity, calming activities can restore composure including eye-hand coordination tasks in a quiet, safe environment.

Reacting to such challenging behaviours with exclusions from the classroom can be re-enacting the early rejection that is driving the behaviours.

For the teacher, too, there is a need to feel safe in the face of challenging behaviours that can be demoralising and exhausting. Your own emotional wellbeing can come under threat in these situations, and it is important that you are ready to 'step back' and resist being drawn into a conflictual relationship that is likely to be a re-enactment of the child's early relationships. The support of other staff and of professional supervision is also critical, and this is explored in detail in Chapter 15. Teacher support groups are regular meetings of staff where the challenging children are discussed and interventions and support are planned (Hanko 1985, 1990, 1995). Such support reduces stress for the teacher and enhances positive interventions for the pupil.

At the extreme end of the continuum the very challenging pupil may well benefit from a small unit where he or she can feel safe and noticed and less challenged by the greater levels of activity and stress. But all children have the potential to develop, grow and change – and it is the mainstream classroom that offers the child with disorganised attachment behaviours the greatest number of positive peer role models.

Final thoughts

Attachment theory can help us to recognise the difficult early experiences that children carry with them into school and inform our responses and interventions. Thankfully, most children have a secure enough background and can cope with the challenges of learning, but for some, this is not the case, and awareness and insight into the behaviours they act out can help the teacher to respond thoughtfully rather than reactively. With this knowledge, teachers can differentiate practice in the classroom to enhance learning.

REFLECTION POINTS

Consider your experience of being in and working in the classroom.

1. To what extent do you believe that you may have observed any of the insecure attachment behaviours described in this chapter?

2. What experience have you had of observing and/or working in classrooms that are supportive of pupils who may exhibit insecure attachment behaviour?

3. What qualities do you possess that might help you to be supportive of pupils who exhibit insecure attachment behaviours? Which qualities do you feel you need to develop further, to help you be more supportive of pupils who may exhibit insecure attachment behaviours?

Bibliography

Ainsworth, M.D.S. and Wittig, B.A. (1969) 'Attachment and Exploratory Behaviour of One-Year-Olds in a Strange Situation.' In B.M. Foss (ed.) *Determinants of Infant Behaviour*, volume 4, 111–136. London: Methuen.

APA (American Psychiatric Association) (2013) *Diagnostic and Statistical Manual of Mental Disorders, 5th Edition (DSM-5)*. Arlington, VA: American Psychiatric Association.

Barrows, K. (1984) 'A child's difficulties in using his gifts and imagination.' *Journal of Psychotherapy 10*.

Bowlby, J. (1944) 'Forty-four juvenile thieves – their character and home life.' *International Journal of Psychoanalysis 25*, 1–57.

Bowlby, J. (1951) *Maternal Care and Mental Health*. World Health Organization Monograph Series 2.

Bowlby, J. (1953) *Child Care and the Growth of Love*. London: Penguin.

Bowlby, J. (1969) *Attachment and Loss. Volume 1: Attachment*. London: Hogarth Press and The Institute of Psychoanalysis.

Bowlby, J. (1973) *Attachment and Loss. Volume 2: Separation: Anxiety and Anger*. London: Hogarth Press and The Institute of Psychoanalysis.

Bowlby, J. (1980) *Attachment and Loss. Volume 3: Loss: Sadness and Depression*. London: Hogarth Press and The Institute of Psychoanalysis.

Fonagy, P. (2001) *Psychoanalysis and Attachment Theory*. London: Karnac.

Geddes, H. (1991) 'An Examination and Evaluation of the Role of Two Teacher Support Groups in Developing More Effective Educational Practice with Pupils with Emotional and Behavioural Difficulties in Mainstream Classrooms.' Unpublished MA dissertation. Roehampton: Roehampton Institute of Higher Education.

Hanko, G. (1985, 1990, 1995) *Special Needs in Ordinary Classrooms. From Staff Support to Staff Development*. Oxford: Blackwell.

Hopkins, J. (1987) 'Failure of the holding relationship: Some effects of physical rejection on the child's attachment and on his inner experience.' *Journal of Child Psychotherapy 13*, 1.

Kohut, H. (1972) 'Thoughts on narcissism and narcissistic rage.' *The Psychoanalytic Study of the Child 27*, 360–400.

Main, M. and Solomon, J. (1982) 'Discovery of an Insecure-Disorganised/Disorientated Attachment Pattern.' In C.M. Parkes and J. Stevenson-Hinde (eds) *The Place of Attachment in Human Behaviour*. London: Routledge.

NSPCC (2001) *Child Abuse and Neglect in the UK Today*. London: NSPCC.

Perry, B.D. (1998) 'Homeostasis, stress, trauma and adaptation: A neurodevelopmental view of childhood trauma.' *Child and Adolescent Psychiatric Clinics of North America 7*, 1, 33–51.

Perry, B.D. (2006) 'Applying Principles of Neurodevelopment to Clinical Work with Maltreated and Traumatized Children.' In N. Boyd Webb (ed.) *Working with Traumatized Youth in Child Welfare* (pp.27–52). New York: The Guilford Press.

Sendak, M. (1963) *Where the Wild Things Are*. New York: Harper.

Sroufe, A. (1983) 'Infant-Caregiver Attachment Patterns of Adaptation in Pre-school: The Roots of Maladaptation and Competence.' In M. Permutter (ed.) *Minnesota Symposium of Child Psychology 16* (pp.41–81). Hillsdale, NJ: Erlbaum.

Sroufe, A. (1986) 'Appraisal: Bowlby's contribution to psychoanalytic theory and developmental psychology: Attachment, separation, loss.' *Journal of Child Psychology and Psychiatry 27*, 6, 841–849.

Varley, S. (2013) *Badger's Parting Gifts*. London: Andersen Press Ltd.

3

Neuroscience and Emotional Development

The Basics Explained

MAISIE SATCHWELL-HIRST

An understanding of the brain is essential if we are to understand the actions and emotions of children and young people in the classroom. Neuroscience is defined as the study of the central nervous system (CNS) that includes the brain and the spinal cord, and refers to the nerve tissues that control the activities of the body. Recent neuroscientific research can enhance our understanding of how and why children behave in the ways that they do. Indeed, our understanding of children and young people may be compromised if it is not informed by some knowledge of the brain changes that underlie the thoughts and feelings of the children we teach. However, the biological development of the brain must be understood in the context of a child's psychological and social development, with none of these three elements more important than the other. While this chapter provides an introduction to neurobiology, it is important to remember that neuroscience is still a new discipline, and we are far from understanding the brain in its entirety.

It is important to understand that the brain is developing and changing throughout infancy, childhood and adolescence – and that it also continues to change during adulthood. At birth, the brain is dominated by the functions of the brain stem and limbic system, as illustrated in Figure 3.1.

The brain stem is a cylindrical mass of nervous tissue that connects the brain with the rest of the body via the spinal cord. It provides many basic reactions, such as survival and reflex reactions, and is sometimes referred to as the 'automated brain'. At birth, the infant is programmed to survive and this part of the brain therefore dominates. The brain stem is vital in controlling muscles, maintaining consciousness, regulating the sleep cycle, regulating heart rate, breathing and eating (e.g. Wang and Ranson 1939).

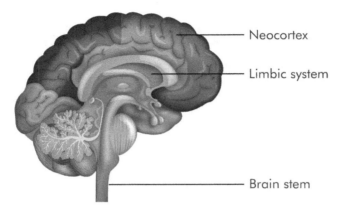

Figure 3.1: The brain stem, limbic system and neocortex

Emanating from the brain stem is a number of cranial nerves, which leave the skull and impact on a number of systems throughout the body. One of these is the vagus nerve (cranial nerve 10), which extends from the brain stem to the abdomen, making it the longest cranial nerve. What is important to recognise here is that not everything is controlled by the brain, and that this vagus nerve has an important role to play as part of the involuntary nervous system. It is involved in regulating emotion by controlling processes such as heart rate and sweating, and is central to the intervention of 'Emotion Coaching' (set out in Chapter 5).

Of equal importance to the brain stem at birth is the limbic system that is fairly central in the brain and is made up of a collection of structures. These include the thalamus, which detects and relays information; the hippocampus, which is involved in memory formation and retrieval; and the amygdala, which processes the emotions of threat and fear. The limbic system's close association with emotional responses will see many chapters in this book refer to it variously as the 'emotional brain', the '999 alarm brain' or the 'downstairs brain'.

An additional area of the limbic system is the hypothalamus that is responsible for producing natural chemical messengers or hormones. The key hormones to be aware of in relation to the emotional development of children include dopamine, serotonin and cortisol.

Dopamine is involved in the brain's pleasure centres and produces a sensation that is pleasant or even euphoric when it is released by the brain. Humans of all ages will naturally seek this sensation through natural or artificial means. Serotonin is a neurotransmitter that maintains mood balance, and variations in serotonin levels can affect social behaviour, mood, sleep patterns and sexual desire. Cortisol is a stress hormone that is released when we need to focus, act and survive. Typically it is the 'nervous' feeling we might get before a presentation, test or confrontation. In small doses, cortisol can be positive as it promotes focus and energy – but in sustained doses, high levels of cortisol can prove toxic for the developing brain.

The neocortex, or 'thinking brain', is the newest part of the brain in evolutionary terms and is made up of four distinct 'lobes'. It is associated with higher-level functions of the brain including decision-making, critical thinking, motor commands and language. The influence of the neocortex on the developing child will increase over time as the initial domination of the 'safety-seeking' brain stem and limbic system gives way to reason, logic and conscious thought.

A particularly important area within the neocortex is the prefrontal cortex, which is part of the frontal lobe. The prefrontal cortex is in part responsible for the task of planning and future thinking (Robbins et al. 1996) and is located behind our foreheads, right at the front. It is important to note that this area of the brain is one of the last to develop, and is often considered not to be fully developed until at least the age of 25 (Casey, Jones and Hare 2008; Sowell et al. 1999). Adolescence is typically associated with emotional mood swings, over reactivity and risky behaviour, and these 'sub-optimal choices' (Casey et al. 2008) may occur because the limbic system develops earlier than the prefrontal cortex; thus adolescents rely on this system more heavily (Casey et al. 2008). As the limbic system is associated with emotion and motivation, decisions made by adolescents may be more biased by the emotional context than adults' decisions. The age at which the prefrontal cortex becomes more engaged than the limbic system will vary between children. For example, children who have experienced trauma, neglect or abuse may have delayed development of the use of the neocortex. There will be a huge variation between children. However, Casey et al.'s suggestion of the 'mismatch' between the limbic system and neocortex for adolescence is not the only explanation for heightened emotional reactions in this age range, as there are many additional likely reasons for such behaviour.

A final concept to be aware of when considering how brains develop is brain 'plasticity'. The brain is made up of billions of neurons (brain cells), and the experiences that children have from birth cause certain neurons to connect together into 'neural pathways'. The more often these pathways are used and reinforced, the greater the efficiency of the pathway. The brain is said to be 'plastic', meaning that the neural pathways can be changed and moulded, rather than having an entirely fixed course of development. Some changes in the brain will be determined by genetics, but the rest will be determined by the environment. In the environment of the classroom, new learning experiences can help develop new neural pathways throughout childhood and adolescence. The capacity of the developing brain is not fixed or static, which means that new experiences that are offered to children can have far-reaching and positive effects, no matter how challenging the children's start in life.

Attachment and brain development

An early, secure attachment between a child and caregiver is essential for healthy brain development. As discussed in Chapter 2, there are generally considered to be four attachment types: secure, insecure-avoidant, insecure-ambivalent and insecure-disorganised. The majority of children form secure attachments with at least one of their parents, which provides them with the best start in life to form healthy relationships with peers and partners. However, forming insecure attachments can have a prolonged and severe effect on development throughout childhood and adolescence. Naturally, this chapter focuses on the differences in the neurobiology of children with secure attachments when compared with those experiencing insecure attachments while evaluating the implications of these differences (taken from Glaser 2000).

Chapter 2 has confirmed that *insecure-avoidant attachment* occurs when the child's caregiver does not show overt affection or comfort in a consistent and reliable way. As a consequence, the child rarely cries on separation from the caregiver, and does not show differences in amount of exploration of the environment when the caregiver is not present. When the caregiver returns, the child may reject them.

Insecure-ambivalent attachment may arise from inconsistent parenting, where the caregiver only sometimes attends to the child's anxiety, meaning the child struggles to know whether exploration of the world is safe. The child is easily distressed, but does not know whether comfort will be provided or not. When the adult tries to comfort the child, the child often rejects help and is difficult to comfort. In later relationships, the adolescent still shows this pattern, showing either a withdrawal from others or high dependency. *Insecure-disorganised attachments* may arise from abusive or neglectful parenting, where the child is left with no meaningful way of relating to other people. The child may also fail to develop the capacity for rational thinking and sensitivity to other people. In a study by Carlson *et al.* (1989), 82 per cent of maltreated 12-month-olds showed a disorganised attachment style, compared with 19 per cent of non-maltreated children. It has been suggested that it is the aspect of fear from the caregiver that causes the disorganised attachment, as the frightened infant seeks comfort from the caregiver, yet this figure is also the source of the fear (Main and Hesse 1990).

Neuroscientific research suggests that the early social and emotional environments of the infant influence the development of brain structures that are later responsible for the individual's social and emotional functioning (Schore 1994). The way the caregiver acts towards the infant and the attachment style the infant develops alters the neurobiological structures that develop during the first two years of life, confirming that there are long-lasting effects of early attachment style (Schore 2001). The brain has two hemispheres, and attachment particularly affects the right hemisphere. The right hemisphere is involved in the processing of social-emotional information, regulating bodily and affective states (Schore 1994, 1998), supporting survival with vital functions, and enabling the organism to cope with stress (Wittling and Schweiger 1993). However, plasticity continues to be available, meaning these issues can be reversed with intervention and future care.

A child's experience of insecure attachment following abuse and neglect can have far-reaching consequences, but the nature of these consequences is difficult to predict. For example, the same experience endured by two different children may produce very different outcomes, while contrasting experiences may lead to similar outcomes. It is also important to note that not all children who have experienced abuse have problems (Kendall-Tackett, Williams and Finkelhor 1993).

Furthermore, we often cannot infer causality, and the maladaptive outcome for a child who has been abused may not necessarily have been caused by the abuse itself. For this reason it is important not to assume that a child has been abused simply because their behaviour infers it.

That said, there is some evidence to suggest that sexual, physical or emotional abuse is associated with depression and anxiety in adulthood (Mullen *et al.* 1996). Mullen *et al.* (cited in Glaser 2000) found certain problems to be associated with particular forms of abuse in that emotional and sexual abuse were associated with eating disorders and sexual difficulties in adulthood, while emotional abuse by the mother was associated with lower self-esteem. Mullen *et al.* also found that physical abuse in childhood was associated with marital breakdown in adulthood.

Hyperarousal, cortisol and the toxic brain

Childhood abuse is also associated with unusual stress responses and the sustained release of cortisol at high levels (Hart, Gunnar and Cicchetti 1996; Kaufman 1991). Cortisol levels that are sustained due to fear and anxiety can be toxic for the brain and have a host of negative effects on a child's functioning. For example, high cortisol levels are associated with hypervigilance, emotional lability and short 'fuses' (Perry 1998, 2006). High levels of irritability can then lead to tantrums and outbursts of anger that appear to be unprovoked.

Another brain area affected by the experience of abuse and neglect is the hippocampus, an area associated with memory. The left hippocampus has been found to have reduced volume in adults who had been abused in childhood, many of whom suffered with post-traumatic stress disorder (PTSD) in adulthood (Bremner *et al.* 1997; Stein *et al.* 1997). However, these reductions were not associated with memory dysfunction; this is possibly due to the plasticity of children's brains, meaning memory functions can be compensated for elsewhere (Stein *et al.* 1997). It is important to remember that plasticity can have effects like this, as it indicates that most early issues are reversible.

The amygdala is part of the brain involved in responding to threat and fear, as discussed earlier. If children have experienced ongoing trauma, they may have associated certain stimuli with the trauma, such as particular sounds or smells. These may then trigger an arousal response in the amygdala (Gallagher and Chiba 1996), meaning the children may become hyperaroused in situations where these stimuli are present, yet they often do not know the cause of their fear. This may manifest as symptoms similar to ADHD (Glaser 2000).

Children who had been maltreated, and who had developed PTSD, were found to have on average 7 per cent smaller cerebral volumes than healthy children who had not been maltreated. The brain volume showed a negative correlation with the duration of the abuse, that is, the longer the abuse went on, the smaller the brain volume (De Bellis *et al.* 1999). This could be due to early traumatic experiences, or a lack of stimulation in the early years. These children may experience lower cognitive functioning, since IQ is correlated with brain size (Glaser 2000).

A longitudinal study indicated that children who experience neglect show social withdrawal, inattention and cognitive underachievement in primary school years (Erickson and Egeland 1996). A child being brought up by a depressed mother also has similar negative effects, with delayed development in cognitive, behavioural and emotional functioning, which last beyond the mother's subsequent normal interaction with her infant.

The impact of experiences

As this section has demonstrated, the early experiences of children can have profound and long-lasting effects on brain development. Children's brains can be affected by their early experiences, with alterations as significant as both size and volume differences. These issues should be borne in mind in the classroom as they may explain some of children's issues relating to attention, learning and emotional control. However, although these early experiences can be very problematic, we must not underestimate the resilience of children to come back from adverse challenges and overcome the issues that can arise. Children's brains are 'plastic', meaning that they are very adaptable, and early intervention may be able to reverse the negative changes that may have occurred in a child's neurology as a result of adversity. As the brain is still forming and developing throughout childhood, we should be optimistic that every child has the potential for change. It is dangerous to 'write off' children who have had adverse early life experiences or to consider them as having 'neurological damage', as these experiences do not *necessarily* lead to behavioural issues – and if the issues do arise, they can be reversed.

The amygdala and emotion recognition

The human face is extremely important in communication and in developing strong affectional bonds (or attachments). Facial movements and expressions provide an enormous amount of information that must be computed in order for conversation and communication to progress smoothly. Very young infants are sensitive to faces, and prefer facial stimuli over other stimuli (Morton and Johnson 1991). Newborn infants imitate the expression on an adult's face (Meltzoff and Moore 1983), suggesting an early sensitivity to the expressions a face can produce, and an early interest. This interest and understanding increases and improves through childhood. Babies are able to recognise their mother over another female stranger (Bushneil, Sai and Mullin 1989), and this recognition of a variety of people in the baby's, and then the child's, life improves.

In addition to recognising the identity of a face, the ability to recognise the emotion on a face improves with age, yet with the different emotions having distinct trajectories of development. For example, the recognition of fear shows a linear improvement, whereas the understanding of anger shows a sharp improvement between adolescence and adulthood (Thomas *et al.* 2007). There is evidence to suggest that adolescents use the amygdala more than adults when processing emotional information (Ernst *et al.* 2005), indicating that the systems that process expressions are still underdeveloped. It is important to remember that a child will not necessarily understand your expression, and that communication between you may therefore be compromised. Although they will interpret expressions to some extent, their capabilities may be less sophisticated than you might be assuming. There will be vast individual differences within one classroom, thus simplistic assumptions about what children 'should' be able to understand must be avoided. It may seem strange, since a vast amount of communication occurs via our expressions, but it may be helpful for feelings such as anger to be verbalised, if it is deemed important that the children know this. In these circumstances it is sensible for the teacher to assume that a lack of recognition of anger is a communication problem (rather than a sign of a child's defiance or indifference), and the teacher should therefore adopt a more direct communication strategy. It is important that, as a beginner teacher, you are as clear and patient as possible when it comes to expressing emotions.

Other difficulties may arise in interpersonal interactions that are also relevant to emotional processing. The areas of the brain used during interpersonal interactions and decision-making can differ between adolescents and adults. For example, there is a tendency for adolescents to use their prefrontal cortices less often than adults, and to rely more on the limbic system. As previously mentioned, the prefrontal cortex is generally used to make complex decisions, whereas the limbic system is more primitive and is thought to be important for processing emotion. Therefore, if adolescents make more use of the limbic system to make decisions, the interactions are more impulsive or based on 'gut' feelings. As a result, the interpretation of emotions is less critical and 'logical' as compared with adults (Arain *et al.* 2013; Choudhury, Blakemore and Charman 2006; Somerville, Fani and McClure-Tone 2011). Similarly, there is evidence to suggest that adolescents tend to focus on emotional information even when it is not relevant to a task, whereas adults are generally more skilled at allocating attention to relevant information (Monk *et al.* 2003).

Interestingly, when there is no emotional information present, adolescents are able to form logical decisions using their prefrontal cortices. Therefore, rather than the prefrontal cortex being underdeveloped, there seems to be a greater salience placed on emotional information (via the limbic system) than on 'logical' information. So even if it is within an adolescent's capabilities to make the more sensible decision, they may well not do so if there is emotional information involved. Naturally, this neurological predisposition in adolescence can be mystifying and frustrating for parents and teachers alike. Unsurprisingly, within one classroom there will be differences between students in their abilities to weigh up information and to make logical decisions, with some having much better impulse control than others. What is important is that, as teachers, we are aware that the adolescents in our classrooms are moving through these neurological changes and that they will be doing so at different paces.

Due to a number of hormonal and physical changes, many adolescents have difficulties with their own emotions. Dopamine levels decrease during adolescence, which can lead to mood swings and difficulties regulating emotion, as dopamine influences brain events that control the emotional response and the experience of pleasure and pain. Serotonin levels also decrease, which is associated with decreased impulse control (Arain *et al.* 2013) and the ability to inhibit the urge to fulfil a desire. These neurotransmitters underlie the classic 'mood swings' that are often associated with adolescents.

Mental health issues in childhood and adolescence

Childhood and adolescence are high-risk periods for the development of a mental health problem, with the peak age for onset for any mental health disorder being 14 (Kessler *et al.* 2005, cited in Paus, Keshavan and Giedd 2008). The development of a paediatric psychiatric disorder leaves the individual at high risk of mental health issues later in life, and therefore early detection and intervention are essential. The most common mental health problems are depression and anxiety, which have wide ranges of severity.

The symptoms of *depression* among children include low mood, lack of motivation, sleepiness, hopelessness, irritability and withdrawal from friends and family (APA 2013). Depression can have a genetic component, which may involve a child being unable to produce as much serotonin as their typically developing peers. Children with a parent experiencing the disorder have up to a 50 per cent chance of developing depression themselves (Weissman *et al.* 2005, 2006). The onset of depression is predicted by an interaction between stressful life events and genetic predisposition.

The first-line recommended intervention for depression is talking therapies (NICE 2015), so a student suspected to be experiencing depression should be directed to the school counsellor. Medication such as antidepressants is only recommended after a talking therapy for more severe forms of depression, as they may result in addiction and other neurological changes. Most antidepressants act on the serotonin receptors in the brain to inhibit the process known as 'reuptake' of serotonin. During reuptake, serotonin is naturally reabsorbed into nerve cells, after being released to send messages between them. Antidepressants (such as selective serotonin reuptake inhibitors, i.e. SSRIs) can inhibit this process, meaning there is more serotonin left in the gap between the nerves, known as the synapse.

Anxiety is also common in adolescents. It is characterised by excessive worry and nervousness, and may prevent an individual from engaging in activities that they used to enjoy (APA 2013). Cognitive behavioural therapy (CBT) is the first recommended treatment for anxiety, which school counsellors will often have training in. There are different CBT interventions, but the main purpose of CBT (as set out in Chapter 1) is to challenge and change the ways that a student may be thinking (or interpreting a situation), which then gives rise to the 'dysfunctional' behaviour of anxiety. CBT seeks to enable the individual to identify and acknowledge their emotional and behavioural responses and the beliefs and attitudes underpinning them. The aim, then, is to help the student to modify their beliefs and attitudes in ways that facilitate positive responses in place of negative ones. Behavioural aspects of CBT involve identifying the fears of the individual, and exposing them to situations where these fears may occur, in order to demonstrate that the fear is unlikely to happen. The rationale here is that the individual will then be less fearful of the outcome and will be able to re-engage in activities. Dysregulation of amygdala activity is associated with depression and anxiety in children (Thomas *et al.* 2001). There has also been shown to be less prefrontal cortex activity in adolescents at risk of anxiety disorders (Pérez-Edgar *et al.* 2007).

Schizophrenia is less common than depression and anxiety in adolescents, which means it often gets overlooked. However, the lifetime prevalence of schizophrenia is one in 100, with single psychotic episodes being much more common during adolescence, making it common enough to deserve recognition. Only in recent years has childhood schizophrenia begun to be taken seriously and subjected to significant research. Symptoms of psychosis are most commonly hallucinations or delusions, and it is characterised by a loss of contact with reality (APA 2013). It is often terrifying for the individual experiencing the episode, and can be associated with a mistrust of everyone, so this person must be approached with a great deal of sensitivity. Risk factors for psychosis include genetics and the use of cannabis (Andréasson *et al.* 1987).

The commonly used statistic is that one in four individuals will experience mental distress at some point in their life. This means that almost everyone will have some directly lived experience of mental health problems, including in a classroom setting. Teachers must be vigilant in looking out for the signs of a student experiencing mental distress, as the earlier the intervention for a child, the better the outcome will tend to be. Furthermore, many students may be carrying out a caring role for a relative with a mental health problem, which could be a great burden on their abilities in school and their own health. Empathy and understanding from a teacher could be invaluable for a student carrying out a young caring role, or experiencing mental health problems themselves.

Final thoughts

This chapter has demonstrated the wide-ranging changes of the brain throughout childhood and adolescence. No individual at school age has a brain that is developed to the same stage as an adult, with many areas continually changing at least until the age of 25. These years are therefore essential for setting the individual up for a healthy adulthood. This chapter has also introduced the concept of plasticity, which illustrates the fluctuating nature of development: there is no fixed course! All experiences the individual meets will influence the way the brain develops. Importantly, it is crucial to be sensitive to difficulties with young people: experiences affect the development of the brain, which in turn affects the ways in which people act. Another crucial point to take away from this chapter is that adverse experiences do not have a deterministic effect on outcomes. Although these experiences may affect brain development adversely for a period, future positive experiences can generate new neural pathways and new ways of acting and responding as the brain continues to be plastic throughout our lives.

An understanding of the brain is an essential part of our understanding of the actions and emotions of children and adolescents, and in Chapter 5, the Emotion Coaching approach will explain how neuroscience can be incorporated into classroom practice. The purpose of this chapter has been to provide a brief introduction to the ways that the different areas of the brain contribute to different aspects of human life. Only 'the basics' have been covered, of course, and there is a range of information that could not be included in this chapter and still a whole host of information that is yet to be discovered about the brain. We are only at the very edge of our discovery and understanding when it comes to the brain, and this should always be borne in mind. Its complexity and delicacy still evades us.

▚ REFLECTION POINTS ▚

Reflect on your own life experiences.

1. When and where did you last have a cortisol 'rush' when you might have felt nervous or anxious (an exam? an interview? a performance?)?

2. How long did the cortisol rush last?

3. Imagine having that level of anxiety as a permanent feeling, a permanent feeling of dread. How would that affect your concentration and learning in class? Some of the children you are teaching will be feeling this way – and their behaviour will communicate this.

Bibliography

Andréasson, S., Engström, A., Allebeck, P. and Rydberg, U. (1987) 'Cannabis and schizophrenia: A longitudinal study of Swedish conscripts.' *The Lancet 330*, 8574, 1483–1486.

APA (American Psychiatric Association) (2013) *Diagnostic and Statistical Manual of Mental Disorders, 5th Edition (DSM-5).* Arlington, VA: American Psychiatric Association.

Arain, M., Haque, M., Johal, L., Mathur, P., Nel, W., Rais, A. *et al.* (2013) 'Maturation of the adolescent brain.' *Neuropsychiatric Disease and Treatment 9*, 449–461.

Bremner, J.D., Randall, P., Vermetten, E., Staib, L., Bronen, R.A., Mazure, C. *et al.* (1997) 'Magnetic resonance imaging-based measurement of hippocampal volume in posttraumatic stress disorder related to childhood physical and sexual abuse – A preliminary report.' *Biological Psychiatry 41*, 1, 23–32.

Bushneil, I.W.R., Sai, F. and Mullin, J.T. (1989) 'Neonatal recognition of the mother's face.' *British Journal of Developmental Psychology 7*, 1, 3–15.

Carlson, V., Cicchetti, D., Barnett, D. and Braunwald, K. (1989) 'Disorganized/disoriented attachment relationships in maltreated infants.' *Developmental Psychology 25*, 4, 525.

Casey, B.J., Jones, R.M. and Hare, T.A. (2008) 'The adolescent brain.' *Annals of the New York Academy of Sciences 1124*, 1, 111–126.

Choudhury, S., Blakemore, S.-J. and Charman, T. (2006) 'Social cognitive development during adolescence.' *Social Cognitive and Affective Neuroscience 1*, 3, 165–174.

De Bellis, M.D., Baum, A.S., Birmaher, B., Keshavan, M.S., Eccard, C.H., Boring, A.M. *et al.* (1999) 'Developmental traumatology part I: Biological stress systems.' *Biological Psychiatry 45*, 10, 1259–1270.

Erickson, M. and Egeland, B. (1996) 'Child Neglect.' In J. Briere, L. Berliner, J. Bulkley, C. Jenny and T. Reid (eds) *The APSAC Handbook on Childhood Maltreatment* (pp.4–20). Thousand Oaks, CA: Sage Publications.

Ernst, M., Nelson, E.E., Jazbec, S., McClure, E.B., Monk, C.S., Leibenluft, E. *et al.* (2005) 'Amygdala and nucleus accumbens in responses to receipt and omission of gains in adults and adolescents.' *NeuroImage 25*, 4, 1279–1291.

Gallagher, M. and Chiba, A.A. (1996) 'The amygdala and emotion.' *Current Opinion in Neurobiology 6*, 2, 221–227.

Glaser, D. (2000) 'Child abuse and neglect and the brain – A review.' *Journal of Child Psychology and Psychiatry 41*, 1, 97–116.

Hart, J., Gunnar, M. and Cicchetti, D. (1996) 'Altered neuroendocrine activity in maltreated children related to symptoms of depression.' *Development and Psychopathology 8*, 1, 201–214.

Kaufman, J. (1991) 'Depressive disorders in maltreated children.' *Journal of the American Academy of Child and Adolescent Psychiatry 30*, 2, 257–265.

Kendall-Tackett, K.A., Williams, L.M. and Finkelhor, D. (1993) 'Impact of sexual abuse on children: A review and synthesis of recent empirical studies.' *Psychological Bulletin 113*, 1, 164–180.

Kessler, R.C., Berglund, P., Demler, O., Jin, R., Merikangas, K.R. and Walters, E.E. (2005) 'Lifetime prevalence and age-of-onset distributions of DSM-IV disorders in the national comorbidity survey replication.' *Archives of General Psychiatry 62*, 6, 593–602.

Main, M. and Hesse, E. (1990) 'Parents' Unresolved Traumatic Experiences Are Related to Infant Disorganised Attachment Status: Is Frightened and/or Frightening Parent Behaviour the Linking Mechanism?' In M. Greenberg, D. Ciccetti and E. Cummings (eds) *Attachment in the Preschool Years* (pp.161–182). Chicago, IL: University of Chicago Press.

Meltzoff, A.N. and Moore, M.K. (1983) 'Newborn infants imitate adult facial gestures.' *Child Development, 54,* 3, 702–709.

Monk, C.S., McClure, E.B., Nelson, E.E., Zarahn, E., Bilder, R.M., Leibenluft, E. *et al.* (2003) 'Adolescent immaturity in attention-related brain engagement to emotional facial expressions.' *NeuroImage 20*, 1, 420–428.

Morton, J. and Johnson, M.H. (1991) 'CONSPEC and CONLERN: A two-process theory of infant face recognition.' *Psychological Review 98*, 2, 164.

Mullen, P.E., Martin, J.L., Anderson, J.C., Romans, S.E. and Herbison, G.P. (1996) 'The long-term impact of the physical, emotional, and sexual abuse of children: A community study.' *Child Abuse & Neglect 20*, 1, 7–21.

NICE (National Institute for Health and Care Excellence) (2015) *Depression in Children and Young People: Identification and Management.* Clinical Guide (CG) 28. London: NICE. Available at www.nice.org.uk/guidance/cg28, accessed on 24 March 2017.

Paus, T., Keshavan, M. and Giedd, J.N. (2008) 'Why do many psychiatric disorders emerge during adolescence?' *Nature Reviews Neuroscience 9*, 12, 947–957.

Pérez-Edgar, K., Roberson-Nay, R., Hardin, M.G., Poeth, K., Guyer, A.E., Nelson, E.E. *et al.* (2007) 'Attention alters neural responses to evocative faces in behaviorally inhibited adolescents.' *NeuroImage 35*, 4, 1538–1546.

Perry, B.D. (1998) 'Homeostasis, stress, trauma and adaptation: A neurodevelopmental view of childhood trauma.' *Child and Adolescent Psychiatric Clinics of North America 7*, 1, 33–51.

Perry, B.D. (2006) 'Applying Principles of Neurodevelopment to Clinical Work with Maltreated and Traumatized Children.' In N. Boyd Webb (ed.) *Working with Traumatized Youth in Child Welfare* (pp.27–52). New York: The Guilford Press.

Robbins, T.W., Weinberger, D., Taylor, J.G. and Morris, R.G. (1996) 'Dissociating executive functions of the prefrontal cortex [and discussion].' *Philosophical Transactions: Biological Sciences 351*, 1346, 1463–1471.

Schore, A.N. (1994) *Affect Regulation and the Origin of the Self: The Neurobiology of Emotional Development.* Hillsdale, NJ: Erlbaum Associates.

Schore, A.N. (1998) 'The Experience-Dependent Maturation of an Evaluative System in the Cortex.' In K. Pribaum (ed.) *Brain and Values: Is a Biological Science of Value Possible?* (pp.337–358). Mahwah, NJ: Erlbaum.

Schore, A.N. (2001) 'The effects of early relational trauma on right brain development, affect regulation, and infant mental health.' *Infant Mental Health Journal 22*, 1–2, 201–269.

Somerville, L.H., Fani, N. and McClure-Tone, E.B. (2011) 'Behavioral and neural representation of emotional facial expressions across the lifespan.' *Developmental Neuropsychology 36*, 4, 408–428.

Sowell, E.R., Thompson, P.M., Holmes, C.J., Jernigan, T.L. and Toga, A.W. (1999) 'In vivo evidence for post-adolescent brain maturation in frontal and striatal regions.' *Nature Neuroscience 2*, 10, 859–861.

Stein, M.B., Koverola, C., Hanna, C., Torchia, M.G. and McClarty, B. (1997) 'Hippocampal volume in women victimized by childhood sexual abuse.' *Psychological Medicine 27*, 4, 951–959.

Thomas, K.M., Drevets, W.C., Dahl, R.E., Ryan, N.D., Birmaher, B., Eccard, C.H. *et al.* (2001) 'Amygdala response to fearful faces in anxious and depressed children.' *Archives of General Psychiatry 58*, 11, 1057–1063.

Thomas, L.A., De Bellis, M.D., Graham, R. and LaBar, K.S. (2007) 'Development of emotional facial recognition in late childhood and adolescence.' *Developmental Science 10*, 5, 547–558.

Wang, S.C. and Ranson, S.W. (1939) 'Autonomic responses to electrical stimulation of the lower brain stem.' *The Journal of Comparative Neurology 71*, 3, 437–455.

Weissman, M.M., Wickramaratne, P., Nomura, Y., Warner, V., Verdeli, H., Pilowsky, D.J. *et al.* (2005) 'Families at high and low risk for depression: A 3-generation study.' *Archives of General Psychiatry 62*, 1, 29–36.

Weissman, M.M., Wickramaratne, P., Nomura, Y., Warner, V., Pilowsky, D. and Verdeli, H. (2006) 'Offspring of depressed parents: 20 years later.' *American Journal of Psychiatry 163*, 6, 1001–1008.

Wittling, W. and Schweiger, E. (1993) 'Neuroendocrine brain asymmetry and physical complaints.' *Neuropsychologia 31*, 6, 591–608.

4

Attachment Aware Schools

JANET ROSE AND LOUISE GILBERT

This chapter explores the idea of Attachment Aware Schools (AAS) and the implications for teachers and practitioners. It draws on the work of two pilot projects recently implemented in two UK local authorities. The aim of the projects was to promote better public understanding of the social and emotional needs that can drive children's behaviour, and to stimulate political debate about inclusive educational provision. In addition, the projects sought to facilitate transformations in schools and in the practice of community-based professionals.

Attachment theory (as set out by Heather Geddes in Chapter 2) and the attachment-based strategies that help to support children's social and emotional development are integral to the AAS project. This chapter documents the positive impact of the AAS project in developing sustainable improvements in systemic school-wide practices relating to children's academic attainment, behaviour, emotional regulation and wellbeing. It concludes with a discussion on how being an AAS translates into everyday practice in the classroom, and provides case studies to illustrate practical applications.

What are Attachment Aware Schools?

AAS aim to promote nurturing relationships that support the socio-emotional development, the learning and the behaviour of all children. Taking cognisance of our innate need for a secure 'sense of belonging' and to feel safe (Bowlby 1969, 1982), AAS focus on the importance of attachment, attunement and trauma-informed practice to address children's individual needs. There is an acknowledgement and acceptance of adults as providing a 'secondary attachment figure' that may both ameliorate insecure-attachment behaviours and encourage development of more secure ones. All staff in AAS have an understanding and insight into attachment theory (Bowlby 1969, 1982), including recent neuroscientific evidence that appears to support the research around the attachment process (Panksepp 2001; Porges 2011; Schore and Schore 2008; Siegel 2012). Staff undertake specific training around Emotion Coaching (Gottman, Katz and Hooven 1997), and are also made aware of the impact of trauma on the developing brain and subsequent behaviour (Balbernie 2001; Heller and LaPierre 2012; Shonkoff and Garner 2012; van der Kolk 2014). Emotion Coaching is an evidence-based strategy that helps children to become more aware of their emotions and to manage their own feelings, particularly during instances of heightened emotions that invariably lead to misbehaviour. It is based on the principle that nurturing and emotionally supportive relationships provide optimal contexts for the promotion of resilience in children. Children's emotions are validated within the relationship with clear limits set, where appropriate, followed by joint problem-solving with the child to develop more effective behavioural strategies (Gus, Rose and Gilbert 2015). Recent research in England suggests that the Emotion Coaching approach can reduce behavioural incidents in school and foster positive relationships between the teacher and pupil (Rose, McGuire-Snieckus and Gilbert 2015). A detailed and practical exploration of Emotion Coaching follows in the next chapter.

By utilising strategies such as Emotion Coaching, the AAS project creates a nurturing infrastructure that binds whole-school strategies into specialised, relational-focused approaches. By facilitating the development of empathetic environments, AAS aims to support children in developing their potential through improving their socio-emotional wellbeing and behaviour. Where this is achieved, evidence suggests that academic achievement improves and the attainment gap decreases (Bergin and Bergin 2009; Cooper and Whitebread 2007; Rose et al. 2016).

The AAS framework draws on a comprehensive review of psychological and educational literature and the preliminary findings from our pilot studies with participating schools. The framework operates on the principles of joined-up thinking and inter-agency collaboration, firmly endorsing the concept of 'the Team Around the Child (TAC)' and community-wide collaboration (Anning 2006; Chivers and Trodd 2011).

Figure 4.1: The Attachment Aware Schools framework
Source: Parker, Rose and Gilbert (2016)

The AAS framework outlined in Figure 4.1 comprises five key elements that enable effective and sustainable implementation. These include a consideration of the whole-school ethos, promotion of setting specific training packages, fostering of universal and specialised attachment-based strategies, developing collaborative partnerships with the wider community and building an evidence base via robust evaluation. This whole-school approach endeavours to develop a sense of 'ownership' by all staff, from the governors and leaders to the teachers and support staff, including admin teams and grounds staff.

This AAS framework also provides a 'pyramid of support' to meet the range of children's needs. At the top of the pyramid is the small number of high-need children who require specialist help, such as referrals to mental health services. In the middle are those children who require some additional support within the school environment, such as one-to-one tutoring or nurture group provision. The base of the triangle represents the entire school community, supported through the provision of whole-school training on relational models and relational actions, such as Emotion Coaching (see Chapter 5).

The strength of the AAS project is that it has a real impact in schools, in classrooms and on the lives of vulnerable children and young people. Evidence from the pilot study is set out in Case study 1 below, which illustrates the kind of impact this approach can have on both socio-emotional development and scholastic attainment.

Case study 1

Child A refers to a Key Stage 2 boy on Pupil Premium, with a troubled family background and a diagnosis of attention deficit hyperactivity disorder (ADHD), who was significantly underperforming in school. He had poor self-esteem, was reluctant to take risks or show task persistence. He regularly refused to comply and was verbally aggressive to staff, frequently fleeing the classroom. There were numerous serious incidents. A number of attachment-based strategies were introduced, which included:

- whole-school training in attachment awareness and trauma

- introduction of a key adult and creation of a 'safe space'

- various practical interventions based on attachment strategies to stabilise anxiety and enable the child to feel safe, secure and able to engage and take risks in learning tasks, such as visual cues

- differentiated learning tasks that addressed his developmental needs

- specialist learning support that facilitated increasing levels of challenge

- consistent use of Emotion Coaching to scaffold emotional regulation when dealing with events that raised his anxiety levels.

In less than a year, Child A was able to remain in class and work independently on many tasks, including attending school events safely such as residential trips. Child A's reading age score rose from 4 to 7 years, a three-year increase in a single year. The frequency of serious incidents dropped to zero.

Why do we need Attachment Aware Schools?

There has been an increasing recognition of the necessity to address child wellbeing from a range of major national and international organisations. One in five children experience a mental health problem each year (RSPH 2015, p.4), and almost £17 billion is spent annually in England and Wales on acute, self-limited, statutory essential services for children and young people experiencing severe difficulties in their lives (Chowdry and Oppenheim 2015). In the UK, those who are born into and live in the most deprived communities will have the poorest mental and physical health and die, on average, 20 years earlier than the rest of the population (DH 2011).

Children from poorer households tend to exhibit poorer self-control and emotional health than wealthier peers, with these differences becoming measurable by the age of three (Feinstein 2015). Chronic and extreme deprivation leads to a greater risk of developing anxiety, depression and cardiovascular problems later in life, and can lead to a compromised ability to learn and to cope with adversity (Allen 2011; Heller and LaPierre 2012; Marmot 2010). A report by the Department of Health (DH 2015) identifies, as a key 21st-century concern, the need to promote positive mental health and wellbeing for all children and young people. This is also echoed in the government's educational priority to close the attainment gap for disadvantaged pupils and to promote the new special educational needs and disability (SEND) reforms (DfE 2013, 2014).

The National Institute for Health and Care Excellence (NICE 2015) confirms that extensive, cross-cultural research demonstrates how attachment is an important influence on children's academic success and wellbeing at school. Traditional attachment theory emphasises the integral role of relationships in child wellbeing, and how children's receptivity to learning is affected by their early relationships with their primary caregivers (Bowlby 1969). Securely attached children are more likely to attain higher academic grades, have greater emotional regulation and social competence, plus a willingness to take on challenges. They will also have lower levels of ADHD and delinquency (Bergin and Bergin 2009). Bergin and Bergin (2009) go on to highlight how one third of all children are likely to have an insecure attachment that can then affect their socio-emotional development, their school performance and their behaviour.

Social baseline theory (Coan, Schaefer and Davidson 2006) recognises as 'essential' the relational component of wellbeing. It proposes that humans are hardwired to seek social proximity as a default strategy for regulating emotional stress, unless experiences have taught them that such social relationships are unavailable or unreliable (Beckes and Coan 2011). With a secure attachment figure in close proximity, not only does an individual register less distress in threatening situations, but the world is also perceived as less daunting. Being with another person with whom we feel secure affects brain processing in a way that conserves rather than depletes energy, allowing engagement of a broader network of brain regions for problem-solving, thereby supporting learning (Coan *et al.* 2006; Pianta 1999). Therefore, although children's wellbeing is seen as relating to and informed by their attachments with their main carers, relationships with their teachers and support staff can also be highly influential.

Literature on attachment offers new insights into educationally based relationships and their consequences on learning and behaviour (Verschueren and Koomen 2012). Davis (2003) highlights various studies that have shown how the quality of teacher–child relationships shapes children's classroom experiences and influences their social and cognitive development. Close, positive relationships in school are believed to foster more effective learning (Kennedy and Kennedy 2004), whilst attachment issues and/or trauma are recognised as adversely affecting children's relationships with peers, teachers and support staff (Cozolino 2013; Pianta 1992). Bergin and Bergin (2009, p.154) evidence how pupils' attachment styles to caregivers can parallel the attachment relationship between teacher and child, noting that 'secure teacher–student relationships predict greater knowledge, higher test scores, greater academic motivation, and fewer retentions or special education referrals than insecure teacher–student relationships'. They suggest a need, within the realms of professional boundaries, to recognise and forge 'attachment-like' relationships between pupil and educator.

Kennedy and Kennedy (2004) draw attention to the evidence that suggests how teachers can misinterpret insecurely attached children's behaviour as uncooperative, aggressive, demanding, impulsive, withdrawn, reactive and/or unpredictable. These judgements of the child's behavioural manifestations, which reflect their underlying interpersonal inner experiences and intrapersonal relationship history, can then adversely affect teachers' attitudes and responses to behaviour. To equip teachers to recognise and effectively engage with the needs actually being communicated by the behaviour, Kennedy (2008) suggests teachers need a better understanding of the complexity of meaning behind such behavioural displays.

The Department for Education (DfE) and NICE have now called for all education professionals to be trained in understanding attachment difficulties, including how they can present, how they can affect learning and behaviour, and how staff can support children and young people with attachment difficulties (NICE 2015). This concurs with Rose *et al.*'s (2012) proposal that all educators need to understand the process of attachment, because:

- the nature of a child's primary attachments (attachments to caregivers) is foundational to the child's socio-emotional wellbeing and capacity to learn

- educators themselves might establish 'attachment-like' relationships with their pupils (i.e. nurturing and responsive), particularly with challenging and vulnerable pupils, to enhance learning opportunities

- secure attachment relationships correlate strongly with higher academic attainment, better self-regulation, wellbeing and social competence.

Nagel (2009) suggests that schools can be prime sites for buffering the impact of stress, building resilience and enhancing all children's capacities for learning. Foundational to the AAS programme is recognition and acceptance that the brain's limbic system (associated with emotions and attachment) takes priority over the brain's neocortex (associated with thinking and exploratory systems). In other words, feeling safe and secure is more important than learning (Sroufe and Siegel 2011), and children will learn most effectively when they feel safe in their environment – and in their relationship with their teacher.

The AAS project promotes 'an attachment-informed approach for all professionals working with children and offers the best prospect for effective early intervention for children, whatever their age or family situation' (Furnivall *et al.* 2012, p.8). Universal whole-school practice and targeted interventions, such as that modelled by AAS, are increasingly being recognised as significant in helping to support children with social, emotional and mental health difficulties (Furnivall *et al.* 2012; NICE 2015; Parker *et al.* 2016). The AAS programme provides a coherent and integrated theoretical framework, discourse and practice for all professionals who work with children and young people. In doing so, it also offers evidence to address the criteria in Ofsted's *The Common Inspection Framework* (2015) that relate to pupils' personal development, behaviour and welfare.

What does an Attachment Aware School look like?

The following case study, told by the Director of Student Support at Bradley Stoke Community School, Bristol, UK, illustrates the changes implemented by a large secondary school once they embarked on the journey to become an AAS.

Case study 2

Bradley Stoke Community School, Bristol, UK, is a fully comprehensive, inclusive all-through school (primary, secondary and post-16 education) within the Olympus Academy Trust. In 2015 we enrolled to be part of the Attachment Aware Schools project; we saw this as an opportunity to re-visit our principles of inclusion.

Although we already had a non-teaching pastoral team with outstanding pastoral and safeguarding care, we quickly became conscious that we needed to reconsider how we were responding to the growing mental health and behavioural needs of our students. Was 'inclusion' actually inclusion or were we sticking plasters where a more strategic view was needed?

Over the last year we have developed the following:

- *Staff training:* We devised a series of six continuing professional development (CPD) sessions and offered this bespoke training to teaching and non-teaching staff. Our aim was to have some 'attachment aware champions' who understood the science, were motivated to use the learning in how they dealt with student behaviour, and who would then share their experience during a whole school INSET. All participants completed evaluations about their training and the impact it has had on their practice. These evaluations were all positive and showed that the knowledge and strategies, such as Emotion Coaching, has had an impact.

- *Whole-school mental health awareness:* Several strands were implemented across the schools and included awareness raising with students, developing staff confidence and training older students to lead peer-to-peer support. Access to information and trusted adults was improved through our 'Talk to me about...' staff stickers, which were commissioned and stuck on to staff laptops so that students could easily identify adults they could talk to about mental health, bullying, being a young carer or LGBT (lesbian, gay, bisexual or transgender).

- *In-school personalised learning opportunities:* We have opened a new personalised learning hub that houses a new Inclusion Centre. This provides a safe place, security and soothing that many students need who cannot manage the whole school day, and who would otherwise be poor attenders or present with challenging behaviour.

In terms of the impact, since becoming an AAS, there has been a significant decrease in our exclusions (from 45 to 7). Staff comments include:

'I wish I had done this training years ago.'

'Made me more patient – look a little deeper.'

'Emotion Coaching is a very effective approach which empowers the teacher and child – teacher can be in control but non-confrontational and the child can be seen, gain security and ultimately learn to self-regulate.'

'An attachment aware approach benefits all students.'

Bradley Stoke Community School has developed an 'Attachment aware checklist' that highlights how all students need to feel *seen, safe, soothed and secure* in school, to ensure that they are 'learning ready'. The model is an adaptation of Siegel's '4 Ss' attachment model' (Siegel 2012a), and these may be ways in which you can develop your own attachment aware pedagogy and practice.

Attachment aware checklist

Being seen

This is more than just being seen visually – it is about perception and letting a child know that they are perceived deeply and empathically, that we 'see' inside the child's mind and what lies beneath their behaviour. Siegel calls this 'mindsight'.

- ✓ Welcome at the door/greetings in corridor
- ✓ Noticing success
- ✓ Differentiation
- ✓ Noticing changes
- ✓ Photographs
- ✓ Work on the wall
- ✓ Smiling/eye contact
- ✓ Giving choices
- ✓ Student voice
- ✓ Saying hello
- ✓ Using names
- ✓ Noticing body language
- ✓ Remembering and mentioning things about them

Feeling safe

This is about helping children have a sense of safety, physically, mentally and emotionally.

- ✓ Providing a safe space/haven in school
- ✓ Seating plans
- ✓ High expectations
- ✓ Staff presence
- ✓ Positive staff-to-staff relationships
- ✓ Mentor/key person for students
- ✓ Challenging inappropriate behaviour
- ✓ Monitoring corridor behaviour and unstructured times
- ✓ Noticing changes to friendships
- ✓ Ensuring routines-predictability-continuity
- ✓ Setting clear expectations and boundaries
- ✓ Parental engagement

Feeling soothed

This is about making sure that we co-regulate children when they are experiencing difficult emotions and stressful situations, helping them to calm down.

- ✓ Staff to model appropriate behaviour
- ✓ Regular check-ins with key staff/mentors
- ✓ Staff in control when students feel on the edge
- ✓ Talking calmly and quietly
- ✓ Maintaining a calm environment
- ✓ Listening
- ✓ Making students feel 'liked' and valued
- ✓ Rapport
- ✓ Not too controlling; using reasoning
- ✓ Appropriate physical contact
- ✓ De-escalation techniques

Feeling secure

This is about providing children with a sense of feeling secure so that they develop an internalised sense of self and personal wellbeing which, in turn, enables them to explore and learn about the world.

- ✓ Developing a sense of belonging
- ✓ All students are part of the class
- ✓ Predictability
- ✓ Clear routines, expectations and boundaries
- ✓ Consistency
- ✓ Calm tone of voice
- ✓ Clean slate every lesson
- ✓ Building positive relationships
- ✓ Supporting with friendship issues
- ✓ Availability of staff

How does being an Attachment Aware School help pupils and teachers?

Preliminary research studies in England indicate that being an AAS and implementing attachment-based strategies can improve behaviour, attendance and academic outcomes (Parker *et al.* 2016; Rose *et al.* 2016), and appears to correlate with claims made elsewhere (Bergin and Bergin 2009; Riley 2009). A significant finding from the pilot studies in England show that being an AAS can help to close the attainment gap, a key government priority (DfE 2014). A number of children were tracked and supported using attachment-based strategies, notably Emotion Coaching, and increases in their academic scores in English, Maths and Reading were noted (Rose *et al.* 2016). Another key impact was the reduction of behavioural incidents, which is likely to be the result of more attuned, sensitive and appropriate behavioural management. Children had an improved ability to manage their feelings and behaviour, increased empathy, an improved ability to problem-solve and to take responsibility for their behaviour, plus better relationships with staff (Rose *et al.* 2016). As one teacher put it, being an AAS 'allows students to understand their emotions, manage them, self-regulate and learn'.

Another benefit was how whole-school approaches and shared strategies improved consistency in communication amongst staff, and between pupils and staff. Staff felt more able to cope and maintain calm in the face of challenging situations. Their confidence increased, perceived stress levels reduced, and they become more understanding of pupils' needs and behaviour. One teacher described how 'my practice has changed by being more patient and calm in certain situations', and another declared, 'I feel like I now look at behaviour differently and can respond in a different and better way' (quoted in Rose *et al.* 2016). More positive vocabulary was used in communicating with pupils, and it was overwhelmingly agreed that attachment-based strategies helped to de-escalate situations. In the words of some teachers who participated in the pilot studies, AAS facilitate staff, 'helps with pupils' needs and supports emotional wellbeing and learning' and 'helps to build trusting and strong relationships between pupils and adults' (quoted in Rose *et al.* 2016).

The following case study shows how a Year 1 child was supported using attachment-based strategies in an AAS.

Case study 3

Child C was a recently adopted boy, aged six, who was new at the school. His adopted mother told the school that he had been taken into care after he was found outside a shopping centre when he was under two years old. At school he would adopt the foetal position during times of high anxiety, and had often been found hiding in cupboards in his previous school. His reading and spelling was below the expected levels by several years. He was very distracted in the classroom, often fidgeting and unable to complete tasks. The school had recently become an AAS and all staff were given training on attachment theory and Emotion Coaching. The school also started a nurture group and established a 'safe base' where the children could relax, talk and feel safe. They also set up a key worker system with support and ancillary staff.

The difference being in an AAS was notable. After only a short time at the school, it was apparent that Child C felt happy and safe in school. He was increasingly able to sit and stay on task. He knew who to talk to when he felt vulnerable. He was able to express his anxiety and used strategies the staff had given him to relieve his stress levels. His reading improved increasingly to age-expected levels, and he himself believed he was now a 'good reader'. He moved from 'emerging' in Maths and Science to 'expected' levels. There was a fundamental improvement in his attitude and self-confidence.

Final thoughts: A cautionary note

An AAS approach does not suggest that teachers become social workers or therapists. Indeed, it is important to maintain professional boundaries (Howes 1999). Moreover, any new strategy adopted within educational practice should generate caution and be undertaken with a critically reflective stance. There are those who urge caution about so-called 'therapeutic education' (Ecclestone, Hayes and Furedi 2005; Gillies 2011) and who express concern about applying such techniques in practice (Mayer and Cobb 2000). However, being an attachment aware teacher does not mean pupils are viewed through a vulnerability lens, but that you are aware and understand pupils' holistic needs. This enables you to 'tune in' more sensitively to foster and empower pupils to achieve their potential. Although research on the AAS programme is relatively limited, strategies adopted can be robustly monitored and evaluated for effectiveness to yield positive outcomes for pupils. Verscheuren and Koonen (2012) suggest that by enhancing pupils' wellbeing at school, via the promotion of close and supportive relationships, teachers may mitigate the risk of negative outcomes for children who may otherwise have difficulty succeeding in school.

In summary, you can be 'attachment aware' by:

- being child-centred and recognising that students may have attachment styles that can adversely affect their learning

- creating nurturing relationships to promote children's learning and behaviour, satisfying the innate need in children and young people to have a secure 'sense of belonging'

- acknowledging your role as a potential 'secondary attachment' figure who can help to reshape insecure attachment behaviours and support the development of more secure ones

- providing appropriate nurturing infrastructures for children with emotional and attachment needs that promote being seen, feeling safe, feeling soothed and feeling secure.

▒ REFLECTION POINTS ▒

Consider the '4 Ss' model of attachment awareness set out in this chapter.

1. What helps you to feel seen, safe, soothed and secure in your own personal and professional life?

2. What aspects of the checklist created by Bradley Stoke Community School do you recognise as familiar practice? Have you noticed any of these activities or processes in any of your school placements?

3. What might you do in your practice to promote the '4 Ss' of attachment?

Bibliography

Allen, G. (2011) *Early Intervention: The Next Steps. An Independent Report to Her Majesty's Government.* London: Cabinet Office. Available at www.dwp.gov.uk/docs/early-intervention-next-steps.pdf, accessed on 2 February 2016.

Anning, A. (2006) *Developing Multi-professional Teamwork for Integrated Children's Services.* Buckingham: Open University Press.

Balbernie, R. (2001) 'Circuits and circumstances: The neurobiological consequences of early relationship experiences and how they shape later behaviour.' *Journal of Child Psychotherapy 27*, 3, 237–255.

Beckes, L. and Coan, J. (2011) 'Social baseline theory: The role of social proximity in emotion and economy of action.' *Social and Personality Psychology Compass 5*, 12, 976–988.

Bergin, C. and Bergin, D. (2009) 'Attachment in the classroom.' *Educational Psychology Review 21*, 141–170.

Bowlby, J. (1969) *Attachment and Loss. Volume 1: Attachment.* London: Hogarth Press and The Institute of Psychoanalysis.

Bowlby, J. (1982) 'Attachment and loss: Retrospect and prospect.' *American Journal of Orthopsychiatry 52*, 4, 664–678.

Brooks, F. (2014) *The Link Between Pupil Health and Wellbeing and Attainment.* Report for Public Health England. London: PHE Publications.

Chowdry, M. and Oppenheim, C. (2015) *Spending on Late Intervention: How We Can Do Better for Less.* London: Early Intervention Foundation Social and Emotional Learning Skills for Life.

Chivers, L. and Trodd, L. (2011) *Interprofessional Working and Practice: Learning and Working Together for Children and Families.* Maidenhead: Open University Press.

Coan, J., Schaefer, H. and Davidson, R. (2006) 'Lending a hand: Social regulation of the neural response to threat.' *Psychological Science 17*, 1032–1039.

Commodari, E. (2013) 'Preschool teacher attachment, school readiness and risk of learning difficulties.' *Early Childhood Research Quarterly 28*, 123–133.

Cooper, P. and Whitebread, D. (2007) 'The effectiveness of nurture groups on student progress: Evidence from a national study.' *Emotional and Behavioural Difficulties 12*, 3, 171–190.

Cozolino, L. (2013) *The Social Neuroscience of Education: Optimizing Attachment and Learning in the Classroom.* London: Norton & Co.

Cozolino, L. (2014) *The Neuroscience of Human Relationships.* New York: Norton & Co.

Cuevas, K., Deater-Deckard, K., Kim-Spoon, J., Watson, A., Morasch, K. and Bell, M. (2014) 'What's mom got to do with it? Contributions of maternal executive function and caregiving to the development of executive function across early childhood.' *Developmental Science 17*, 2, 224–238.

Davis, H. (2003) 'Conceptualizing the role and influence of student–teacher relationships on children's social and cognitive development.' *Educational Psychologist 38*, 207–234.

DfE (Department for Education) (2010) *Literacy and Numeracy Catch-up Strategies.* London: DfE.

DfE (2013) *Increasing Options and Improving Provision for Children with Special Educational Needs (SEN).* London: DfE.

DfE (2014) *Pupil Premium: Funding for Schools and Alternative Provision.* London: DfE.

DH (2011) *No Health Without Mental Health: A Cross-government Mental Health Outcomes Strategy for People of All Ages.* London: DH.

DH (Department of Health) (2015) *Future in Mind. Promoting, Protecting and Improving our Children and Young People's Mental Health and Wellbeing.* London: DH.

Driscoll, K. and Pianta, R.C. (2010) 'Banking time in Head Start: Early efficacy of an intervention designed to promote supportive teacher–child relationships.' *Early Education and Development 21*, 1, 38–27.

Dweck, C. (2008) 'Brainology: Transforming students' motivation to learn.' *Independent School 67*, 2, 110–119.

Dweck, C. (2012) *Mindset: How You Can Fulfil Your Potential.* New York: Constable & Robinson.

Ecclestone, K., Hayes, D. and Furedi, F. (2005) 'Knowing me, knowing you: The rise of therapeutic professionalism in the education of adults.' *Studies in the Education of Adults 37*, 182–200.

Feinstein, L. (2015) *Social and Emotional Learning: Skills for Life and Work.* London: Early Intervention Foundation.

Fullan, M. (2005) *Leadership and Sustainability: Systems Thinkers in Action.* Thousand Oaks, CA: Corwin Press.

Furnivall, J., McKenna, M., McFarlane, S. and Grant, E. (2012) *Attachment Matters for All – An Attachment Mapping Exercise for Children's Services in Scotland.* Glasgow: Centre for Excellence in Looked After Children in Scotland, University of Strathclyde.

Geddes, H. (2006) *Attachment in the Classroom. The Links Between Children's Early Emotional Wellbeing and Performance in School.* London: Worth.

Gillies, V. (2011) 'Social and emotional pedagogies: Critiquing the new orthodoxy of emotion in classroom behaviour management.' *British Journal of Sociology of Education 32*, 185–202.

Goleman, D. (1995) *Emotional Intelligence.* New York: Bantam Books.

Gottman, J., Katz, L. and Hooven, C. (1997) *Meta-emotion: How Families Communicate Emotionally.* New York: Psychology Press.

Gus, L., Rose, J. and Gilbert, L. (2015) 'Emotion Coaching: A universal strategy for supporting and promoting sustainable emotional and behavioural well-being.' *Journal of Educational and Child Psychology* 32, 1, 31–41.

Heller, L. and LaPierre, A. (2012) *Healing Developmental Trauma: How Early Trauma Affects Self-regulation, Self-image, and the Capacity for Relationships.* Berkeley, CA: North Atlantic Books.

Hohnen, B. and Murphy, T. (2016) 'The optimum context for learning: Drawing on neuroscience to inform best practice in the classroom.' *Educational and Child Psychology* 33, 1, 75–90.

Howe, D. (2011) *Attachment Across the Lifecourse: A Brief Introduction.* London: Palgrave.

Howes, C. (1999) 'Attachment relationships in the context of multiple caregivers.' In J. Cassidy and P.R. Shaver (eds) *Handbook of Attachment: Theory, Research and Clinical Applications* (pp.671–687). New York: The Guilford Press.

Immordino-Yang, M.H. (2011) 'Implications of affective and social neuroscience for educational theory.' *Educational Philosophy and Theory 43*, 1, 98–103.

Jennings, P.A. and Greenberg, M.T. (2009) 'The prosocial classroom: Teacher social and emotional competence in relation to student and classroom outcomes.' *Review of Educational Research 79*, 1, 491–525.

Kennedy, B.L. (2008) 'Educating students with insecure attachment histories: Toward an interdisciplinary theoretical framework.' *Pastoral Care in Education 26*, 4, 211–230.

Kennedy, J.H. and Kennedy, C.E. (2004) 'Attachment theory: Implications for school psychology.' *Psychology in the Schools 41*, 2, 247–259.

Kohlrieser, G. (2012) *Care to Dare: Unleashing Astonishing Potential Through Secure Base Leadership.* San Francisco, CA: John Wiley & Sons.

Lendrum, A., Humphrey, N. and Wigelsworth, M. (2013) 'Social and emotional aspects of learning (SEAL) for secondary schools: Implementation difficulties and their implications for school-based mental health promotion.' *Child and Adolescent Mental Health 18*, 3, 158–164.

Marmot, M. (2010) *Fair Society, Healthy Lives (The Marmot Review).* Available at www.instituteofhealthequity.org/projects/fair-society-healthy-lives-the-marmot-review, accessed on 23 March 2011.

Martin, A.J. and Dowson, M. (2009) 'Interpersonal relationships, motivation, engagement, and achievement: Yields for theory, current issues, and educational practice.' *Review of Educational Research 79*, 1, 327–365.

Mayer, J. and Cobb, C. (2000) 'Educational policy on emotional intelligence: Does it make sense?' *Educational Psychology Review 12*, 163–183.

McLaughlin, C. and Clarke, B. (2010) 'Relational matters: A review of the impact of school experience on mental health in early adolescence.' *Educational and Child Psychology 27*, 1, 91–103.

Milkie, M. and Warner, C. (2011) 'Classroom learning environments and the mental health of first grade children.' *Journal of Health and Social Behavior 52*, 1, 4–22.

Murray-Harvey, R. (2010) 'Relationship influences on students' academic achievement, psychological health and wellbeing at school.' *Educational and Child Psychology 27*, 1, 104–113.

Nagel, M. (2009) 'Mind the mind: Understanding the links between stress, emotional wellbeing and learning in educational contexts.' *International Journal of Learning 16*, 2, 33–42.

NICE (National Institute for Health and Care Excellence) (2015) *Children's Attachment: Attachment in Children and Young People Who Are Adopted from Care, in Care or at High Risk of Going into Care.* NICE Guidelines (NG) 26. London: NICE.

Ofsted (2015) *The Common Inspection Framework: Education, Skills and Early Years.* London: Ofsted.

Panksepp, J. (2001) 'The long term psychobiological consequences of infant emotions: Prescriptions for the twenty-first century.' *Infant Mental Health Journal 22*, 1–2, 132–173.

Parker, R., Rose, J. and Gilbert, L. (2016) 'Attachment Aware Schools: An Alternative to the Behaviourist Paradigm.' In H.E. Lees and N. Noddings (eds) *The Palgrave International Handbook of Alternative Education* (pp.463–484). London: Palgrave.

Pianta, R. (1999) *Enhancing Relationships Between Children and Teachers*. Washington, DC: American Psychological Society.

Pianta, R.C. (ed.) (1992) *Beyond the Parent: The Role of Other Adults in Children's Lives*. San Francisco, CA: Jossey-Bass.

Porges, S. (2011) *The Polyvagal Theory*. New York: Norton.

Riley, P. (2009) 'An adult attachment perspective on the student–teacher relationship and classroom management difficulties.' *Teaching and Teacher Education 25*, 626–635.

Roffey, S. (2010) 'Content and context for learning relationships: A cohesive framework for individual and whole school development.' *Educational and Child Psychology 27*, 1, 156–167.

Roorda, D.L., Koomen, H.M., Spilt, J.L. and Oort, F.J. (2011) 'The influence of affective teacher student relationships on students' school engagement and achievement. A meta-analytic approach.' *Review of Educational Research 81*, 4, 493–529.

Rose, J., McGuire-Snieckus, R., and Gilbert, L. (2015) 'Emotion Coaching – A strategy for promoting behavioural self-regulation in children and young people in schools: A pilot study.' *European Journal of Social and Behavioural Sciences 13*, 1766–1790.

Rose, J., Gilbert, L. and Smith, H. (2012) 'Affective Teaching and the Affective Dimensions of Learning.' In S. Ward (ed.) *A Student's Guide to Education Studies* (pp.178–188). London: Routledge.

Rose, J., McGuire-Snieckus, R., Wood, F. and Vatmanides, O. (2016) *Impact Evaluation of the Attachment Aware Schools Project for B&NES and Stoke on Trent Virtual Schools: Phase 1 Pilot Study – Combined Summary Report*. Bath: Institute for Education, Bath Spa University.

Rose, J. and Wood, F. (2016) 'Child Development.' In D. Wyse and S. Rogers. *A Guide to Early Years and Primary Teaching* (pp.85–104). London: Sage.

RSPH (Royal Society for Public Health) (2015) *Minded to Change: The Link Between Mental Wellbeing and Healthier Lifestyles*. London: RSPH. Available at www.rsph.org.uk/resourceLibrary/minded-to-change-the-link-between-mental-wellbeing-and-healthier-lifestyles.html, accessed on 17 March 2017.

Schaffer, R. (2004) *Introducing Child Psychology*. Oxford: Blackwell Publishing.

Schore, J. and Schore, A. (2008) 'Modern attachment theory. The central role of affect regulation in development and treatment.' *Clinical Social Work Journal 36*, 1, 9–20.

Sebba, J., Berridge, D., Luke, N., Fletcher, J., Bell, K., Strand, S. *et al*. (2015) *The Educational Progress of Looked After Children in England: Linking Care and Educational Data*. Oxford: Rees Centre.

Shonkoff, J. and Garner, A. (2012) 'The lifelong effects of early childhood adversity and toxic stress.' *American Academy of Pediatrics 129*, 1, 232–246.

Siegel, D. (2012) *The Developing Mind* (2nd edn). New York: The Guilford Press.

Siegel, D. (2012a) *The Whole Brain Child*. New York: Bantam Books.

Smith, D. (2006) *School Experience and Delinquency at Ages 13 to 16*. Edinburgh: Centre for Law and Society, University of Edinburgh.

Smyth, J. (2007) 'Teacher development against the policy reform grain: An argument for recapturing relationships in teaching and learning.' *Teacher Development 11*, 2, 221–236.

Sroufe, A. and Siegel, D. (2011) 'The Verdict Is In: The case for Attachment Theory.' Available at www.drdansiegel.com/uploads/1271-the-verdict-is-in.pdf, accessed on 26 December 2014.

van der Kolk, B. (2014) *The Body Keeps the Score: Brain, Mind and Body in the Healing of Trauma*. New York: Penguin Books.

Verschueren, K. and Koomen, H.M.Y. (2012) 'Teacher–child relationships from an attachment perspective.' *Attachment and Human Development 14*, 205–211.

Vogel, S. and Schwabe, L. (2016) 'Learning and memory under stress: Implications for the classroom.' *Science of Learning 1*, 1–10.

Vygotsky, L.S. (1978) *Mind in Society*. London: Harvard University Press.

5

Emotion Coaching

LICETTE GUS AND FELICIA WOOD

Emotion Coaching is a central feature of the Attachment Aware Schools (AAS) initiative described in the previous chapter. Here we critically explore Emotion Coaching in greater detail as a practical means of promoting positive teacher–pupil relationships and supporting children with effective emotion regulation strategies.

Emotion Coaching stems from the work of John Gottman, the American psychologist, who used the phrase to describe a parenting style he observed in his research. Gottman, Katz and Hooven (1996) found that parents fell into one of two broad groups: those who gave guidance to their children about the world of emotions, and those who did not. Having warm, positive relationships with children and young people, although clearly vital, did not necessarily mean that parents also taught their children how to deal effectively with negative emotions. This process of parents identifying and empathising with negative emotions, discussing them with the child, setting limits on behaviour if needed, and finding alternatives ways to respond, formed the basis of Gottman *et al.*'s (1996) definition of Emotion Coaching.

Importantly, Gottman *et al.* (1996) found that children who experienced Emotion Coaching were better able to regulate their emotions, control impulses and delay gratification. They could self-soothe when upset, and had better attention and motivation than children who did not experience an Emotion Coaching style of parenting (Gottman and Declaire 1997). Further comparisons between the two groups demonstrate that Emotion Coached children achieved more academically, were more popular, displayed fewer behavioural problems, were healthier and were more emotionally stable and resilient when adverse life events did occur.

Rose, Gilbert and Richards (2015) explored the relevance of Emotion Coaching to the school environment, and suggest that when successfully applied to educational settings, the learning of pupils is improved. They found the use of Emotion Coaching in education and community settings resulted in a decrease of disruptive behaviour and an increase in pro-social behaviour in children and young people. Significantly, the need for the use of the traditional behaviourist approach of rewards and sanctions was reduced and social and emotional competencies were increased. Gus and Kilby (2016) also report improved emotional regulation and accelerated pupil attainment.

This chapter seeks to reiterate the core idea that emotions are key to learning and that emotions can affect the body's central nervous system in significant ways. The importance of relationships as a fundamental support and learning structure for emotional regulation is clearly linked with pupils' potential academic success. But we also contend that recent findings from neuroscience supports the evidence from educational research that a relational approach to behaviour actively creates new connections within the brain, leading to positive behavioural change.

The need for Emotion Coaching in schools

Public Health England (2015) reminds practitioners that in an average class of 30 15-year-old pupils:

- three could have a mental disorder

- ten are likely to have witnessed their parents separate

- one could have experienced the death of a parent

- seven are likely to have been bullied

- six may be self-harming.

Schools have become increasingly accountable for the planning and delivery of social, emotional and mental health (SEMH) input for their entire population (DfE 2015). Current ways of thinking about SEMH promotion suggest that whole-school approaches are effective ways of improving outcomes for pupils and staff (Banerjee, Weare and Farr 2014). However, it is acknowledged that professionals within education should receive training to support these outcomes (Public Health England 2015). We propose Emotion Coaching as a whole-school approach to supporting sustainable emotional health and wellbeing (Rose, McGuire-Snieckus and Gilbert 2015). It is a style of communicating with pupils that is simple, inclusive and sustainable (Gus, Rose and Gilbert 2015).

The benefits to children whose parents used a predominantly Emotion Coaching style when dealing with their emotions were seen socially, academically and in health; in particular, these children were found to regulate their own emotions more successfully (Gottman and Declaire 1997). These findings have been seen in educational settings where Emotion Coaching strategies have been used (Gus and Kilby 2016; Rose, McGuire-Snieckus and Wood 2015, 2016) and the authors would contend that rather than encouraging the self-obsession suggested by Craig (2007), Emotion Coaching supports children and young people to acknowledge their emotions, handle them and empowers them to find solutions to problems rather than obsess about them. Indeed, one hallmark of the evidence base so far is the improved relationship between teachers and their pupils (Rose, McGuire-Snieckus and Wood 2016).

Emotions and behaviour

As Chapter 1 has already contended, emotions are universal, and Ekman (1972) identified six primary emotions that are hardwired into the human brain from birth to ensure survival: fear, joy, sadness, surprise, anger and disgust. These automated emotions cannot be helped and they cannot be erased. They can, of course, be regulated, and the raw expression of emotion in the infant or toddler eventually gives way to a self-awareness and self-management of emotions in the well-regulated child. However, difficulties in regulating strong emotional responses can be problematic for some children in school, especially if they have particular vulnerabilities following neglect, trauma or abuse. Evidence suggests that our ability to regulate emotions effectively develops from birth through a significant attachment relationship that uses co-regulation to help the developing child in managing dysregulation (Schore 2001).

When we are born we need people to help us, or provide us with a scaffold, to enable us to learn to do things. We need this support to survive. For example, a baby needs to eat. Initially we feed babies, and over time, the child takes on more and more of the feeding role until they are eating independently: the baby moves from needing the support of an adult to becoming independent. In the same way, a baby looks to and needs a main carer to support the feelings that arise in them until they are able to manage these feelings themselves. For example, a baby may need an adult's help to soothe them and help them calm the feeling of fear they experience when hearing a sudden loud noise. Without the adult's support, the baby would remain in a state of fear. As the baby matures and understands that the loud noise was a long way away and that they are not in any danger, the child may startle upon hearing the sudden noise but be able to stay calm independently. The child has moved from needing the adult to co-regulate their fear to being able to self-regulate the fear. Where children have not had sufficient access to emotional co-regulation, Emotion Coaching in school may offer a means of 'catching up' with these important social skills (Rose *et al.* 2016).

The emotional world of children and young people is complicated, and naturally they are less practised at regulating potentially overwhelming feelings than adults (Saarni 1999). Traditional behaviour management strategies often focus upon observable behaviours and the use of rewards and sanctions to modify them (Rose *et al.* 2015). However, when we consider the underlying complexity of the emotional world that lies behind behaviour, simple sanctions and rewards may not offer an adequate response. An understanding of what is driving the behaviour therefore becomes an intrinsic part of solving what is actually the visible manifestation of emotion. If behaviour is communication (Watzlawick, Beavin Bavelas and Jackson 1967), then the quest of the Emotion Coach is to decipher the code behind the behaviour in collaboration with the child in question.

To assist with this quest, we can think about an iceberg as a model that displays the relationship between emotion and behaviour. The part that we can see above the water – the behaviour – is only a small part of its overall mass. There is substantial weight below the waterline, namely, the emotion that gives rise to the behaviour. This raises some important questions regarding challenging behaviours we may see in schools. If we only use behaviourist principles and implement rewards and sanctions for visible behaviour, we are ignoring the emotions that lie beneath. If we ignore emotions that lie beneath, are we then communicating to children that their feelings, which cannot be helped, are wrong, inappropriate or invalid?

The neuroscience of emotion

As Chapter 3 of this book has indicated, neuroscience is a field of study that is developing at an incredible rate. If we are to understand emotions and how we are best able to regulate them, knowing how the brain creates the structures that control our emotions and helps them develop is key to creating well-balanced and well-regulated human beings. We know that brains grow through experience and sensory information from the outside world, and that the brain is, therefore, a social organ (Cozolino 2013).

A newborn baby's brain contains approximately 80–100 billion neurons (Howard-Jones 2010). Neurons connect together into neural pathways, like connecting roads, which develop as we learn from the world around us. There are, of course, key connections we are born with, for example, basic motor connections that let babies move, demonstrate reflex actions such as sucking, and, of course, crying, a key survival behaviour (Ward 2010). The remaining connections develop over time and each brain is unique because of individual life and learning experiences. For example, if you practise a musical instrument, your brain will develop synaptic connections that link the different parts of your brain needed to play, and these will include areas responsible for listening, fine motor movement and rhythm. With increased iteration (or repetition) of exercises, the associated neural pathways become stronger and myelinated, creating a fatty white sheath that enables impulses to travel faster and more efficiently between neurons (Ward 2010). This means that after five years of piano practice, you can play much better than your friend who has never learned. Your brain has established highly tuned and well-used synaptic connections that enable you to do so.

The establishment of these pathways depends on their use. Without iteration, connections will grow weaker and may even be pruned away, or be lost altogether. It is important to remember that our brains have a 'plasticity' that involves the ability to both grow and prune synaptic pathways. If we therefore consider that we learn emotional regulation through positive, warm and nurturing relationships (Cozolino 2013), neuroscience now tells us that children who have not experienced this vital connection with an adult will have key deficits in the connectivity of their brains, and may lack the circuitry needed to cope with the social and emotional world around them (Siegel 2011). Emotion Coaching is, therefore, a strategy that helps to build connections in the brain that will promote socio-emotional development and enable the regulation of emotions. This will, in turn, impact on the way that children and young people express their emotions through their behaviour in the classroom (Gottman and Declaire 1997; Havighurst *et al.* 2009; Rose *et al.* 2015).

Emotions and the brain – Siegel's hand model

In this section, aspects of neuroscience that were first introduced in Chapter 3 are now developed in more detail. Siegel's (2011) hand model of the brain involves using the wrist, thumb and fingers to help illustrate the way that the human brain is organised (see Figure 5.1).

In simple terms, the brain can be thought of as a three-layered organ that has developed from the inside out:

- The first and deepest area is the brain stem (or automated brain). In terms of human evolution, this is the earliest part of the brain and is responsible for automatic bodily processes such as breathing, eating and sleeping. In Siegel's (2011) hand model, this is represented by the wrist.

- The second layer is the limbic system (or emotional brain) that contains key areas such as the amygdala (the seat of our fear response system) and hippocampus (important for memory). This is what Siegel calls the 'downstairs' brain, where emotions based on interactions with the environment are processed. It is also the seat of our survival responses of 'fight, flight or freeze'. In the hand model, this area is represented by the thumb that should be tucked in to demonstrate its position deep within the brain.

- The third and final layer is the neocortex (or thinking brain). This represents the 'upstairs brain' in which the executive functions reside. The prefrontal cortex at the front of the brain is specifically linked to controlling impulses, regulating emotion and decision-making as well as working memory and motivation, all of which are key skills for learning in the classroom. In Siegel's model, fingers represent the thinking brain and when folded over, cover the limbic system (or thumb) completely.

The prefrontal areas of the thinking brain have strong and reciprocal connections to limbic regions of the emotional brain (Kaufer 2007), and it would therefore be apposite to conclude that emotions and thinking are very closely related. Sensory information tells us what is going on in the outside world, but it goes to the limbic system faster than the neocortex (LeDoux 2012), so every interaction we have with the external environment has an impact on how we feel before we are able to rationalise it.

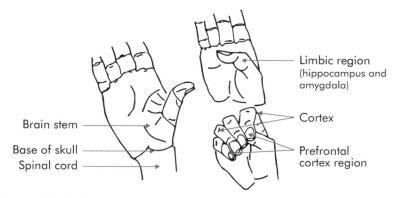

Brain stem

Base of skull
Spinal cord

Limbic region
(hippocampus and amygdala)

Cortex

Prefrontal
cortex region

Figure 5.1: Siegel's hand model of the brain
Source: Siegel (2011), illustrated by Christopher Walker

As part of this learning process, create Siegel's hand model of the brain for yourself. To do this, place your thumb across your palm and close your fingers around it to make a fist. Your fist now represents a model of a calm and regulated brain with the 'downstairs' brain (limbic system and emotions) enclosed by the 'thinking' brain (neocortex).

In this scenario, emotional stimuli can be calmly considered by the thinking brain, and regulation allows a measured response that is 'permitted' by the thinking brain. Rationality is in charge.

If, however, something in the environment triggers a stress response, the decision-making process in the brain can change rapidly. This can be visually represented if you now straighten the four fingers of the hand model. At this point, our limbic system and neocortex have disconnected; emotions are no longer controlled by rational thought, and the person has, in effect, 'flipped their lid'. Our decision-making is suddenly ruled by our emotions, and the thinking part of our brain has little or no input.

This is exactly what is happening when a child has a tantrum, for example, or when a person loses their temper, becomes hysterical with joy or overcome by sadness. Reconnecting and maintaining the thinking and emotional parts of the brain, particularly in times of stress, is the goal of Emotion Coaching.

Vagal tone and the regulation of emotion

Our brains and body have evolved to help us to survive, and two key 'systems' in our brain and body help us to achieve this goal – the stress response system and the social engagement system.

Real and perceived threats trigger the fight, flight or freeze stress response in our nervous system, resulting in various bodily responses such as pupil dilation, increased heart rate, activation of sweat glands, faster breathing and appetite suppression. The stress hormone floods the body and prepares it for immediate action in response to a threat. In times of stress and when survival is at stake, the responses that have helped us to survive as a species for millions of years take over instantly. When the 'lid has flipped' and the thinking brain is disconnected, it is emotions that take control.

Conversely, the social engagement system is part of the nervous system that has evolved to balance the stress response system (Porges 2011). This system primarily depends upon the largest nerve in the body, the vagus nerve, first introduced in Chapter 3. Together with the adjoining nerves, the vagus nerve activates the muscles of the face, throat, middle ear and voice box (Porges 2011). Human contact can activate the vagus nerve that enables the stress response system to calm and for bodily stress responses to return to their normal level of function. Use of the social engagement system is promoted through attuned relationships with others, and helps explain why people experiencing dysregulated emotional states benefit from having calm and regulated people around them.

The vagus nerve is like the paramedic who comes to our rescue when we have 'flipped our lid'. It is the longest cranial nerve and contains motor and sensory fibres. The vagus nerve passes through the neck and thorax to the abdomen, and has the widest distribution in the body, helping to send messages to our brain and body to calm it down. Vagal tone refers to how well our survival responses (fight, flight and freeze) and the vagus nerve are working together. To have good vagal tone is to be able to assess and respond to threats, and then to be able to return the body and brain back to a normal functioning state soon after the event. Effective vagal tone is linked to better emotional balance, clearer thinking, improved attention, a more efficient immune system and greater resilience (Gottman *et al.* 1996).

Children who have poor vagal tone are less able to regulate the body's response from the state of stress back to a normal resting state (Gottman *et al.* 1996). Think about the different responses and recovery rates for pupils in your class to unexpected events such as fire alarms, supply teachers or any changes to routines. Some pupils will remain excited and overtly dysregulated far longer than others, and this could be due to the difficulty they find in activating their vagus nerve that returns the body and brain back to normal functioning.

Emotion Coaching is one of the key strategies through which we can help children and young people to regulate themselves and their responses in the classroom (Gottman *et al.* 1996; Rose *et al.* 2015). Emotion Coaching helps to trigger the vagus nerve via the social engagement system and to put the 'lid' back on (Gottman and Declaire 1997). Furthermore, Emotion Coaching encourages the development of empathy for others, which, in turn, encourages the development of more socially and academically appropriate behaviours within schools.

How, then, do we help our pupils achieve emotional self-regulation and good vagal tone?

Emotion Coaching in the classroom

For young children, vagal tone is initially activated and developed via access to safe and secure relationships, nurturing environments and secure enough attachments. Usually these are provided by the child's main carers whose contingent responses attune to their child's distress and respond to their needs. By showing empathy and offering physical and psychological attunement through co-regulation, the child's stress response system is soothed physiologically, and psychologically they return to a calmer state. This helps children to 'practise' vagal tone from infancy until they are able to self-regulate.

As children grow older, and through frequent opportunities to learn through co-regulation and repetition, children begin to self-soothe and self-regulate. Positive nurturing experiences help children to develop a vagal system that helps to restore the calm after a storm and to re-engage the thinking brain (or neocortex) to the limbic system after 'flipping the lid'.

Emotion Coaching is an 'in the moment' relational approach to behaviour that teaches pupils about the world of emotions and encourages the development of self regulation. It can be considered to be a long-term, ongoing intervention capable of being implemented immediately by all adults who come into contact with pupils. It is a natural form of communication requiring no timetabling, manual or special equipment. You might Emotion Coach in the classroom, in the corridor or out in the playground – whenever you notice low-level indicators of a difficult emotion being felt by the pupil. The more often a pupil is supported to regulate their feelings, the more likely they will be able to do this for themselves.

It is helpful to think of Emotion Coaching as consisting of four steps:

1. becoming aware of and empathising with the emotion

2. labelling and validating the emotion

3. limit setting

4. problem-solving.

1. Becoming aware of and empathising with the emotion

Often we ignore low-level signs of emotion and only deal with the behaviour emanating from very strong emotions – when a pupil has 'flipped their lid'. Instead, Emotion Coaching requires practitioners to look for and notice physical and verbal signs of the emotions being felt by the pupil. When emotions are being felt, the body often responds. You may notice changes in the child's facial expression, posture, level of moment (fidgeting, squirming), colouring (flushing) or tone of voice. Try and think of what might be the reason for this behaviour. What is the outward behaviour communicating?

Once you are aware of a possible feeling the pupil may be experiencing, empathise with the child and demonstrate that you see things from their point of view. Check you're not being judgemental ('There's no need to be angry about such a trivial thing!') and rather, recognise that emotions are not a matter of choice or logic ('I can see that what happened has made you really cross and that's understandable'). You do not need to condone the pupil's behaviour, but you do need to empathise with the feelings that gave rise to it.

2. Labelling and validating the emotion

Letting the pupil know that you understand their emotional situation and that you don't blame them for feeling that way is very important. This helps soothe their emotional brain. An example of this could be as simple as: 'I can see you're getting frustrated by the amount of writing that needs to be done, it's hard to stick with things we don't enjoy very much.' Remember, none of us can help the way we feel – there is nothing wrong with feeling emotions. It is how we display them that is often the issue!

Often we feel empathy for our pupils but don't acknowledge it or label it – we try to make the emotion go away through our words and interactions. A common concern adults have with labelling emotions is that somehow this will make the emotions worse. However, labelling emotions has been shown to alter brain activation and allow the prefrontal cortex to dampen the emotions triggered by the amygdala within the limbic system (Lieberman *et al.* 2007). In other words, labelling emotions helps re-engage the prefrontal cortex.

In addition, labelling and validating the emotion helps pupils to feel safe by developing a trusting relationship between them and their teacher. Through this trusting relationship pupils accept and internalise the language used with them about their emotions. The social engagement system is activated.

3. Limit setting

Limit setting involves discussion about what the rules or norms are regarding appropriate behaviour. There are occasions when strong emotions do not result in poor behaviour, and in these situations, limit setting may not be relevant. However, for those occasions where emotions have caused challenging responses, this third stage is important. It can only begin once the individual is calm and the thinking and emotional brains are reconnected. Clear communication about the expected boundaries of behaviour is then important, for example: 'You're angry that I've taken the phone away from you, but you can't use your phone in class. These are the rules everyone has to follow. I will keep it safe for you.'

4. Problem-solving

Help your pupil to think about what they will do the next time they feel like this. The emphasis should be put on pupils offering their own solution, where feasible. It is really tempting to jump in and offer alternatives, but it is important that pupils try to learn to find solutions for themselves or work with you to find alternative ways of behaving. This is the point at which pupils are learning that they can be empowered: they can find alternatives to challenging behaviours, even when they feel strong emotions. For example: 'Next time you feel really cross, what do you think you could to that might help? It might be useful to let a teacher know. How could you do that?'

In the case study below, a teacher in a special school for pupils with complex learning difficulties (Charlotte Read, Science Coordinator, Equality Advocate and Emotion Coaching Lead) describes how paying attention to the pupil's emotions, far from acting as 'fuel to the fire', helped the pupil to regulate the feeling much more quickly.

Case study: Emotion Coaching

Violet is 15 years old with significant developmental delay. She often complains of something or other, and is thought by staff to be attention seeking. I had just finished dealing with a very difficult situation with another pupil and needed to get on to my next lesson. Violet was waiting for me with tears slowly rolling down her face. My instinct was to dismiss Violet's tears, and to tell her to get on with it; she would soon feel better.

However, I said, 'I can see you feel really sad; you really look unhappy; do you know what these tears are for?' and I gave her a school-approved 'good greeting' (a sideways hug). Violet told me she was crying because she didn't want to go to boarding that night. I validated her feelings by saying that, 'It's okay to feel sad, and I bet you just wish you could make this Monday disappear.'

I then told her that I had felt like that this morning when I woke up after lots of bad dreams.

I agreed that it was okay to feel like she felt – that she didn't want to go to boarding, I understood that. Her tears stopped.

I suggested Violet went to her first lesson, as we were at school and at school you have to go to your lesson (rule reminders) and we would talk at break. She agreed that this was a good suggestion, picked up her bag and went.

I feel this was a really positive way of handling Violet's feelings and behaviour. It took no longer, perhaps less time than other alternatives, and we were both left feeling happier about ourselves – Violet felt understood, felt that her feelings were okay and was better able to cope. For me, I felt like a better teacher.

Given that Emotion Coaching aims to help children to understand the different emotions they experience, why they occur and how to handle them, adults should be aware of their own emotions. This idea is called meta-emotion philosophy (Gottman and Declaire 1997; Rose *et al.* 2015) and has been shown to be key in the initial stage of the Emotion Coaching process. Children learn about emotions by watching adults, so managing our own emotions is vital for pupils as their brains mirror the adults they interact with. A person's meta-emotion philosophy is the beliefs they hold about emotions and their expression. Each person's meta-emotion philosophy is different and is formed as a result of their early personal or family/community experiences. Please undertake the task at the end of this chapter because reflecting on your own meta-emotion philosophy can give you insights into your own emotional repertoire and this will, in turn, prepare you for Emotion Coaching in the classroom.

Final thoughts

When reflecting on the changes made to their practice following Emotion Coaching training, school staff often highlight that while only a small tweak was needed in their practice, the difference it made to the children and their relationships with them was significant and surprising. Gottman and Declaire (1997) note that Emotion Coaching is not needed on every occasion for it to have an effect. In fact, there are situations when Emotion Coaching is not appropriate, for example, when you have an audience, if you are too tired for coaching to be productive or if you need to address serious or dangerous misbehaviour.

Some people are natural Emotion Coaches and have developed an awareness of the benefits of consciously using the strategy more often. Others (like us) are not. Some school staff comment that talking about emotions in this way with children is almost 'frightening', and the language in the different steps can feel quite robotic and unnatural. However, having the four steps, as set out above, does give structure to the process and helps those who do not often use Emotion Coaching in their usual interactions with others. People have found that over time they become used to new ways of speaking and have become comfortable discussing emotions openly.

To help you start Emotion Coaching, select one pupil and start a diary. Divide the page into four columns, as set out below, and record a few examples that relate to the pupil.

Behaviour	What you (or others) do or say	Pupil's response	Reflect – what emotion do you think gave rise to the behaviour you observed?

You may want to share these observations and interpretations with a trusted colleague. Once you feel you have an idea of the emotion underlying what you see, try labelling the emotion with the pupil, letting the pupil know (through words, actions and tone of voice) that you empathise with how they are feeling. Then set limits (if needed) and help the pupil to problem-solve the situation for the future.

Emotion Coaching is a mechanism that will allow you to develop trusting teacher–pupil relationships and support the development of emotion regulation in your pupils. It will also support you in being the teacher you want to be.

▨ REFLECTION POINTS ▨

Awareness of your own emotions will help you appreciate your pupil's emotional experiences. 'Being aware' means that you recognise when you are feeling an emotion, you can identify your feelings and you are sensitive to the presence of emotions in other people. Think back over yesterday. Name an emotion you experienced (if you're having trouble doing this, use photos in a magazine/online as a prompt to find one that might represent how you felt).

1. What was the feeling?
2. What made you feel that way?
3. How did you know you were feeling that?
4. What thoughts went through your head?

Becoming a teacher who is able to support the emotional development of pupils begins with self-examination. Think about some of the messages you received from your parents, siblings, extended family, friends and community about emotions and their expression. Write down some of the messages you received about emotions as you grew up. How might your meta-emotion philosophy about these emotions influence your response to your pupil's emotions? Awareness of your personal responses to emotional situations will help you pause before responding to a child's emotional state and behaviour.

Consider sadness and anger: Is anger wrong? Is sadness something one has to get over and ride out? Does anger deserve a time-out? Is sadness a way of getting attention?

For further help with reflection on your meta-emotion philosophy, an adaptation of John Gottman's questionnaire about assessing your responses to emotions (anger and sadness) can be found at www.emotioncoachinguk.com

Bibliography

Banerjee, R., Weare, K. and Farr, W. (2014) 'Working with "Social and Emotional Aspects of Learning" (SEAL): Association and school ethos, pupils' social experiences, attendance and attainment.' *British Educational Research Journal 40*, 718–742.

Clarke, A.M., Morreale, S., Field, C.A., Hussein, Y. and Barry, M.M. (2015) *What Works in Enhancing Social and Emotional Skills Development During Childhood and Adolescence? A Review of the Evidence on the Effectiveness of School-based and Out-of-School Programmes in the UK.* A report produced by the World Health Organization Collaborating Centre for Health Promotion Research, National University of Ireland, Galway.

Cozolino, L. (2013) *The Social Neuroscience of Education.* New York: W.W. Norton & Co.

Craig, C. (2007) *The Potential Dangers of a Systematic, Explicit Approach to Teaching Social and Emotional Skills (SEAL).* Glasgow: Centre for Confidence and Wellbeing.

DfE (Department for Education) (2015) *Counselling in Schools: A Blueprint for the Future. Departmental Advice for School Leaders and Counsellors.* Available at www.gov.uk/government/ uploads/system/uploads/attachment_data/file/497825/Counselling_in_schools.pdf, accessed on 8 September 2016.

DfES (Department for Education and Skills) (2005) *The National Strategies Early Years Excellence and Enjoyment: Social and Emotional Aspects of Learning.* London.

Ecclestone, K. and Hayes, D. (2008) *The Dangerous Rise of Therapeutic Education.* London: Routledge.

Ekman, P. (1972) 'Universals and Cultural Differences in Facial Expressions of Emotions.' In J. Cole (ed.) *Nebraska Symposium of Motivation* (pp.207–282). Lincoln, NB: University of Nebraska Press.

Gardner, H. (1993) *Frames of Mind: The Theory of Multiple Intelligences.* New York: Basic Books.

Goleman, D. (1996) *Emotional Intelligence.* London: Bloomsbury.

Gottman, J. and Declaire, J. (1997) *Raising an Emotionally Intelligent Child. The Heart of Parenting.* New York: Simon & Schuster.

Gottman, J.M., Katz, L.F. and Hooven, C. (1996) 'Parental meta-emotion philosophy and the emotional life of families: Theoretical models and preliminary data.' *Journal of Family Psychology 10,* 3, 243–268.

Greenberg, M.T. (2010) 'School-based prevention: Current status and future challenges.' *Effective Education 2,* 1, 27–52.

Gus, L. and Kilby, R. (2016) 'The emotion coaching approach.' *SPECIAL,* May, 35–36.

Gus, L., Rose, J. and Gilbert, L. (2015) 'Emotion Coaching: A universal strategy for supporting and promoting sustainable emotional and behavioural well-being.' *Educational & Child Psychology 32,* 1, 31.

Gutman, L.M. and Schoon, I. (2013) *The Impact of Non-cognitive Skills on Outcomes for Young People.* Education Endowment Foundation. Available at https://educationendowmentfoundation. org.uk/public/files/Publications/EEF_Lit_Review_Non-CognitiveSkills.pdf, accessed on 9 September 2016.

Havighurst, S.S., Wilson, K.R., Harley, A.E. and Prior, M.R. (2009) 'Tuning in to kids: An emotion-focused parenting program – Initial findings from a community trial.' *Journal of Community Psychology 37,* 8, 1008–1023.

Hawkey, K. (2006) 'Emotional Intelligence and mentoring in pre-service teacher education: A literature review.' *Mentoring and Tutoring: Partnership in Learning 12,* 2, 137–147.

Howard-Jones, P. (2010) *Introducing Neuroeducational Research.* Abingdon: Routledge.

Kaufer, D.I. (2007) 'The Dorsolateral and Cingulate Cortex.' In B.L. Miller and J.L. Cummings (eds) *The Human Frontal Lobes* (pp.44–58). New York: The Guilford Press.

LeDoux, J. (2012) 'Rethinking the emotional brain.' *Neuron 73,* 4, 653–676.

Lieberman, M.D., Eisenberger, N.I., Crockett, M.J., Tom, S.M., Pfeifer, J.H. and Way, B.M. (2007) 'Putting feelings into words affect labeling disrupts amygdala activity in response to affective stimuli.' *Psychological Science 18,* 5, 421–428.

Porges, S. (2011) *The Polyvagal Theory. Neurophysiological Foundations of Emotions, Attachment, Communication and Self-Regulation.* New York: W.W. Norton & Company.

Public Health England (2015) *Promoting Children and Young People's Emotional Health and Wellbeing: A Whole School and College Approach.*

Rose, J., Gilbert, L. and Richards, V. (2016) *Health and Well-being in Early Childhood.* London: Sage Publications. (Includes a stand-alone chapter on Emotion Coaching.)

Rose, J., McGuire-Snieckus, R. and Gilbert, L. (2015) 'Emotion Coaching – A strategy for promoting behavioural self-regulation in children/young people in schools: A pilot study.' *European Journal of Social and Behavioural Sciences 13,* 1766–1790.

Rose, J., McGuire-Snieckus, R. and Wood, F. (2016) *Impact Evaluation of the Attachment Aware Schools Project for Stoke and B&NES Virtual Schools: A Pilot Study.* Bath: Institute for Education, Bath Spa University.

Saarni, C. (1999) *The Development of Emotional Competence.* New York: The Guilford Press.

Salovey, P. and Mayer, J.D. (1990) 'Emotional Intelligence.' *Imagination, Cognition and Personality 9.*

Schore, A. (2001) 'Effects of a secure attachment relationship on right brain development, affect regulation and infant mental health.' *Infant Mental Health Journal 22,* 102, 201–269.

Siegel, D.J. (2011) *Mindsight: The New Science of Personal Transformation.* New York: Bantam Books.

Siegel, D.J. and Bryon, T.P. (2011) *The Whole-Brain Child.* London: Constable & Robinson Ltd.

Ward, J. (2010) *The Student's Guide to Cognitive Neuroscience* (2nd edn). New York: Psychology Press.

Watzlawick, P., Beavin Bavelas, J. and Jackson, D.D. (1967) *Pragmatics of Communication: Studies of Interactional Patterns, Pathologies and Paradoxes.* New York: W.W. Norton & Co. Inc.

6

Promoting Resilience in Schools

The Importance of Both Training and Reflection for Teachers and School Staff

MIKE SOLOMON

The word 'education' comes from the Latin 'educere', meaning 'to lead out'. Teachers, on behalf of society, have the role of 'leading out' learners, helping them to develop not just learning skills and knowledge, but also crucial social skills and relationship-building skills that will be a key part of later life. In this sense, the task of education can be thought of in terms of socialising the next generation. Each new year group represents a cohort of children and young people who are growing up in society under the guidance of parents, carers and schools, while becoming progressively more equipped for the journey into adulthood.

Promoting the resilience of children and young people is a key part of this role that teachers and schools have. Schools themselves can be emotionally intense environments, and by learning and developing resilience in school settings, learners can experience progress in their own development and build experiences and skills for their future adult life.

This chapter outlines the concepts of resilience and mentalising, and shows how they both contribute to improved mental health (Allen, Fonagy and Bateman 2008; Bak 2012; Bateman and Fonagy 2012; Midgley and Vrouva 2012; Moffit *et al.* 2011; Stein 2006). 'Mental health is defined as a state of well-being in which every individual realises his or her potential, can cope with the normal stressors of life, can work productively and fruitfully, and is able to make a contribution to her or his community' (WHO 2014). This chapter outlines the concept of resilience (Bak 2012), the ability to cope with the stresses of life that is included in this World Health Organization (WHO) definition of good mental health. The chapter also introduces the idea of mentalising (Bateman and Fonagy 2012), which is a key component of building resilience (Stein 2006), as it encapsulates how we relate to one another (Allen *et al.* 2008; Midgley and Vrouva 2012; Moffitt *et al.* 2011).

The chapter then outlines a specific training programme that is a brief systemic approach based on empirical understanding and knowledge from research. The training programme builds the capacity of teachers and staff teams in schools to promote the resilience of learners, while also having useful applications for the teachers themselves and the whole school community. Some practical examples are included that can be easily incorporated into the classroom and into school life generally.

In addition, another approach is outlined, one that highlights the importance of developing observational skills for teachers while recognising that the behaviour of children always communicates aspects of their emotional state. This second approach emphasises the importance of times for school staff to share their experiences, observations and thinking, in order to facilitate emotionally informed thinking in the daily life of schools.

Resilience

We can think of resilience in terms of being able to cope with the challenges that life presents, especially when life is hard. Components of resilience include: feeling good enough about ourselves; having the ability to 'bounce back' from setbacks; having good relationships both with the self and with others; and being on track and having the ability to focus.

Resilience is something in our minds, and something that takes place and develops between people. It has been defined as successful adaptation to adversity, including successful recovery from adverse life events, and sustainability in relation to life challenges, individually and on group and community levels (Zautra, Hall and Murray 2010).

We can further think about resilience in relation to four key aspects: *people* – relationships with other people; *tasks* – things I must do, my attitude to tasks; *temptations* – what is good and not good for us; and *suffering* – we will suffer, life involves suffering (illness, sickness, chronic disease, loss and losses of people, and relationships), so how can I carry on, do what I need to do? All of these aspects of resilience are relevant to school life, to children and young people in schools, the adults who work with them, and to whole school communities.

Resilience is useful in many situations. It makes it easier to be open to experience something exciting, to learn something new, to make good decisions, and it prevents stress and conflicts. This makes it essential in school settings, where the task of learning can only be achieved if learners have sufficient resilience to manage the inherent challenges involved. This has crucial implications for schools and the adults who foster the development of resilience in children and young people.

So how can teachers and adults in schools help to promote the mental health and resilience of children and young people? How can teachers help children to grow up to become more resilient adults?

Most children and young people spend a substantial proportion of their time in schools. So while mental health professionals and clinicians continue to meet with children, young people and families in clinical settings, there is also a growing body of practice and evidence for providing a range of clinically informed interventions in schools.

Some models are along the lines of 'the clinic goes to school', providing direct clinical work in school settings. Direct work with children and families can be appropriate and very helpful at times, and there is much evidence and literature that indicates this effectiveness (DCSF 2008; Dowling and Osborne 1994).

However, there are also other ways of supporting schools to be places that foster resilience and improved mental health, and such approaches can be characterised in two ways. In the first, teachers can be supported to promote the resilience and mental health of children and young people through being trained to teach specific skills to the learners (e.g. 'mentalising', breathing techniques, attention 'muscles' or brain awareness sessions). This approach is delivered through didactic training for teachers and school staff, based on empirical knowledge and skills-based practice. The training intervention can be very brief and is therefore time- and cost-effective.

The second approach has a focus on building resilience in the community as a whole through opportunities for sharing staff observations, reflections and thinking about particular children, families and situations in school. Teachers can be supported to reflect upon their own capacities to understand mental states (their own and that of colleagues and students). They can be supported to meet together, often with an external professional, to combine theoretical and empirical knowledge with reflections on their observations and personal and emotional experience in schools. Providing staff with these kinds of opportunities can promote the resilience and emotional wellbeing of the community as a whole.

Approach 1: Training teachers to teach learners the skills of resilience

Resilience is something that can be taught, learned and developed (Bak 2012). There is a growing body of international evidence showing the effectiveness of resilience training (Bak *et al.* 2015; Valle *et al.* 2016).

According to Bandura's social learning theory (Bandura 1977), our behaviour is determined by our expectations of our own self-efficacy, and our expectations of the outcome/s of our behaviour. That is to say, our belief about whether we can succeed in a task will often determine whether we do succeed – and this applies to all people of all ages. This self-efficacy is determined by our personal experience and our personally relevant knowledge, namely, our own thoughts and our own attachment figures.

While children arrive at school with personal experiences that have already shaped their developing sense of self-efficacy, school-based interventions can be highly effective in influencing and shaping their thoughts and feelings about themselves. Schools, teachers and support staff can have a profound influence on how children and young people develop their 'personal relevant knowledge' that then influences their sense of self-efficacy. While personal experience, attachment figures and early experiences of attachment relationships are outside our control, nevertheless the learners' personally relevant knowledge and their own thoughts and feelings can be influenced, and the skills associated with resilience can be taught. Schools are a key site for such interventions that include the concept of 'mentalising'.

Mentalising, attachment and schools

The concept of mentalising can be extremely useful for putting into practice ways of promoting resilience and mental health. Mentalising can be thought of as the skill and ability to understand mental states, one's own and those of others. An increased capacity to mentalise helps children (and adults) to develop several strategies to respond to the difficulties in life, thus increasing their resilience (Stein 2006).

We can describe mentalising in terms of 'thinking about thinking'. To what extent can I reflect on my own thoughts, 'mind-read' myself and see myself as if from the outside? Can I see myself as others see me? To what extent can I adjust the direction of my thinking? To what extent can I be curious about what might be going on in someone else's mind? To what extent can I hold another's mind in my mind? Can I understand others' mental states? Can I identify emotions and where they come from?

Whenever any of us have felt understood by another person, we have had the experience of mentalising, and have benefited from the other person having this capacity. Our own capacity to mentalise becomes even more important when being with someone who can't mentalise. For example, parents mentalise with their newborn babies, trying to understand what might be going on, and hopefully finding ways to ease distress and interact more happily as a result. A parent may wonder aloud if a baby is crying because the baby is hungry, tired, needs changing etc. Another example is the process of an adult helping an adolescent who is worried about their exams, trying to name and articulate their worries, and helping them to feel understood as a result. For learners in schools to have the chance to experience being thought about, and to have structures in which they can experience seeing, hearing and understanding multiple perspectives, can be extremely important in developing their capacity to mentalise, which helps to build their resilience.

The developmental model suggested by Allen *et al.* (2008) argues that the mentalisation process is rooted in the attachment relationship established with the first caregiver in infancy and early childhood. However, teachers and adults in schools can and do play a crucial role in helping children and young people to develop their capacity to mentalise, whatever their starting point. By promoting young people's capacity to mentalise, teachers and all professionals in education can help learners to develop understanding of their own mental states and those of others around them, and how these link to behaviour. This can foster understanding of what they and others do, inside and outside the classroom, what happens in relationships and in the world around them. Crucially, Mary Main has emphasised that attachment states of mind should not be viewed as fixed and unalterable: 'these... categorical placements...must be understood to reference only current, and potentially changeable, states of mind with respect to attachment' (Main 2000, p.1094).

By applying ideas from attachment theory, we can see not only how parents can mentalise with their newborn babies, and with young children (and, of course, with adolescent and grown-up children!), but also how teachers, as potential attachment figures in schools, can mentalise with pupils and students in the classroom and beyond. Teachers and education professionals have key roles in developing young people's capacity to mentalise. 'It is likely that a teacher who has an increased understanding of mental functioning, and who can talk about it in the classroom, is able to help children to increase their mentalizing skills' (Valle *et al.* 2016, p.9). For example, a child who behaves aggressively or violently in school may be feeling anxious about the unpredictability or uncertainty inherently involved in a learning task or a social situation, and may therefore be helped by a teacher who tries to help them to feel understood (Solomon 2009).

This supports the role of teachers in supporting children and young people to become more securely attached as a result of their experiences of relationships with adults in schools. Specifically, children can be supported to become more 'earned-secure' in adult life. Adults with an 'earned-secure' attachment style are described as having an insecure attachment style in infancy that develops into a secure attachment pattern later (Main 1995). The primary characteristics of 'earned-secure attachment' are metacognitional and integrative thinking. This includes the capacity to elaborate a theory of the other's mind, the ability to reflect on one's mental states, and the establishment of a sense of mastery and personal efficacy. These are all elements of the capacity to mentalise. Research evidence indicates that adults with 'earned-secure attachments' have had experience of emotionally supportive relationships with alternative support figures. These alternative support figures are reported to have been able to listen, comfort and reassure children, particularly at times of distress (Saunders *et al.* 2011).

Ideas from attachment theory, developed by John Bowlby at the Tavistock Clinic (Bowlby 1969, 1973, 1980), provide teachers with ways of understanding the early experiences of the pupils and learners in their classrooms. Crucially, teachers and school staff can also use their own experience to understand patterns of attachment relationships. Relationships happen between people, and by using personal emotional experiences of their relationships with their pupils, teachers can better understand the 'model in the mind' that learners have about relationships.

The development of mentalisation-based approaches is a growing area in mental health promotion and research, as well as clinical practice (Midgley and Vrouva 2012). They are also applied widely in schools and education settings (Solomon and Thomas 2013). There are many examples in education where daily practices promote mentalising, including class agreements, circle time activities, restorative approaches (Hopkins 2004), assemblies, parent/carer meetings and other regular times in the routine school schedule. These provide structures in which students – and staff – can hear the perspectives of others. People can be helped to see that there are multiple perspectives on situations and on people, themselves and others, and so can be helped to develop their capacity to mentalise.

Incorporating mentalisation techniques into your classroom: practical examples

By using a range of techniques, teachers can incorporate resilience building into everyday classroom practice. This can include simple exercises, stories and lessons as well as simple displays for classrooms and corridors.

The 'Thoughts in Mind Project' or 'Resilience Programme' (Bak 2012) addresses mentalising, resilience and self-control concepts using simple language, metaphors and pictures available on a dedicated website (see http://myresilience.org, adapted for the UK at https://tavistockandportman.nhs.uk/training/cpd-courses/robust-ed-promoting-resilience-young-people-staff-and-communities).

Self-control is strongly linked to resilience and good mental health, and evidence suggests that assisting children to have self-control as a central element of building resilience has been shown to be a significant predictor of health, wealth and public safety in adulthood (Moffitt *et al.* 2011).

Using the Tavistock Robust-Ed resources, school staff teams can be trained in relatively brief training sessions, quickly becoming competent and able to make use of a range of resources. One key element of the training is the picture of the brain in two 'modes' that can be easily explained to most school-aged children (see Figure 6.1).

Figure 6.1: The Thinking Brain and the 999 Alarm Brain

The Thinking Brain and the 999 Alarm Brain

As Chapter 3 has explained, in the frontal part of our brain (or neocortex), thoughts and feelings for other people are created. This part of the brain holds helpful resources (problem-solving skills, decision-making, self-regulation, planning and other helpful experiences). In the centre of our brain is the brain's alarm centre (or limbic system), which checks on dangerous and uncomfortable situations. Insecurity and guilt activate the alarm centre. This turns down the thinking brain. Then it becomes difficult to think and to learn. Fear, anger and sadness can take over, and the body may become sick.

Teachers can use the 'thinking brain' and 'alarm brain' models as a classroom tool to develop mentalising, in terms of situations when the alarm brain takes over, for example. The sessions with children and young people can then introduce useful strategies for helping the thinking brain to recover. This helps children to identify when they or classmates may be in 'alarm brain' thinking mode, and when they are using their 'thinking brain'.

Breathing

The most important strategy for recovering from 'alarm brain thinking' is quick, free, almost invisible, has no side effects and needs no equipment. All mammals sigh. Many cultures have different practices that involve the act of breathing deeply. Examples include yoga and meditation, and more recently, mindfulness. It can be the most basic tool at our disposal, yet it is important not to underestimate its value. Breathing is connected to the heart, and to the brain. Deep and calm breathing slows the heart, so that the thinking brain can start again.

However, like most things, this requires practice if we want it to work. The more practice and repetition we can have, the more valuable and useful this can become. Teachers can help with arranging even very brief times for regular breathing exercises in the classroom. Even encouraging people to take just three deep breaths can help to slow things down, and can help the thinking brain to begin to recover.

Developing an 'attention muscle'

We can all think about an 'attention muscle' in our brain that focuses attention on different thoughts coming from different areas. A bit like going to the gym to train other muscles, our 'attention muscle' needs training, usually through practice and repetition. We can train and control our 'I', meaning that we can, over time, become more able to adjust the direction of our attention and develop the capacity to choose some thoughts over others.

For example, teachers can physically point to different parts of the brain or head, to demonstrate where the learner is currently focusing their thoughts, and can indicate where to redirect their thoughts if that would be more helpful. Someone in 'alarm brain thinking' is likely to be attending to thoughts at the back of their head, while choosing to focus more on the thinking of the thinking brain would involve moving attention to the front part of their brain or head.

Thought bubbles

It is possible to conceptualise thinking in terms of just two kinds of thoughts. We can have either helpful or destructive thoughts. Teachers can draw out large, blank thought bubbles, and print them in different colours, to highlight the difference. In any kind of conversation, the thought bubbles can be pointed to, or held up, to indicate which kind of thought is being articulated at any given time. Thought bubbles can be particularly useful in whole group discussions to facilitate class groups generating ideas about thoughts that are more helpful in a given situation (often it is the destructive thoughts that are generated more 'automatically').

Stories and metaphors

Stories can be a powerful way to illustrate the idea of choosing to focus thoughts in different directions. The story of the House of Thoughts (see http://myresilience.org) is one such example, in which different thoughts live in different rooms in a house. The listener is invited to explore different rooms, to discover different thoughts along the way, rather than be stuck in the same room with the same (often destructive) thoughts. Questions can then be explored further, such as how I move from one room to another, how I can focus my attention on more helpful thoughts. Project work in schools has included children drawing or making models of their houses, and teachers using particular culturally relevant examples (e.g. from television or film) to provide further illustrations.

Such stories provide ways for teachers to help to develop the capacity to mentalise in whole classes of learners, to help them to become more curious about their own thinking, and about the thinking process in general. Experience also shows that teaching professionals can be encouraged to use these tools for themselves, and to develop their own capacity to reflect on their thinking, both individually and particularly in staff teams as a whole.

Applications to whole-school settings

The concepts of resilience and mentalising can be extended and applied to whole-school settings and communities. Evidence is beginning to emerge that supports the idea that 'the creation of a mentalizing community promotes the mentalization abilities of its members' (Valle *et al.* 2016, p.1).

For good mental health, it is vital to be accepted by others. We might say that the core of being a human being is to be valued by others. In a community like a school, bullies and those who are bullied are in the same boat of insecurity. Both can be thought of as being in a state of 'fight/flight' survival modes. So it is likely to be important to include resilience-building elements into a school's anti-bullying policy and practice. For example, providing education through sharing the mechanisms of bullying is likely to be very helpful. People are often willing to pay a high price to be accepted, including behaviour that can be damaging to themselves and to others. Sharing such understanding with whole communities can help to build a shared understanding and ways of talking together, building resilience across a community. Furthermore, focusing on the use of language itself can be very helpful, emphasising the value of using ordinary, decent language with each other, something that is likely to need practice and time in a community. Celebrating diversity actively also helps to foster community-wide resilience.

Importantly, there is growing evidence that training school staff in these and related strategies is effective in promoting resilience (Bak *et al.* 2015). While the primary focus of training is for professionals working with children, young people and families, with schools being a key element of this, such training inevitably also prompts teachers, individually and collectively, to consider what affects their own resilience and capacity to mentalise. In our experience from training school staff, many staff teams enjoy adopting new techniques and practices, and applying new resources to themselves.

Approach 2: Building resilient communities through reflection-based thinking for school staff

A second approach to promoting resilience in school communities focuses on the importance of teachers and school staff having ongoing, regular time and space to reflect on their experiences.

The processes of teaching and learning involve complex human interactions and intense psychological experiences, for pupils and staff alike (e.g. Hinshelwood 2009; Salzberger-Wittenberg, Williams and Osborne 1983; Youell 2006). Working within any education setting inevitably has an emotional impact on all of us.

Teachers and other professionals working in schools are subject to intense experiences as a result of communications from pupils and students, and also parents and carers. These can be overt and clear, and can be managed. Other communications may be experienced in ways that we are less aware of. That is, they create a 'feeling', an experience in the recipient, without an obvious awareness of how it may have got there (Hinshelwood 2009; Salzberger-Wittenberg *et al.* 1983; Youell 2006). In terms of being seen as potential attachment figures in schools (Geddes 2006), teachers, support staff and other colleagues in schools are commonly on the receiving end of feelings projected onto them. It becomes vitally important for staff to have an opportunity to think and reflect with others on what might be going on. Often this may happen informally in the staffroom (or the pub!), but formal times and spaces for discussion can also be vitally important. There are different models of how this may work (Solomon and Nashat 2010), including work discussion groups (Hanko 2002; Jackson 2008) and consultation to schools (Maltby 2008).

Initial training and awareness raising for trainee teachers is clearly vitally important for new colleagues entering the profession. However, at the Tavistock Clinic we know, from our experience of providing training and clinical services in schools, that all staff working in schools and educational settings greatly value opportunities for ongoing support. The teaching profession does not have a tradition of supervision as in the mental health professions, but we know that school staff appreciate times to think together with colleagues about their experiences and observations, mental health themes and child development, in order to inform their ongoing work with children and young people. Feedback we receive demonstrates that children in schools and their families benefit from such reflective spaces used by the school staff with whom they have ongoing relationships.

Typically, many schools are good at behavioural approaches, that is, using rewards and sanctions to influence learners' behaviour. However, we find that often this isn't enough, as children's behaviour is communicating something of their internal, emotional state. It is important for teachers to observe closely and to try to understand what may be being communicated, in order to make sense of it, and so how best to support a learner and/or make meaningful interventions. This is usually best accomplished together with others, as part of a team, and this process may be facilitated. External facilitation often helps to keep curiosity alive, with questioning from a 'not-knowing' position helping new and different ideas to emerge, rather than rushing to premature certainty.

Teachers, support staff and others in school are the key people who form important attachment relationships, often over many years. For some children, this includes key school staff such as secretaries and caretakers. Children with less secure attachment patterns from home and family can form crucial attachment relationships with schools, and other community settings, and those people within them, notably teachers and other school staff. These relationships are often vitally helpful in making children feel less insecure. For many children, this can be provided by routine, predictable school life, and the sustained interest, curiosity and understanding of teachers and key staff. For those children who come to school feeling less secure about the world and relationships in it, teachers may benefit from external support in developing shared understanding of more complex needs, what different behaviours may be communicating, and so tailoring specific interventions accordingly.

The emotional experience in schools – as felt by individual teachers, staff teams and/or whole school communities – can be used as 'intelligence' (Armstrong 2004) to better understand organisational life and 'what might be going on'. Opportunities for sharing experiences and reflecting with others can be vital for enhancing understanding of complex situations, and so jointly and collaboratively formulating interventions and shared strategies.

For some schools, support available from local Child and Adolescent Mental Health Services (CAMHS) can be requested, and clinical colleagues can speak on the phone or visit schools. In a research study of nearly 300 schools, education staff reported that 'most teachers were short of informal support systems for advice when they were concerned about a child's mental health…many teachers valued the opportunity to talk over concerns or ask for advice from CAMHS on an informal basis, rather than make a formal referral' (Gowers, Thomas and Deeley 2004, p.423).

Moreover in some areas, commissioners and service providers have established clinical services embedded within schools. CAMHS clinicians, embedded and integrated within schools, are in a potentially useful position to develop ideas and practice about thinking and learning in schools that can integrate with existing educational work. By being present in schools on a regular basis, therapeutic professionals can work alongside school staff and, in effect, join the system. They can be on hand to offer and promote insights and to work towards 'an extra dimension of self-reflection' among teachers (Hinshelwood 2009, p.519). They are in a position to support teachers on a daily basis to think about teaching and learning in the context of relationships (Salzberger-Wittenberg et al. 1983; Youell 2006), and to offer informal, spontaneous opportunities to reflect on specific interactions that can promote 'reflection-in-action' (Schon 1983). The combination of different perspectives, roles and positions helps to develop more fully understanding of young people and their needs (see Solomon and Nashat 2010 for more details and specific examples).

Whatever the exact arrangements, providing opportunities for teachers and school staff to reflect on their experiences, to share their observations with colleagues and to think and be curious together is a vitally important way to promote resilience across a staff team and thus a school as a whole.

Final thoughts

This chapter has outlined two approaches for supporting teachers and school staff to become more able to support resilience building in schools. One approach is a brief training programme for teachers, equipping them with easy-to-use strategies for using with groups of children and young people in class and in schools as a whole, helping them to develop their capacities for mentalising, and so helping to build resilience for individuals and groups, with the aim of promoting their mental health. A second approach is the provision for time and space for teachers and adults in schools to share their observations, emotional experiences, reflections, thoughts and ideas, in order to develop specifically tailored approaches for working in particular situations, emphasising the central importance of the relationships that children, young people and families have with teachers, school staff and schools.

These two approaches are by no means mutually exclusive. They can offer different and complimentary ways of developing the capacity of school communities to become more resilient, promoting more thoughtful, reflective and ultimately more effective responses to situations that inevitably arise in the emotional lives of schools. In these ways they can contribute to ways in which schools can play a crucial role in promoting the mental health of children and young people and their communities.

▨ REFLECTION POINTS ▨

1. Think of one practical tool or strategy to build resilience that you could introduce into your school or classroom. What would be the next step to make this happen?

2. Think of one striking emotional experience in which you were made to feel something unfamiliar. See if you can create an opportunity to discuss this with a colleague, or preferably a group of colleagues, in a safe, confidential setting. Is it helpful? If so, what do you think contributed to making it helpful?

Bibliography

Allen, J.G., Fonagy, P. and Bateman, A.W. (2008) *Mentalizing in Clinical Practice.* Washington, DC: American Psychiatric Publishing.

Armstrong, D. (2004) 'Emotions in Organizations: Disturbance or Intelligence?' In C. Huffington, D. Armstrong, W. Halton, L. Hoyle and J. Pooley (eds) *Working Below the Surface: The Emotional Life of Contemporary Organizations* (pp.11–27). London: Karnac Books.

Bak, P.L. (2012) '"Thoughts in Mind": Promoting Mentalizing Communities for Children.' In N. Midgley and I. Vrouva (eds) *Mentalization-based Interventions with Children and Families.* London: Routledge.

Bak. P.L., Midgley, N., Zhu, J.L., Wistoft, K. and Obel, C. (2015) 'The resilience program: Preliminary evaluation of a mentalization-based education program.' *Frontiers in Psychology 6, 753*, 1–6.

Bandura, A. (1977) *Social Learning Theory.* Upper Saddle River, NJ: Prentice Hall.

Bateman, A.W. and Fonagy, P. (eds) (2012) *Handbook of Mentalizing in Mental Health Practice.* Washington, DC: American Psychiatric Publishing.

Bowlby, J. (1969) *Attachment and Loss. Volume 1: Attachment.* London: Hogarth Press and The Institute of Psychoanalysis.

Bowlby, J. (1973) *Attachment and Loss. Volume 2: Separation: Anger and Anxiety.* London: Hogarth Press and The Institute of Psychoanalysis.

Bowlby, J. (1980) *Attachment and Loss. Volume 3: Loss: Sadness and Depression.* London: Hogarth Press and The Institute of Psychoanalysis.

DCSF (Department for Children, Schools and Families (2008) *Targeted Mental Health in Schools Grant Project (TaMHS) – Evidence-based Guidance Booklet.* Available at www.gov.uk/government/uploads/system/uploads/attachment_data/file/184060/DFE-RR177.pdf, accessed on 17 March 2017

Dowling, E. and Osborne, E. (eds) (1994) *The Family and the School: A Joint Systems Approach to Problems with Children.* London: Routledge.

Geddes, H. (2006) *Attachment in the Classroom.* Belper: Worth Publishing Ltd.

Gowers, S., Thomas, S. and Deeley, S. (2004) 'Can primary schools contribute effectively to tier 1 child mental health services?' *Clinical Child Psychology and Psychiatry 9*, 3, 419–425.

Hanko, G. (2002) 'Making psychodynamic insights accessible to teachers as an integral part of their professional task: The potential of collaborative consultation approaches in school-based professional development.' *Psychodynamic Practice 8*, 3, 375–389.

Hinshelwood, R.D. (2009) 'Do unconscious processes affect educational institutions?' *Clinical Child Psychology and Psychiatry 14*, 4, 509–522.

Hopkins, J. (2004) *Just Schools: A Whole School Approach to Restorative Justice.* London: Jessica Kingsley Publishers.

Jackson, E. (2008) 'The development of work discussion groups in educational settings.' *Journal of Child Psychotherapy 34*, 1, 62–82.

Main, M. (1995) 'Recent Studies in Attachment: Overview with Selected Implications for Clinical Work.' In S. Goldberg, R. Muir and J. Kerr (eds) *Attachment Theory, Social, Developmental and Clinical Perspectives* (pp.407–474). London: Analytic Press.

Main, M. (2000) 'The organized categories of infant, child, and adult attachment: Flexible vs. inflexible attention under attachment-related stress.' *Journal of the American Psychoanalytic Association 48*, 4, 1055–1096.

Maltby, J. (2008) 'Consultation in schools: Helping staff and pupils with unresolved loss and mourning.' *Journal of Child Psychotherapy 34*, 1, 83–100.

Midgley, N. and Vrouva, I. (eds) (2012) *Minding the Child: Mentalization-based Interventions with Children, Young People and their Families.* London: Routledge.

Moffitt, T.E., Arseneault, L., Belsky, D.W., Dickson, N., Hancox, R.J., Harrington, H.L. *et al.* (2011) 'A gradient of childhood self-control predicts health, wealth, and public safety.' *PNAS (Proceedings of the National Academy of Sciences of the USA) 108,* 108, 2693–2698.

Salzberger-Wittenberg, I., Williams, G. and Osborne, E. (1983) *The Emotional Experience of Learning and Teaching.* London: Karnac Books.

Saunders, R., Jacobvitz, D., Zaccagnino, M., Beverung, L.M. and Hazen, N. (2011) 'Pathways to earned-security: The role of alternative support figures.' *Attachment & Human Development 13,* 4, 403–420.

Schon, D. (1983) *The Reflective Practitioner: How Professionals Think in Action.* New York: Basic Books.

Solomon, M. (2009) 'A Psychodynamic Perspective.' In C. Arnold, J. Yeomans, S. Simpson and M. Solomon, *Excluded from School: Complex Discourses and Psychological Perspectives* (pp.31–42). Stoke on Trent: Trentham Books.

Solomon, M. and Nashat, S. (2010) 'Offering a "therapeutic presence" in schools and educational settings.' *Psychodynamic Practice 16,* 3, 289–304.

Solomon, M. and Thomas, G. (2013) 'Supporting behaviour support: Developing a model for leading and managing a unit for teenagers excluded from mainstream school.' *Emotional and Behavioural Difficulties 18,* 1, 44–59.

Stein, H. (2006) 'Does Mentalizing Promote Resilience?' In J.G. Allen and P. Fonagy (eds) *Handbook of Mentalization-based Treatments* (pp.307–326). Chichester: John Wiley & Sons Ltd.

Tavistock and Portman NHS Foundation Trust, The (no date) *Robust-Ed: Promoting Resilience in Young People, Staff and Communities.* Available at https://tavistockandportman.nhs.uk/training/cpd-courses/robust-ed-promoting-resilience-young-people-staff-and-communities, accessed on 30 March 2017.

Valle, A., Massaro, D., Castelli, I., Sangiuliano Intra, F., Lombardi, E., Bracaglia, E. and Marchetti, A. (2016) 'Promoting mentalizing in pupils by acting on teachers: Preliminary Italian evidence of the "Thought in Mind" project.' *Frontiers in Psychology 7,* 1213, 1–12.

WHO (World Health Organization) (2014) *Mental Health: A State of Well-being.* Available at www.who.int/features/factfiles/mental_health/en, accessed on 17 March 2017.

Youell, B. (2006) *The Learning Relationship: Psychoanalytic Thinking in Education.* London: Karnac Books.

Zautra, A.J., Hall, J.S. and Murray, K.E. (2010) 'Resilience, a New Definition of Health for People and Communities.' In J.W. Reich, A.J. Zautra and J.S. Hall (eds) *Handbook of Adult Resilience* (pp.3–34). New York: The Guilford Press.

7

Emotional Development and Missed Early Experiences

The Nurture Group Approach

DAVID COLLEY

Nurture groups are classrooms in mainstream schools where small groups of children with a range of emotional and attachment difficulties are offered specialist support (Bennathan and Boxall 2000). Nurture groups acknowledge that learning and emotions are inextricably linked (Gerhardt 2004). For this reason, the nurture group actively attends to the emotional needs of the children as a priority, with the understanding that this is the foundation for effective learning in the mainstream classroom.

By way of an introduction to nurture group practice, this chapter begins with a descriptive overview of the 'classic' nurture group in action. This is followed by a detailed analysis of the unique aspects of nurture group intervention that support the emotional development and attachment needs of children and young people in school.

The classic nurture group in action

Let me introduce you to the 'classic' nurture group that is both well led and well taught (Ofsted 2011). Based in a large, urban primary school, the Rainbow Room is a standard primary classroom with a difference – and that difference is apparent as soon as you enter the room. For all visitors there is a warm welcome upon arrival and the room has a homely feel with soft furnishings, curtains, a comfortable seating area and a large breakfast table. There are also formal work areas, a play box, a full-length mirror, a quiet reading table and a cooking area. A colourful rainbow made by the children adorns the wall along with an array of high-quality, academic and creative displays. The

'Six principles of nurture' are on display in the classroom (these core principles of nurture group practice will be explored in more detail as the chapter develops).

As you enter the Rainbow Room, there are ten children from Key Stage 1 (aged 5–6) working in subgroups with two members of staff. At one table, a group of six is completing a literacy task with a specific focus on vocabulary and language development. The adult models the skills required to listen and contribute while encouraging the children to regulate their urges to talk over one another. The activity is vibrant and interactive. A quieter member of the group is gently encouraged to make their own contribution while the adult skilfully creates the time and space within the discussion for that child to play their part.

In another work area, a maths session is being led by the second member of the nurture team. With only four children in the group, the adult is able to focus with great care and flexibility on both the conceptual learning that is taking place, but also on the children's emotional responses to the learning task. Without warning, anger and frustration is expressed by one of the children. Objects are thrown and shouting and tears follow. This is managed firmly by the nurture team, but with calm assurance and empathy. The outburst is understood by staff to be symptomatic of this child's emotional and attachment needs, and this behaviour offers an ongoing example of how emotional difficulties are affecting the child's learning (and jeopardising his place within the school community). In this case, the child has not yet learned how to manage the rush of frustration that sometimes overwhelms him when learning is challenging. As a consequence, he has been hurting other children in these moments and running out of the mainstream classroom. For this reason, the nurture team has specific SMART targets for this child with a focus on emotional regulation and the self-management of anger. When these outbursts occur, staff members have a clear and consistent response that involves a calm, firm rejection of the behaviour (but not the child), and a series of alternatives for the child to explore. This might include a form of co-regulation between adult and child that is usually experienced in early attachment relationships; employing a particular calming technique (slow breathing, counting to five, having a glass of water); or talking through the experience and identifying the triggers that have caused the outburst. In the nurture group, staff have the time to do this.

Central to the philosophy of nurture group practice is the belief that children learn to value themselves through the experience of being understood, valued and cared for by others. Following this outburst, staff will support the recovery process with care, warmth and good humour. The child is not rejected, despite the challenging nature and ferocity of the outburst. Indeed, where the child has made progress in terms of choices and responses (no matter how small this progress may appear), this will be praised and celebrated. But the nurture group is not a soft option where 'unruly' children are appeased. When the boundaries set for appropriate classroom behaviour have been crossed, this will be challenged firmly by staff as part of the process of co-regulation and emotional learning. Where harm has been caused by the outburst, to either friends or staff, the child will be encouraged to repair the harm done at an appropriate point in the day.

Each child attending the Rainbow Room has a series of specific targets relating to their emotional development. The Boxall Profile (Bennathan and Boxall 1998) is an assessment instrument that is closely linked to nurture group practice and seeks to identify the missed early experiences that are acting as emotional barriers to the child's learning in school. The individual targets for each child are informed by this assessment and more details of the Boxall Profile follow.

Following the morning's first work-based session in the Rainbow Room, a circle time activity (see Moseley 1996) involving all ten children and the two staff precedes the nurture breakfast. The children are familiar with this routine. Every nurture group session follows the same structure to promote a sense of predictability and safety. During the circle time session, children comply with the circle time rules around speaking and listening. On occasions, individuals are reminded that their time will come and that listening to others is important and of value. Individuals are thanked for their contributions.

A board game is then chosen and five children play this game under the supervision of a member of staff. Difficulties with winning, losing, cooperating, accepting and sharing are often indications of missed early learning experiences, and the nurture staff are trained to be on high alert during these 'informal' and 'fun' activities. The second group of five children are tasked with preparing the nurture breakfast, under staff supervision. This involves setting the table, preparing the soft drinks, washing the fruit and making the toast. Again, staff are highly vigilant at these times to ensure that 'fairness' issues are transparent and that cooperative skills are explored. Extra places are set as the headteacher and a number of parents are expected to join the group for breakfast.

Sharing food together is an important experience in the Rainbow Room on a number of levels. Apart from providing sustenance, the food is also comforting and, at another level, might be viewed as symbolic of the adults' care for the children. The children might not perceive this consciously (at Key Stage 1), but non-consciously and at a primal level it could be argued that the sharing of food is an experience that has long been associated with safety, belonging and human inter-connectedness.

A number of parents arrive in time to join the breakfast and a member of the group is sent to remind the head of her appointment. During the course of this communal activity, children are encouraged to use language effectively and to communicate with peers and adults appropriately. They have the opportunity to listen with interest and to reflect on the contributions that others have made; to get the joke, to laugh along and to make others laugh. The children learn that they can be interesting and that they also have something interesting to say. They project to the future and think about aspirations; they draw on the past and compare their experience with others.

Clearly, the nurture breakfast is a complex and multi-layered interaction that deliberately sets out to help children catch up with the missed early learning experiences of active listening – and of being actively listened to. It is a key learning activity in the nurture room, and anyone labelling this activity pejoratively as 'just tea'n'toast' betrays their own fundamental lack of understanding.

Following the nurture breakfast, the parents stay and engage with a group activity while five children and a member of staff undertake the washing up, drying and clearing away. 'Fairness', roles and cooperation again come under strain within the group during this activity. One child refuses to take part in the washing up, preferring to join the game activity. However, staff do not let this child's decision pass unchallenged. Reference is made to the washing up chart on display that clearly sets out the different roles for each child. Staff encourage and cajole the child to comply with the role, as do the parents and the other children. The game itself is postponed until the child complies with the requirement to take part in the washing up. Finally the child agrees, and this is praised and celebrated by the group.

Break time follows and the transition into the playground is again afforded careful attention by the nurture team. Staff ensure that the children are prepared for break time in terms of their coats, games and activities. Pep talks and guidance may be offered to specific children regarding who to play with (or who to avoid), and children may be guided as to which parts of the playground to locate themselves in. The nurture team may then make an appearance in the playground to monitor key children and their interactions with their peers.

The post-playtime 'fall out' that often follows break times in large urban primary schools can be managed in the Rainbow Room with the required time and consideration. Given the small numbers of children attending the nurture room, in addition to the double staffing, an upsetting incident that has been experienced or caused by a nurture group member can be handled immediately by one member of staff. Finding a resolution promptly to such incidents can ameliorate emotional challenges that might otherwise interfere with the primary goal of the nurture group – learning.

Following break time, a further formal learning session routinely follows in the Rainbow Room with a focus on academic tasks drawn from the mainstream curriculum. Links between the mainstream staff and the nurture team are critical in the effective nurture group. Social and emotional targets are shared in both settings across the term, and mainstream tasks are undertaken in the nurture room to ensure that children do not fall behind in terms of their academic progress. The nurture curriculum (with a focus on emotional needs) and the mainstream curriculum (with a focus on academic progress) work together symbiotically.

Following the second learning session, the ten children who have attended the Rainbow Room that morning will return to their mainstream classrooms for the remainder of the day. The Rainbow Room sessions will take place for these children on Monday, Wednesday and Friday mornings only, because nurture group intervention is designed to be part time and short term. Children should only require this intervention for two or three terms maximum, and a return to full-time, mainstream provision is the goal for all children.

In the afternoon, a new group of 12 Key Stage 2 children attend the Rainbow Room. Each child has specific targets generated by the Boxall Profile assessments and will attend for three afternoons each week over a two-term period. The focus is again on the emotional and attachment needs of the individual children, and research suggests that this kind of early intervention can improve socio-emotional functioning, improve confidence and reduce displays of disruptive behaviour (Cooper and Whitebread 2007; Ofsted 2011; Pyle and Rae 2015; Reynolds, MacKay and Kearney 2009; Seth-Smith *et al.* 2010).

The Boxall Profile assessment (Bennathan and Boxall 1998) is undertaken at regular termly intervals to monitor the developmental progress that children are making and to gauge the timing of an appropriate return to full-time mainstream provision. Given the number of references already made to this instrument, it will be apparent that the Boxall Profile is central to how the nurture group assesses, targets and monitors the emotional development and attachment needs of the children and young people in attendance. For this reason, a more detailed understanding of the Boxall Profile is now required.

The Boxall Profile

The Boxall Profile is a diagnostic instrument that aims to help staff target specific social and emotional skills that may be missing or only partially mastered by the individual child. The Profile comprises two sections – the Developmental Strands (Section I) and the Diagnostic Profile (Section II) – and both sections provide rich, detailed information about the socio-emotional development of the child being assessed. The time taken to complete the Profile is time well spent. As part of the process, staff are required to think carefully and critically about each individual child, and when this is undertaken as a team, the assessment generates an in-depth discussion that pools professional knowledge and promotes an empathetic understanding of needs.

The Boxall Profile was developed by teachers for teachers, and its practical classroom application is its strength (Bennathan and Boxall 2000). It sets out to be a *guide* to staff in schools, and does not claim to predict the presence of psychiatric disorders. It does, however, claim to provide the basis for a diagnosis of an individual child's functioning with a view to planning an individual intervention programme (Bennathan and Boxall 1998). To be succinct, it allows the nurture team to follow the Assess-Plan-Do-Review cycle in relation to the emotional and attachment needs of the individual children, as recommended in the *SEND Code of Practice* (DfE/DH 2015).

When deciding on priorities for intervention, it is recommended that practitioners consider the results generated in Sections I and II of the Boxall Profile together. Overall, the scores displayed on the Profile offer staff the opportunity to break down the needs of children into manageable parts; to identify areas of developmental need; to prioritise target areas; and to monitor progress through a repeat of the assessment after a period of time (Bennathan and Boxall 1998). To support effective intervention, the publication *Beyond the Boxall Profile* (Evans 2006) provides strategies and resources that link directly to developmental areas identified by the Profile results.

Due to the development of nurture groups in secondary schools (Colley 2009), the Boxall Profile was revised for an older age group in 2010. *The Boxall Profile for Young People* (Bennathan, Boxall and Colley 2010) has adapted the language and focus of the original items for the secondary setting, and the histogram norms in the updated version relate to young people aged 11–14. Strategies and resources to support the interventions in the secondary school nurture group are collated in *Beyond the BPYP* (Rae 2012).

The Boxall Profile handbooks (*The Boxall Profile*, Bennathan and Boxall 1998; *The Boxall Profile for Young People*, Bennathan *et al.* 2010) provide detailed guidance on the use and interpretation of the Profile data, and the Boxall Profile Online is available at https://boxallprofile.org.

Six principles of nurture

The 'classic' nurture group, based on the pioneering work of Marjorie Boxall (Benathan and Boxall 2000; Boxall 2002), is a rigorous and structured educational intervention, informed by the psychological theory of Bowlby (1969), Maslow (1954) and Vygotsky (1978). Key features such as double staffing, formal training, assessment through the Boxall Profile, professional reflection, parental involvement and a focus on the emotional development and attachment needs of the children are all central to the 'classic' Boxall nurture group. But variants on the 'classic' model do exist, including those that contravene, undermine or distort the classic model, offering containment and control in place of developmental support (Cooper and Whitebread 2007; Cooper and Tiknaz 2007). To ensure that the 'classic' nurture group model can be distinguished from aberrant variants, the 'Six principles of nurture' were established by The Nurture Group Network (www.nurturegroups. org) and articulated by Colley (2012). The six principles form the basis of the Boxall Quality Mark Award that represents the 'gold standard' for nurture group practice.

When considering critically the quality of the 'nurture group' provision that is on offer in a particular setting, a simple quality control task might suffice – can the nurture team articulate the six principles of nurture, or not?

Principle 1. Learning is understood developmentally

In addition to Bowlby's attachment theory (1969, 1973, 1980) and Maslow's hierarchy of human needs (1954), nurture group theory and practice is informed by the developmental psychology of Piaget (1951, 1954) and Vygotsky (1978). Nurture groups understand that certain children may have skill sets and emotional needs that are not necessarily commensurate with their chronological ages. Nurture staff are therefore trained to respond to children not in terms of national curriculum expectations, but in terms of the child's developmental progress. The response to the individual child is 'as they are', underpinned by a non-judgemental and accepting attitude (Bennathan *et al.* 2010).

Principle 2. The classroom offers a safe base

A central aim of 'classic' nurture groups is to provide students with a secure and safe environment that provides the conditions necessary for them to develop emotionally, socially and cognitively (Boxall 2002). This principle is clearly informed by Bowlby's attachment theory (Bowlby 1969, 1973, 1980), where the safe and secure base is described as being the cornerstone of secure attachment and of positive mental health.

A sense of safety and security within the nurture group is developed for children through a variety of means:

- Relationships are understood to be the key to successful school placements, and the relationships between children and staff are forged through a balance of educational and domestic experiences.

- Double staffing is a key non-negotiable in the 'classic' nurture group, and staff model good relationships for the children. At all times staff seek to reassure children in a variety of ways that the nurture environment is both physically safe and free of psychological fear and anxiety.

- The working day is deliberately predictable with slow moving, established routines and an emphasis on order and repetition.

- Boundaries for behaviour are set clearly and maintained firmly with warmth, care and empathy.

- Great attention is paid to detail, and the adults are expected to be reliable and consistent in their approach to the children.

- A trusting relationship is established that offers reassurance, constancy, interest and commitment that in turn models constructive relationships and appropriate interactions (Lucas, Insley and Buckland 2006).

Principle 3. The importance of nurture and self-esteem

Research has found that a common feature of students with social, emotional and behavioural difficulties is low self-esteem (DfE 2015), and that environments that are supportive of learner autonomy have been found to be associated with higher self-esteem (e.g. Deci and Ryan 1995). The classic nurture groups seek to promote learner autonomy through the implementation of choice in activities and opportunities for cooperative learning (The Nurture Group Network 2016).

Dweck (2000) defines self-esteem as being 'a positive way of experiencing yourself when you are fully engaged and are using your abilities to the utmost in pursuit of something you value' (Dweck 2000, p.4). Nurture teams take cognisance of Dweck's definition, and are encouraged to plan activities that promote self-esteem development through challenges met (The Nurture Group Network 2016), while praise and affirmation are regular features of the nurture group (Bani 2011).

Principle 4. Language as a vital means of communication

The theory and practice of nurture groups pays particular attention to the crucial role of language development in promoting quality relationships and the expression of feelings, be they positive or negative (The Nurture Group Network 2016). Research by Colwell and O'Connor (2003) confirmed that the verbal and non-verbal communications made within the nurture group were more positive than in the mainstream, and more likely to enhance the self-esteem of students. This research was later confirmed by the work of Bani (2011).

Bennathan *et al.* (2010) suggest that language is more than a skill to be learned; it is a way of putting feelings into words. They suggest that nurture group children often 'act out' their feelings, lacking as they do the vocabulary to 'name' how they feel. In nurture groups the informal opportunities for talking and sharing that include welcoming the children into the group or having breakfast together are as important as the more formal lessons that explicitly teach language skills.

Principle 5. It is understood that all behaviour is communication

Nurture group theory and practice suggests that when a child is presenting with negative, troublesome or inappropriate behaviour, it is vital that staff separate the behaviour from the child and seek to understand the underlying messages contained within the behaviour (The Nurture Group Network 2016). Social, emotional and attachment difficulties may be understood from a variety of psychological perspectives, but for nurture group staff the principle remains that all behaviour is understood as a form of communication. Staff will therefore endeavour to remain vigilant as to the causes and drivers of problem behaviour and will ask themselves, 'given what I know about this child and their development, what is this child trying to tell me?' (Bennathan *et al.* 2010).

Understanding the messages that a child is trying to communicate through their behaviour helps staff to respond in a firm but non-punitive way without being provoked or discouraged. If the child can sense that their feelings are understood, this can help to diffuse difficult situations, as the adult makes the link between the external/internal worlds of the child. A variety of strategies may then be employed by nurture staff to de-escalate challenging situations, and the behaviour will be 'understood rather than judged' (Lucas *et al.* 2006).

Principle 6. The importance of transition

Colley (2009) reports that nurture groups have been found to be particularly successful in supporting the transition of students from primary school into secondary school. But nurture groups also recognise that the less obvious transitions occurring regularly throughout the school day can cause certain children anxiety and precipitate behavioural problems. Nurture staff are therefore trained to pay particular attention to the subtle transitional periods in the school day that might involve the child changing from one activity to another in the nurture group, going out to play or break, lunchtimes or the return from lunch – and preparing for entry or egress from school.

In preparation for any transition, be it major or minor, the nurture team anticipates the problems posed by the change in routine and prepares the children accordingly (Lucas *et al.* 2006).

Parents/carers and the 'classic' nurture group

Cooper and Tiknaz (2007) note that 'parental involvement is extremely important to the success of the nurture group provision', and that the nurture group environment is ideal for less formal discussions with parents/carers regarding a child's progress (Cooper and Tiknaz 2007, p.138). The nurture team's approach is one of 'we're in this together' (Boxall 2002, p.165), and this attitude transmits to the family as a commitment, despite the challenges posed. In this way the students themselves receive a powerful message that 'home and school visibly become one' (Bennathan and Boxall 2000, p.34).

Relationships with parents/carers were identified as a particular strength in the 'classic' nurture group by the Ofsted survey of nurture group provision across the UK (Ofsted 2011). Of the 95 parents and carers interviewed by Ofsted, the vast majority expressed their appreciation of how the nurture group intervention had helped their children. Parents/carers spoke of their children being calmer, happier and more confident, both at school and at home, and of their own greater confidence in managing their children's behaviour. One parent stated that, 'without the group our children would be expelled or lost' (quoted in Ofsted 2011, p.37), while another described the difference that attending the nurture group made to her child: 'He is much calmer now and there are no problems getting him to school. He is keen to come now' (quoted in Ofsted 2011, p.37).

Positive outcomes in the home are confirmed by Pyle and Rae (2015), who explored parental perceptions of the impact of nurture group practice on parent–child relationships. The key findings of this research included the parental perception that child anxiety had decreased and confidence had grown as a result of the nurture group intervention. Parents also perceived their children to be more communicative, more affectionate and having fewer emotional outbursts in the home (Pyle and Rae 2015).

When children are assessed for nurture group placements, the information that parents/carers can provide is crucial and influential (Cooper and Tiknaz 2007) and, when motivated, the parents/carers frequently participate in supporting the nurture group with their own time and resources. It should be noted, however, that parental agreement must be secured before nurture group intervention can be implemented.

Criticisms of nurture group practice

A defining feature of the 'classic' nurture group is the way in which children access a separate, specialist learning environment away from the mainstream classroom. For some, the idea of separating children through 'alternative educational environments' contravenes the notion of 'inclusion for all'. Indeed, Howes *et al.* (2002) conclude that, 'on a day to day basis, a nurture group is not an inclusive mode of provision' (cited in Farrell and Ainscow 2002, p.102).

Critics of nurture group practice contend that children who are withdrawn from their mainstream class each day are separated from peers whose potentially positive influence on them is reduced. They suggest that this separation may lead to negative labelling and a perception by the rest of the school that these are a group of children whose behaviour warrants their isolation (Farrell and Ainscow 2002). Critics also warn that alternative educational environments such as nurture groups may reduce the sense of responsibility that mainstream staff have in differentiating their planning and teaching to meet the needs of all the children in their mainstream class (Howes *et al.*, quoted in Farrell and Ainscow 2002). When the new *SEND Code of Practice* (DfE/DH 2015) is urging mainstream staff to take full responsibility for all learners in their classrooms, why should certain children be withdrawn and taught by 'specialist' teams?

Nurture group theorists have countered that these critics assume the children accessing the nurture group provision would otherwise be fully engaged with learning in the mainstream setting (Bennathan *et al.* 2010). In reality, mainstream staff have already identified that a child is in difficulty and struggling with the demands of the mainstream classroom, despite their best efforts. Advocates would argue that the aim of a short-term, nurture group placement would be to intervene in the current cycle of failure and to try another approach. The nurture group placement would seek to reduce tensions, enhance the child's confidence, boost developmental attainment and encourage engagement with the learning process. In this sense, nurture groups could be said to be an *inclusive* model because they are designed to reduce suspensions, exclusions and educational disengagement at an early age by removing barriers to learning (Cooper and Tiknaz 2007).

A further criticism levelled at the nurture group approach is the perception that nurture groups cultivate a 'diminished self' that encourages children to perceive themselves as fragile, uncertain and damaged (Ecclestone and Hayes 2008). Bailey (2007) goes further and argues that nurture group practice disempowers children, staff and parents through its 'multiple positions of vulnerability' (Bailey 2007, p.11).

But nurture groups are not therapeutic interventions; they are educational interventions. While staff may indeed encourage children to reflect on their feelings as part of the emotional co-regulation that is central to the work, the ultimate goal of the nurture group is to promote educational engagement in children at risk of total disengagement.

A final criticism of nurture group provision is the costs involved. The 'classic' Boxall nurture group is staffed by two adults, one of whom may be a teacher and the other, a nurture support assistant. The joint salary cost for staffing a full-time nurture group would therefore be in the region of £33,000 + £22,000= £55,000 p.a. at the time of writing (2016). The set-up costs to furnish a nurture room and invest in initial resources would be in the region of £7,000, and the ongoing costs for consumables and learning resources might be in the region of £1,500 p.a. (The Nurture Group Network 2016).

For many schools, under pressure to make savings in the current economic climate, such a cost is prohibitive and a nurture group is not something they can afford to run. Conversely, over 1500 schools across the UK have prioritised nurture group intervention in their settings and have found the resource streams, such as Pupil Premium funding, to allow the provision to be funded effectively (The Nurture Group Network 2016).

Evidence of impact

The success of nurture groups has been recognised in a range of research papers (e.g. Colley 2009; Cooper and Whitebread 2007; Pyle and Rae 2015), Ofsted guidance (e.g. 2005, 2011) and government documents (DCSF 2009; DES 1978; DfEE 1998).

The Ofsted report *Managing Challenging Behaviour* (Ofsted 2005) reflected that 'nurture groups...have proved effective in helping younger pupils to improve their concentration, behaviour and ability to learn' (Ofsted 2005:14), while the influential Steer Report (DfES 2005) confirmed the growing research evidence in support of nurture group intervention, stating:

> Nurture Groups are an important early intervention for emotionally vulnerable children, providing a safe and supportive environment for those who lack confidence and enthusiasm at school. Nurture Groups offer a safe and contained environment, where a pupil can spend much of the school day, while also keeping in contact with their class. By offering pupils more intensive support to overcome particular obstacles to emotional development, Nurture Groups help children re-establish good relationships with adults, and begin to see school as a place where they experience success. (DfES 2005, p.70)

In 2007, the national nurture group study by Cooper and Whitebread (2007) collected data over a two-year period and found that children improved significantly in their social, emotional and behavioural functioning following access to nurture group provision. Interestingly, the study went on to find that schools with nurture groups also achieved significantly higher gains for children across the school, and that a school with a nurture group dealt with mainstream behavioural issues more effectively than a school without this facility.

Research evidence generated by Glasgow City Council in 2007 has led to significant investment in nurture groups across the city. The council undertook a formal evaluation of nurture group provision in the city that matched 16 control schools with 16 nurture groups, and the council report concluded that nurture groups represent:

> …an extremely effective intervention strategy to identify and address additional needs which fall into the category of social, emotional and/or behavioural difficulties. (GCC 2007, p.4)

Children accessing nurture groups were found to make significant changes in both their behaviour and their ability to access the national curriculum when compared with the control group. This encouraged the council to invest further in the provision with an additional 11 nurture groups established in January 2010 to complement the 58 nurture groups already in place in the city.

In 2011, Ofsted published a survey entitled *Supporting Children with Challenging Behaviour Through a Nurture Group Approach* (Ofsted 2011), and found that:

- when nurture groups were working well, they made a considerable difference to the behaviour and the social skills of the students who attended them

- the nurture groups gave parents practical support

- nurture groups can generate academic progress where previously there had been none

- all children retained contact with their mainstream classes.

Research evidence in support of nurture group intervention is current and ongoing. Bennett (2016) has undertaken a systematic review of nurture group effectiveness, while Chiappella (2015) has found that nurture groups in secondary schools can impact positively on the emotional difficulties experienced by students. Professor Tommy MacKay has reflected carefully on how nurture groups might form part of a broad, four-level model of nurture in education (2015). MacKay's model ranges from universal applications in nurturing schools to the children whose needs are so extreme as to be beyond the reach of school-based nurture groups.

In addition, the Department of Education in Northern Ireland has published their report on nurture group intervention in the province (CESI 2016), concluding that the intervention has been highly successful in its primary aim of achieving improvements in social, emotional and behavioural skills.

Final thoughts

Nurture groups began in 1970 with a small number of pilot facilities in the infant schools of London's East End. Based on the understanding that missed early experiences affected emotional development and attachment, nurture groups sought to ameliorate emotional difficulties through the process of careful attunement. The number of nurture groups nationally now exceeds 1500, and nurture groups feature internationally in countries such as Malta, New Zealand and Canada (The Nurture Group Network 2016).

Informed by the psychological theory of Bowlby (1969), Maslow (1954) and Vygotsky (1978), nurture groups have developed from infant settings into primary and secondary school settings because they work. That is to say, both professional intuition and empirical evidence confirm that the intervention promotes emotional regulation, fosters empathy and meets attachment needs.

It should be no surprise to learn that nurture groups are now being developed on university campuses (Chimbganda 2016) and in the workplace (Marshall 2011), for nurture and nurturing is a fundamental human need that spans both age and setting.

REFLECTION POINTS

Explore nurture group theory and practice further by logging on to The Nurture Group Network website at www.nurturegroups.org. Reflect critically on:

1. The content of the three-day training in nurture group theory and practice.

2. The criteria set to attain the Boxall Quality Mark Award in 'classic' nurture group practice.

Bibliography

Bailey, S. (2007) 'So What's All the Fuss About Nurture Groups?' Conference Paper. British Educational Research Association Annual Conference. London: Institute of Education, University of London.

Bani, M. (2011) 'The use and frequency of verbal and non-verbal praise in nurture groups.' *Emotional and Behavioural Difficulties 16*, 1, 47–67.

Bennathan, M. and Boxall, M. (1998) *The Boxall Profile: A Guide to Effective Intervention in the Education of Pupils with Emotional and Behavioural Difficulties.* Maidstone: Association of Workers for Children with Emotional and Behavioural Difficulties.

Bennathan, M. and Boxall, M. (2000) *Effective Intervention in Primary Schools* (2nd edn). London: David Fulton Publishers.

Bennathan, M., Boxall, M. and Colley, D. (2010) *The Boxall Profile for Young People.* London: The Nurture Group Network.

Bennet, T. (2016) *Developing Behaviour Mangement Content in Initial Teacher Training.* London: DfE.

Bishop, S. (2008) *Running a Nurture Group.* London: Sage Publications.

Booth, T., Ainscow, M., Black-Hawkins, K., Vaughan, M. and Shaw, L. (2000) *Index for Inclusion: Developing Learning and Participation in Schools.* Bristol: Centre for Studies on Inclusive Education (CESI).

Bowlby, J. (1969) *Attachment and Loss. Volume 1: Attachment.* London: Hogarth Press and The Institute of Psychoanalysis.

Bowlby, J. (1973) *Attachment and Loss. Volume 2: Separation: Anxiety and Anger.* London: Hogarth Press and The Institute of Psychoanalysis.

Bowlby, J. (1980) *Attachment and Loss. Volume 3: Loss: Sadness and Depression.* London: Hogarth Press and The Institute of Psychoanalysis.

Boxall, M. (2002) *Nurture Groups in School. Principles and Practice.* London: Paul Chapman Publishing.

Cefai, C. and Cooper, P. (2009) *Promoting Emotional Education. Engaging Children and Young People with Social, Emotional and Behaviour Difficulties.* London: Jessica Kingsley Publishers.

Centre for Evidence and Social Innovation (2016) *The Impact and Cost Effectiveness of Nurture Groups in Primary Schools in Northern Ireland.* Belfast: CESI.

Chiappella, J. (2015) 'Part-time secondary school nurture groups.' *The International Journal of Nurture in Education 1*, 1.

Chimbganda, T. (2016) 'Investing in student success through nurturing universities.' *The International Journal of Nurture in Education 2*, 1.

Colley, D. (2009) 'Nurture groups in secondary schools.' *Emotional and Behavioural Difficulties 14*, 4, 291–300.

Colley, D. (2012) 'Setting Up a Nurture Group in Your Secondary School.' In J. Visser, H. Daniels and T. Cole (eds) *Transforming Troubled Lives: Strategies and Interventions for Children with Social, Emotional and Behavioural Difficulties* (pp.121–138). Bingley: Emerald Books UK.

Colwell, J. and O'Connor, T. (2003) 'Understanding nurturing practices – A comparison of the use of strategies likely to enhance self-esteem in nurture groups and normal classrooms.' *British Journal of Special Education 30*, 3, 119–124.

Connolly, M., Hubbard, S. and Lloyd, L. (2008) *Evaluation Summary: Nurture Group Pilot Study: Year 2.* West Dunbartonshire Council.

Cooke, C., Yeomans, J. and Parkes, J. (2008) 'The Oasis: Nurture group provision for Key Stage Three pupils.' *Emotional and Behavioural Difficulties 13*, 4, 291–303.

Cooper, P. and Lovey, J. (1999) 'Early intervention in emotional and behavioural difficulties: The role of nurture groups.' *European Journal of Special Needs Education 14*, 2, 122–131.

Cooper, P. and McIntyre, D. (1996) *Effective Teaching and Learning: Teachers' and Pupils' Perspectives.* Buckingham: Open University Press.

Cooper, P. and Tiknaz, Y. (2005) 'Progress and challenge in nurture groups: Evidence from three case studies.' *British Journal of Special Education 32*, 4, 211–221.

Cooper, P. and Tiknaz, Y. (2007) *Nurture Groups in School and at Home. Connecting with Children with Social, Emotional and Behavioural Difficulties.* London: Jessica Kingsley Publishers.

Cooper, P. and Whitebread, D. (2007) 'The effectiveness of nurture groups on student progress: Evidence from a national research study.' *Emotional and Behavioural Difficulties 12*, 3, 171–190.

Cooper, P., Arnold, R. and Boyd, E. (1999) *The Nature and Distribution of Nurture Groups in England and Wales.* Cambridge: University of Cambridge School of Education.

Cooper, P., Arnold, R. and Boyd, E. (2001) 'The effectiveness of nurture groups: Preliminary research findings.' *British Journal of Special Education 28*, 4, 160–166.

DCSF (Department for Children, Schools and Families) (2009) *Learning Behaviour: Lessons Learned. A Review of Behaviour Standards and Practices in our Schools.* London: The Stationery Office.

Deci, E.L. and Ryan, R.M. (1995) 'Human Autonomy: The Basis for True Self-esteem.' In M. Kernis (ed.) *Efficacy, Agency and Self-esteem* (p.3149). New Yor: Plenum.

DES (Department for Education and Science) (1978) *Special Educational Needs. Report of the Committee of Enquiry into the Education of Handicapped Children and Young People (The Warnock Report).* London: HMSO.

DfE (Department for Education) (2011) *Ensuring Good Behaviour in Schools.* London: DfE.

DfE and DH (Department of Health (DH)) (2015) *SEND Code of Practice: 0 to 25 years.* London: The Stationery Office.

DfEE (Department for Education and Employment) (1998) *Meeting Special Educational Needs: A Programme of Action.* Sudbury: DfEE Publications Centre.

DfES (Department for Education and Skills) (1999) *Social Inclusion: Pupil Support.* London: The Stationery Office.

DfES (2002a) *Intervening Early. A 'Snapshot' of Approaches Primary Schools Can Use to Help Children Get the Best from School.* London: The Stationery Office.

DfES (2005) *Learning Behaviour: The Report of The Practitioners' Group on School Behaviour and Discipline (The Steer Report).* London: The Stationery Office.

DfES (2005a) *Excellence and Enjoyment: Social and Emotional Aspects of Learning (SEAL).* London: The Stationery Office.

Doyle, R. (2005) *'I Hate You. Please Help Me': A Case Study from a Classic Boxall Nurture Group.* Pastoral Care, pp.3–11.

Dweck, C.S. (2000) *Self Theories: Their Role in Motivation, Personality, and Development.* Philadelphia, PA: Psychology Press.

Ecclestone, K. and Hayes, D. (2008) *The Dangerous Rise of Therapeutic Education.* Abingdon: Routledge.

Estyn Report (2007) *Evaluation of the Implementation by Schools and Local Education Authorities of Guidance on Exclusions.* Her Majesty's Inspectorate for Education and Training (Wales).

Evans, M. (ed.) (2006) *Beyond the Boxall Profile.* London: The Nurture Group Network.

Farrell, P. and Ainscow, M. (2002) *Making Education Inclusive.* Abingdon: David Fulton Publishers.

Garner, J. (2010) 'The Role and Contribution of Nurture Groups in Secondary Schools: Perceptions of Children, Parents and Staff.' Unpublished EdD thesis. London: University of East London.

GCC (Glasgow City Council) (2007) *Nurture Groups Report: Report to Education Services Policy Development and Scrutiny Committee.* Glasgow: GCC.

Gerhardt, S. (2004) *Why Love Matters.* Hove: Routledge.

Howes, A., Emanuel, J. and Farrell, P. (2002) 'Can Nurture Groups Facilitate Inclusive Practice in Primary Schools?' In P. Farrell and M. Ainscow (eds) *Making Special Education Inclusive.* Abingdon: David Fulton Publishers.

Izatt, J. and Wasilewska, T. (1997) 'Nurture groups: An early intervention model enabling vulnerable children with SEBD to integrate successfully into school.' *Educational and Child Psychology 14*, 3, 63–70.

Lucas, S., Insley, K. and Buckland, G. (2006) *Nurture Group Principles and Curriculum Guidelines. Helping Children to Achieve.* London: The Nurture Group Network.

MacKay, T. (2015) 'Future directions for nurture in education.' *The International Journal of Nurture in Education 1*, 1.

Marshall, T. (2011) *Nurturing a 21st Century Workforce.* Training Journal June 2011 (pp.29–32). www.trainingjournal.com.

Maslow, A.H. (1954) *Motivation and Personality.* New York: Harper & Row.

Moseley, J. (1996) *Quality Circle Time in the Primary Classroom: Your Essential Guide to Enhancing Self-esteem, Self-discipline and Positive Relationships.* London: LDA.

Nurture Group Network, The (2016) www.nurturegroups.org.

O'Connor T. and Colwell, J. (2002) 'The effectiveness and rationale of the "nurture group" approach to helping children with emotional and behavioural difficulties remain within mainstream education.' *British Journal of Special Education 29*, 2, 96–100.

Ofsted (2005) *Managing Challenging Behaviour.* London: Ofsted.

Ofsted (2006) *Improving Behaviour.* London: Ofsted.

Ofsted (2011) *Supporting Children with Challenging Behaviour Through a Nurture Group Approach.* Available at www.ofsted.gov.uk/resources/supporting-children-challenging-behaviour-through-nurture-group-approach, accessed on 17 March 2017.

Piaget, J. (1951) *The Origin of Intelligence in Children.* New York: International Universities Press.

Piaget, J. (1954) *The Construction of Reality in the Child.* New York: Basic Books.

Pyle, A. and Rae, T. (2015) 'Nurture groups and parent–child relationships.' *The International Journal of Nurture in Education 1*, 1.

Rae, T. (ed.) (2012) *Beyond the Boxall Profile for Young People.* London: Nurture Group Network.

Reynolds, S., MacKay, T. and Kearney, M. (2009) 'Nurture groups: A large-scale, controlled study of effects on development and academic attainment.' *British Journal of Special Education 36*, 4, 204–212.

Rose, J. (2010) *How Nurture Protects Children: Nurture and Narrative in Work with Children, Young People and Families.* London: Responsive Solutions UK Ltd.

Scott, K. and Lee, A. (2009) 'Beyond the "classic" nurture group model: An evaluation of part-time and cross-age nurture groups in a Scottish local authority.' *Support for Learning 24*, 1, 5–10.

Seth-Smith, F., Levi, N., Pratt, R., Fonagy, P. and Jaffey, D. (2010) 'Do nurture groups improve the social, emotional and behavioural functioning of at risk children?' *Educational and Child Psychology 27*, 1, 21–34.

Vygotsky, L. (1978) *Mind in Society: The Development of Higher Psychological Processes.* London: Harvard University Press.

8

Understanding the Impact of Trauma on Children in the Classroom

BETSY DE THIERRY

Trauma is an experience that causes powerlessness and terror. This chapter represents the views of two organisations that work as a group of psychotherapists, therapeutic mentors and trauma-informed teachers in the support of children who have experienced trauma. Collectively, these professionals believe that when the impact of trauma on emotions, learning, behaviour and relationships is understood by all, then teachers become less stressed and the children have the potential to recover with reduced shame.

The Trauma Recovery Centre (TRC) offers therapy with parenting support groups and alternative education centres in buildings that are not on school sites. This alternative setting offers a neutral, homely environment for those who need to find a safe place to recover that is not associated with schools or clinical settings.

The Therapeutic Mentoring Rooms work from the same theoretical framework as the TRC and yet work within the school setting, offering a different but complementary service. The Therapeutic Mentoring Rooms do not work as intensively with the parents, but can offer more frequent sessions of support from a known and especially trained staff member at school, requiring less out of school time and less transport challenges.

Two Trauma Recovery Centre projects

At the TRC and in the Therapeutic Mentoring Rooms that are located in schools across the UK, we recognise that the brains of children who have been traumatised by life events are completely preoccupied by trying to survive. Their subconscious is dominated by working out how to feel safe, how to manage their strong emotions and how to have their primary needs met. Whilst their brain is chronically engaged with trying to survive in what they perceive to be an unsafe, scary world, the children often have little ability to focus on learning. So we have created places for them to recover rather than 'be managed'.

I developed the concept of having Therapeutic Mentoring Rooms within mainstream schools as a solution to the growing need for teachers and education staff to be able to work alongside a specialist, trauma-informed psychotherapist on the school site. A trauma-informed psychotherapist is a professional who has usually completed counselling or psychotherapy training and additional trauma training. Psychotherapy allows the person to look deeper into the problems and worries, and deal with feelings of confusion and thoughts that cause sadness, anxiety or unsettled behaviour. Psychotherapy usually involves talking, but with children especially, other modalities are used – for example, art, music, play, drama and movement. Through a partnership with a specialist psychotherapist who is confident and familiar with the journey of recovery for a child who has been traumatised, mainstream staff can develop their own professional skills with confidence. In these rooms the therapeutic mentor will work with children who have been traumatised on a range of activities that have been suggested on a treatment plan. The activities will have been written by the trauma psychotherapist, and the sessions take place for a specified amount of time each week. As part of the process, the specialist trauma psychotherapist will assess the children regularly and also give clinical supervision to the teacher mentor every half term.

To open a Therapeutic Mentoring Room in a mainstream school led by a member of staff already employed by the school, the teacher has to complete the BdT Ltd Certificate in Therapeutic Mentoring, which is a 14-day intensive training in trauma recovery. In this approach, schools can upskill the current staff who already have positive relationships with the children. The school can then be flexible about the hours spent on each child and enable recovery to take place in the school context without the need to employ new staff.

A second project that I have also founded is the Trauma Recovery Centre, which has special buildings away from mainstream school sites in various cities across the UK. Here, children and young people come out of school or after school to access trauma-informed creative therapy in a fun, playful, homely environment whilst the parent is supported in a trauma-informed parenting group. In each TRC there are smaller therapy rooms that look enticing to any child, welcoming entrances with sofas and friendly faces and specially trained professionals.

Both projects are based on theories that are foundational to the work of psychotherapists and which maintain that the process of recovery includes processing the traumatic experience, which may need the help of a clinical trauma specialist. As a teacher and a psychotherapist I know the importance of both professions working well together and the centrality of both the clinician's professional training (in understanding the subconscious where the impact of trauma resides) and the teacher's ability to build a consistent relationship and nurturing culture in the classroom. I believe that education staff are positioned to be able to focus on the importance of relationships and emotional literacy and the vital underpinning philosophy that 'behaviour is communication'. Meanwhile, the partner clinicians can unpick and unravel the subconscious and unconscious aspects that may be driving behaviour and reactions because this has become stuck and muddled due to the trauma.

The other primary theories that underpin the work in both projects that I have started are those that are central to play and arts therapy such as Axline (1947, 1964) and Oaklander (1997) alongside contemporary research regarding neuroscience and relationships from other clinicians such as Bruce Perry (2006; Perry and Szalavitz 2011) and the life works of Bessel van der Kolk (1984, 1987, 1996, 2014) and Dan Siegel (1999). These clinicians offer research findings and practical frameworks for all who work with the traumatised child, but also offer an ideal framework for a team around the child of teacher, parent and clinician to work together with similar emphasis but differing roles. The foundational child development theories also offer a strong foundation to our work as we can then identify behaviour that is inappropriate to the child's biological age, and could therefore indicate a possible conflicting emotional age of the child.

When working with complex trauma we work within the TRC 'Complex Trauma Framework', which is a synergy of the structural dissociation theory of van der Hart, Nijenhuis and Steele (2006) along with Watkins and Watkins' ego state theory (1979) and my own Daisy Theory (de Thierry 2015).

What is trauma and the trauma continuum?

Stress is a natural experience that can facilitate positive momentum if the context is warm and encouraging but can become toxic when there is no solution to that stress (Neves de Jesus and Conboy 2001). The impact of stress on healthy brain development has been discussed in Chapter 3. Trauma is an extreme form of stress and can be defined as a 'psychologically distressing event that is outside the range of usual human experience, often involving a sense of intense fear, terror and helplessness' (Perry 2007 p.15), while Levine and Kline (2006) suggest that 'trauma happens when any experience stuns us like a bolt out of the blue; it overwhelms us, leaving us altered and disconnected from our bodies. Any coping mechanisms we may have had are undermined, and we feel utterly helpless and hopeless' (Levine 2006, p.4). Trauma in childhood causes fear, pain and turmoil, and will impact on a child's body, brain, memory, emotions, relationships, learning and behaviour (de Thierry 2015). It is also vital to understand that trauma primarily lies in the body and in the subconscious and that this needs discharging appropriately.

Traumatic experiences, and our responses to them, vary widely and the trauma continuum (de Thierry 2013, p.97) seeks to classify the impact of trauma on specific individuals. The trauma continuum (see Figure 8.1) identifies three 'trauma types'.

For beginning teachers, knowledge of traumatic stress and how it develops, presents and affects the lives of the children may be the first step towards being able to interact positively with those affected by trauma.

TYPE I TRAUMA
SINGLE INCIDENT
TRAUMA

TYPE II TRAUMA
MULTIPLE
TRAUMAS

TYPE III TRAUMA
MULTIPLE PERVASIVE
TRAUMAS FROM
EARLY AGE THAT
CONTINUE OVER
LENGTH OF TIME

Figure 8.1: The trauma continuum
Source: © Betsy de Thierry

The Type I (single incident or 'simple) trauma is usually defined as a one-off traumatic incident or crisis. Simple trauma is difficult and painful and has the potential to cause injury to the child. This level of trauma, however, usually has less stigma associated with the experience, and therefore other people are often responsive and supportive to those who have experienced these traumatic incidents. This results in Type I trauma being placed at the beginning of the trauma continuum, especially if this is an experience within the context of a stable family where processing difficulties is a normal cultural expectation. This kind of supportive environment could significantly limit the damage of the simple trauma experience – for example, a car accident where the emergency services are involved but there is no long-term harm, or a child who has to adapt to their parents' divorce but this was handled with care, thereby limiting the emotional damage to the child.

The continuum progresses according to the degree of trauma experienced, the frequency of different traumatic experiences, and the level of social support and family attachment a child has to enable them to process the trauma and recover.

Type II trauma is trauma that is not a single event but has been an ongoing experience over a period of time where the child has endured multiple trauma such as sexual abuse, physical abuse, domestic violence or some other traumatic occurrence. These multiple traumas will often fracture the core family relationships and simultaneously create terror and powerlessness for the child.

Type III or multiple pervasive (complex) trauma is positioned at the furthest end of the continuum (see Figure 8.1) and refers to a child who experiences multiple abuse and/or neglect over many years, without a family setting in which the traumatic experience could be processed or spoken about in a recovery-focused manner. This may be due to parents' absence, neglect or inability themselves to cope with the trauma. Complex trauma usually involves interpersonal violence, violation or threat, and is often longer in duration. It is almost always an experience that causes a strong sense of shame due to community stigma, which can lead to the child feeling isolated and different – for example, repeated sexual abuse, trafficking, torture, organised abuse, repeated care placements that break down or severe neglect.

The parenting capacity continuum

It is important that the trauma continuum in Figure 8.1 is considered together with the parenting capacity continuum as set out in Figure 8.2. The parenting (or environmental) capacity continuum illustrates the level of support that is currently available in the child's environment and the experiences they may have had in the foundational years of their life.

Figure 8.2: The parenting (or environmental) capacity continuum
Source: © Betsy de Thierry

The first point of the parenting or environmental capacity continuum (warm, caring, verbal) indicates an environment where the child is probably experiencing a long-term relationship with a caring consistent adult. The adult may also be nurturing and enables the child to process verbally any concerns, worries or fears they may have. At this stage of the continuum there is a consistent, warm and genuine emotional connection between the adult and the child that can facilitate a natural recovery from a traumatic event. The middle stage of the continuum represents the child experiencing a lack of emotional connection, a brushing off, or even the possibility of being bullied for expressing some emotions. These children may be dissuaded from exploring their feelings and responses to situations, and therefore any natural processing through words or play may be curtailed by the adult. The furthest, most negative end of the continuum, is where the child may be punished if they ever talk or explore any responses to the trauma they have experienced, and they may live with a degree of fear regarding the adult who is meant to be caring for them. The further that a child is moved towards this end of the continuum, the more the child will experience a challenge in processing their trauma experience within their primary relationships, and therefore the impact of the trauma will be more significant and longer lasting.

Evidence suggests that the weaker the relational support that is available to the child currently and historically (for example, the relationships with parents, grandparents, long-term relatives etc.), the greater the degree of impact the traumatic experience may have. Conversely, the more relationally rich the child's life has been, the less the impact of the trauma. Other factors that need to be reflected upon when using the continuum are the combined factors of the trauma experienced; the trauma symptoms manifest; the current environment of the child (primarily the parenting capacity); and the support system including the length of time that the support system has been in place.

Professionals are therefore encouraged to reflect on both the trauma continuum (Figure 8.1) and the parenting capacity continuum (Figure 8.2) simultaneously in relation to individual children. This, in turn, enables a professional discussion to be had that leads to an agreed place on the continuum for that child at that time. Having agreed this together, the team around the child can then plan an appropriate intervention to meet the child's needs.

The impact of trauma on emotional development: responding to threats (or perceived threats)

Abuse and neglect in childhood affects a child's psychological functioning, their neurological (brain) responses, their spirit, their relationships and their capacity for hope (see *Teaching the Child on the Trauma Continuum*, de Thierry 2015). It is known that from early infancy through to adulthood, trauma can change how we perceive ourselves and the world around us, how we process information, and how we behave in response to our environment (Cozolino 2006). Without appropriate intervention these altered cognitive processes and behavioural responses can lead to long-term problems, such as difficulties in learning, self-regulation and/or behaviour (Cattanach 1992).

As earlier chapters have illustrated, it is in times of great stress, or trauma, that the brain activates its deeply instinctive 'fight, flight or freeze' survival responses. These responses to threat are ancient, primal mechanisms that prioritise surviving over the thinking, judging or evaluating that takes place in the prefrontal cortex (neocortex). The responses to threat or perceived threat are located in the brain stem, which is the area of the brain that is fully formed by birth. It is responsible for breathing, heart rate, body temperature and also these automated threat responses. The brain stem, on alert, immediately sends messages to an area of the brain called the amygdala that is located in the limbic area, just above the brain stem.

In our work in the Therapeutic Mentoring Rooms and at the TRC, we spend time with the children exploring how the brain is working and how it is processing information and stimuli from the environment. We tell the children that the amygdala is like a smoke alarm, and alerts the body to the threat (perceived threat or clear danger), and that adrenaline and cortisol gets pumped around the body so that it is ready to have enough energy to react in an emergency.

When the limbic areas of the brain are fully alert and active, the consequence is that the prefrontal cortex goes 'off line'. As trained therapists, we explain to the children that when this happens, our ability to be rational, reasonable and thoughtful is hindered. We believe that this physiological response to trauma needs to be explained to the children to reduce the shame and shock that they often feel about their responses.

Too often, an adult's first reaction to an incident of high emotion, hurt or aggression in school is to say to the child, 'Why are you doing this?' The problem here is that most children are desperately wanting to say, 'I don't know, you tell me – you're the adult! I am more terrified than anyone else by what I am doing; I did not want to do this and I'm scared!!' They cannot articulate this as their ability to reflect or be rational is still 'off line'. As adults, we need to wait until the 'emotional brain' has calmed and the 'thinking brain' has re-engaged before we can begin to reflect on the incident.

Trauma symptoms and interventions that work

When any of us have been traumatised, it impacts our behaviour, relationships, emotions and learning. The changes in these areas can often be seen as symptoms of the trauma. When they are understood in that framework, they are less negative and facilitate a more empathic and understanding response, and subsequently the symptoms can be reduced and the child can recover.

Type I 'simple' trauma, or the first third of the trauma continuum, suggests that children at this level need opportunities and interventions that enable them to develop positive attachments and growth in their understanding of emotional literacy. At this stage on the trauma continuum, a child could be experiencing a single trauma symptom, such as sudden anger outbursts, or being continually agitated. For these children, any provision in schools facilitating emotional growth and recovery will be a necessary addition to their curriculum. This might include an understanding of the brain and how it works, work on emotional literacy, Emotion Coaching, breathing exercises and a focus on relationship approaches such as kindness, empathy and listening to each other.

Moving towards the middle of the trauma continuum and Type II trauma suggests that a child or young person at this level has been significantly impacted by the trauma experience, with the trauma symptoms now interrupting normal functioning on a daily basis. In this case, a child may experience multiple trauma symptoms, such as flashbacks, nightmares, self-harming, aggression, shut-down responses or outbursts of prolonged anger. Conversely, these children may also demonstrate compliance due to the level of coercive control in their home life, so that the risk of them not doing what is required is intrinsically linked to their life or death. This is not an exaggeration. Sometimes children we work with have been sadly threatened with horrible scenarios if they don't behave well in school, because their home life is hiding something, and this can cause worryingly high levels of compliance in the children.

In Type II trauma, two primary adaptive response patterns often follow, namely, hyperarousal responses (acting out, visible behaviours) and hypo-arousal (acting in, withdrawn) behaviours. Schools often give more attention to the hyperaroused responses due to the impact on the other children and the disruptive nature of such a response. A lot of the hyperaroused behaviour is due to the changes that the brain of a traumatised child has made in order to focus on survival. These children need to learn to self-regulate using techniques to calm their system, such as breathing and grounding techniques. They need to be able to slowly identify which behaviours, emotions, responses, reactions and experiences are actually trauma symptoms in the context of a warm and empathetic adult who they trust. This can slowly reduce many of the symptoms.

Trauma symptoms that are hypo-arousal (acting in, withdrawn) behaviours can be less disruptive in a classroom but usually indicate that the child has been exposed to things that caused significant terror and that help has not been found to process it. The more silent and internal the symptoms, the more concerning they are for long-term emotional wellbeing. Staff need to keep an eye out for those quieter, more internalised trauma responses that cause less disruption to others but cause huge disruption to a child's life. This kind of trauma may only become explicitly apparent when they are quite entrenched. Usually these children cannot risk being angry and volatile as this would mean their needs may not be met and so they shut down. Behaviours such as freezing, numbness, dissociation, lethargy, daydreaming or disengagement from the here and now can all indicate that the child may be living in a state of fear and confusion. For these children to recover they are dependent on taking time to build a relationship with an adult they can trust who can enable them to slowly process and explore their feelings and worries. This is usually where a professional clinician (psychotherapist) would need to be involved, as the impact of the trauma is affecting the whole physiological system and the unconscious and subconscious is therefore overwhelmed. School staff need to be aware of the level of vulnerability and therefore the impact of the smallest negativity, failure, rejection or teasing, as this could cause a huge outburst. These children need warm, empathetic, kind, key adults who treat them with respect for being so brave.

When a child is not safe and so develops additional maladaptive coping mechanisms to survive, a child moves further along the trauma continuum towards complex trauma. The complex trauma response represented by Type III is the internalised adaptation that enables a child to survive despite an overwhelming traumatic experience and an unmet need. This would indicate that the child needs help to unpack their non-conscious mind, which may be full to overflowing with negative experiences. It is important to note here that any interventions would need to include a trauma specialist who is trained to work with unconscious processes. These particular children need targeted support from education staff or therapy staff using trauma-informed interventions, which are very different to more traditional cognitive and behavioural approaches commonly advocated for use in school. Indeed, superficial cognitive and behavioural interventions may be inappropriate or actively harmful for children with Type III level trauma (de Thierry 2015; Bombèr and Hughes 2013).

Metaphors and muddy buckets

An illustration that I use in my work in both the TRC and Therapeutic Mentoring Rooms to explore the impact of trauma on a child, young person or adult refers to the 'buckets' that we all carry around with us internally. I explain that every child (and adult) has a shiny, golden bucket that collects love, happy moments, feelings of success and affirmations. The more that is in the shiny bucket, the more stable and secure a child can feel. Then there is the muddy bucket. This is where all the negative experiences collect, and when life is too busy, the lid goes on and the contents of the bucket simmer until there is time to process the contents. Children seem to recognise when they have 'full buckets' and need help emptying them.

As adults we know far too well what it is like to have a catastrophic event occur and then have to put those thoughts, feelings and worries in a bucket so that we can assume our professional roles during the day. At the end of the day, hopefully, there is time to attend to the feelings or worries and to be able to process the bucket's contents. But if we don't have time and more and more has gone into the bucket, then we can leak! When we leak as adults we can become grumpy, irritable, tired or sad – and when we leak this can be communicated to our colleagues and to the children with whom we work.

By way of illustration, I was recently delivering training in a school where the Year 6 cohort (aged 10–11) were suddenly escalating their negative behaviour and the staff were struggling to cope with the extent of their challenging behaviour. I offered support to the staff and some debriefing around the golden and muddy buckets that we all carry. The training went on to include ideas on self-regulation that were relevant to the emotional age of these children. The headteacher emailed me the following day with the title, 'The staff have shiny, golden buckets now and the children are settling down again.'

It is important to note that, as adults working in schools, we all need time to debrief and process the tough times in our classrooms and our home lives. Professional supervision is important, and this is discussed later, in Chapter 12. Processing our own experiences will then enable us to be emotionally resilient and to be calm and emotionally engaged with our students. If we were told to just 'reframe our thinking' or 'make good choices' (as many children are advised in school), then we would either shut down emotionally, disengage from relationships or struggle to control our emotions – which generally leads to some kind of explosion! We all need time to 'empty our buckets' and, as adults, many of us find ways of doing this – we talk with friends, we play sport or music, we meditate or focus on the power of now. We know that when an adult can respond with kindness and empathy to children's behaviour that is unpleasant, then the child can begin to build trust that they are not 'too bad' and can heal and recover. One of the most powerful and effective approaches to enable a child who has been traumatised is to refrain from being shocked, horrified, upset or cross when their behaviour is challenging, but this is only possible when our own buckets are not full to overflowing!

For many children following trauma, all they know they have is strong feelings and behaviours they don't feel in control of – and these feelings are challenging (anxiety, fear, sadness, rejection, failure). These feelings are hard for the children to articulate or explain and they reside in the child's subconscious. The more negative emotions that pile up in the muddy bucket, the deeper in the subconscious these feelings will be until there seems to be little link between the negative behaviour being witnessed and the child's experiences. At an early stage (Type I or II trauma) a teacher, friend or friendly person might help empty the child's muddy bucket with attuned support. However, the fuller the bucket gets, the more the child will need specialist help as the bucket contents get increasingly murky and are driven deeper into the subconscious.

Common interventions that will not work for traumatised children

The primary work that I lead tends to be with the children and young people in trauma Type III and who require one-to-one support. These children have usually caused high levels of anxiety to staff in schools. The number of traumatised children requiring one-to-one support is rising, and the majority of whole-school, mainstream approaches do not necessarily help these children engage in learning or settle down in the classroom. In fact, whilst many mainstream approaches can equip staff with some tools that are helpful for children exhibiting unsettled behaviour, sadly, the same interventions can become counter-productive for the most traumatised. A lot of these mainstream approaches are based on cognitive approaches that, whilst being helpful in the later stages of recovery, are not sufficient interventions for the most traumatised in our schools. To be effective, there needs to be the understanding that trauma primarily lies in the body and in the subconscious, and that this needs discharging appropriately. Many of the mainstream approaches are reliant on the cognitive, 'thinking' part of the brain, and this can be immensely difficult for deeply traumatised children to access. As discussed earlier, the traumatised and frightened brain has been rewired for survival, which often reduces the child's access to the area of their brain responsible for reflection, thinking, negotiating and being rational. Asking traumatised children to work through cognitive behavioural interventions can be highly inappropriate, and can then cause further shame and failure for these most vulnerable students.

Indeed, simplistic understandings of needs based on attachment theory can also be misleading when working with traumatised children.

In one TRC case, a referred child had always had a very secure attachment to her mother but was then sexually abused by her father in a way that used coercive control as part of the manipulation. The manipulation, that was central in the abuse, actually depended on the child having a strong attachment relationship with her mother and, consequently, this is a child who is traumatised but who does not have a history of poor attachment. School staff working with this child were confident that they were adopting an evidence-based, cognitive psycho-education model of support and intervention that would meet the needs of the child. Sadly, the school believed that their framework was enough to help the traumatised child and declined advice from the TRC that emphasised the in-body, subconscious nature of the trauma. This led to this child's behaviour escalating due to feeling unsafe and misunderstood in school. For the TRC team, this child needed to have an emotional connection with a member of staff who understood that the impact of trauma resides in their subconscious and body. These children have hidden needs. The staff working with the traumatised child need to take notice of these needs, not just what is presented. If this child had been able to have a 'known safe adult' who understood trauma and who knew some of her history, this escalation may have been avoided.

For further ideas and strategies, please see *The Simple Guide to Understanding Trauma: What It Is and How to Help* (de Thierry 2016).

Staff training

TRC and Therapeutic Mentoring Rooms firmly believe that trauma-trained psychotherapists or psychologists need to be involved in the life of a school because they are trained in working with the subconscious and unconscious. Once this training is combined with specific trauma training, this professional involvement may be what is needed to enable traumatised children to recover and subsequently engage in learning.

The training for education staff in the support of traumatised children can be undertaken through BdT Ltd, the organisation that provides the theoretical underpinning and training to all the staff of the TRC and Therapeutic Mentoring Rooms. The 14-day training programme includes a thorough exploration of the impact of trauma, listening skills, neuroscience of relationships and the brain, creative arts tools to use in the classroom, and an understanding of the journey of recovery.

Following the completion of this course, staff in schools can open a Therapeutic Mentoring Room that provides the qualified teacher with a clinical supervisor and individual development plans for the most traumatised children. This ensures that the children have appropriate support that aids recovery and not just the mainstream, whole-school approaches to 'behaviour management'. This seems to be a great balance between education staff and therapy staff working as a team.

For more information please see www.betsytraininguk.co.uk and www.trc-uk.org.

Final thoughts

> I really am grateful to my TA [teaching assistant] Mrs S. She has coped with me being really horrid. I didn't want to be that awful but I couldn't seem to do anything else until she helped me know what to do with the strong feelings that would explode in me. I was scared at first but Mrs S. helped me know I wasn't a bad person, just a bit messed up. Now I'm not. I can do stuff to stop me exploding and know that it's going to be okay. (Steven, age 11)

Children who have experienced trauma will be in your classrooms and will be in need of your professional understanding and support. Trauma can differ significantly from attachment insecurity, and mainstream interventions that might be appropriate for the behaviour management of the majority might be counter-productive for those who have experienced significant trauma.

Steven's reflection on the work of Mrs S. (above) confirms that progress, recovery and change can take place for all children, given the right support.

This chapter has sought to enable the beginning teacher to grasp the importance of understanding the different levels of trauma, and what the most effective strategy can be to each stage. This chapter is also bringing the voice of the clinician as the professional who is trained to understand the impact of trauma. The clinician can work safely with the unconscious and subconscious to facilitate recovery, alongside the important work of the teacher who creates the culture of safe relationships in the classroom. The Therapeutic Mentoring Room and the TRC work in partnership with schools and staff to ensure that the classroom culture is trauma-informed and the child is able to process their subconscious safely as they move towards recovery.

REFLECTION POINTS

1. What are the key characteristics of a teacher who facilitates a trauma-informed environment in their classroom?

2. Can you name ten trauma symptoms that may present in classrooms?

3. How might these symptoms be mislabelled and misunderstood?

4. Reflect on the behavioural presentation of one child and discuss with a colleague where they might fit on the trauma continuum. Remember to discuss the known trauma history, trauma symptoms and parenting or environmental capacity.

Bibliography

Alisic, E. (2010) *Toolkit Kind en Trauma. Informatie voor Leerkrachten van Groep 5 t/m 8* [*Toolkit Child and Trauma. Information for Teachers in the Last Four Grades of Primary School*]. Utrecht: University Medical Center Utrecht. Available at http://trauma-recovery.net/over/, accessed on 5 March 2013.

Alisic, E. (2012) 'Teachers' perspectives on providing support to children after trauma: A qualitative study.' *School Psychology Quarterly 27*, 1, 51–59.

Alisic, E., Bus, M., Dulack, W., Pennings, L. and Splinter, J. (2012) 'Teachers' experiences supporting children after traumatic exposure.' *Journal of Traumatic Stress 25*, 98–101.

Axline, V. (1947) *Play Therapy.* New York: Ballatine.

Axline, V. (1964) *Dibs in Search of Self.* New York: Ballatine.

BBC News UK (2013) 'One in ten young people "cannot cope with daily life".' 2 January. Available at www.bbc.co.uk/news/uk-20885838, accessed on 18 March 2013.

Bombèr, L.M. and Hughes. D. (2013) *Settling Troubled Pupils to Learn: Why Relationships Matter in School.* Belper: Worth Publishing Ltd.

Cafcass (2009) 'Care Statistics Continue to Rise.' Press release, 8 May. London: Cafcass. Available at www.cafcass.gov.uk/news/archive/2009/care-statistics.aspx, accessed on 12 June 2013.

Cattanach, A. (1992) *Play Therapy with Abused Children.* London: Jessica Kingsley Publishers.

Cozolino, L. (2006) *The Neuroscience of Human Relationships. Attachment and the Social Brain.* New York: Norton Publishers.

de Thierry, B. (2015) *Teaching the Child on the Trauma Continuum.* London: Grosvenor House Publishing Ltd.

de Thierry, B. (2016) *The Simple Guide to Understanding Trauma. What It Is and How to Help.* London: Jessica Kingsley Publishers.

DfE (Department for Education) (2004) *Every Child Matters: Change for Children.* London: The Stationery Office. Available at http://webarchive.nationalarchives.gov. uk/20130401151715/https://www.education.gov.uk/publications/standard/ publicationdetail/page1/dfes/1081/2004, accessed on 16 November 2013.

Donnelly, L. (2013) 'Children as young as five suffering from depression.' *The Daily Telegraph,* 30 September. Available at www.telegraph.co.uk/health/healthnews/10342447/Children-as-young-as-five-suffering-from-depression.html, accessed on 21 October 2013.

Levine, P.A. and Kline, M. (2006) *Trauma Through a Child's Eyes: Awakening the Ordinary Miracle of Healing.* Berkeley, CA: North Atlantic Books.

Neves de Jesus, S. and Conboy, J. (2001) 'A stress management course to prevent teacher distress.' *International Journal of Educational Management 15,* 3.

Oaklander, V. (1997) 'The therapeutic process with children and adolescents.' *Gestalt Review 1,* 4, 292–317.

Perry, B. (2006) *Applying Principles of Neurodevelopment to Clinical Work with Maltreated and Traumatized Children.* New York: The Guilford Press.

Perry, B. (2007) *Stress, Trauma and Post-traumatic Stress Disorders in Children: An Introduction.* Available at https://childtrauma.org, accessed on 30 November 2016.

Perry, B. and Szalavitz, M. (2011) *Born for Love: Why Empathy Is Essential – and Endangered.* New York: HarperCollins.

Siegel, D. (1999) *The Developing Mind: Towards a Neurobiology of Interpersonal Experience.* New York: The Guilford Press.

Solomon, E.P. and Heide, H.P. (1999) 'Type III trauma: Toward a more effective conceptualization of psychological trauma.' *International Journal of Offender Therapy and Comparative Criminology 43,* 2. Available at http://ijo.sagepub.com/content/43/2/202. short, accessed on 20 March 2017.

Terr, L.C. (1991) 'Childhood traumas: An outline and an overview.' *The American Journal of Psychiatry 19,* 91, 148, 10–20.

van der Hart, O., Nijenhuis, E. and Steele, K. (2006) *The Haunted Self: Structural Dissociation and the Treatment of Chronic Traumatisation.* New York: Norton.

van der Kolk, B.A. (ed.) (1984) *Post-traumatic Stress Disorder: Psychological and Biological Sequelae.* Washington DC: American Psychiatric Press.

van der Kolk, B.A. (1987) *Psychological Trauma.* Washington, DC: American Psychiatric Press.

van der Kolk, B.A., McFarlane A.C., Weisaeth, L. (eds) (1996) *Traumatic Stress: The Effects of Overwhelming Experience on Mind, Body and Society.* New York: Guilford Press.

van der Kolk, B.A. (2014) *The Body Keeps the Score: Brain, Mind, and Body in the Healing of Trauma.* New York: Viking Press.

Watkins, J.G. and Watkins, H.H. (1979) 'The Theory and Practice of Ego State Therapy.' In H. Grayson (ed.) *Short Term Approaches to Psychotherapy* (pp.176–220). New York: Human Sciences Press.

9

People Meet in a Classroom and Say 'Hello'

A Psychoanalytic Perspective on the Emotional Relationship between the Teacher and Student

PETER WILSON

The learning experience in the classroom can be strongly influenced by a range of emotional tensions and conflicts that reside within the teacher–student relationship. Many of these are irrational and unconscious and can have a disturbing effect on how learning takes place. In this chapter, an illustration is given of this which highlights a particular 'meeting' between one teacher (Mrs Parker) and one student (Jimmy) in which they say, in effect, 'hello' to each other – from widely different backgrounds and perspectives.

The concepts of 'transference' and 'counter-transference' in psychoanalytic theory and of the 'internal working model' in attachment theory are used to help throw light on the quality of the interaction between the two. Misunderstandings and misperceptions can be more fully understood with reference to the experience of both individuals outside the classroom and from the past. The importance of support for both is underlined, not least for the teacher, in the form of work discussion groups and consultations in which all kinds of feelings and sensibilities can be expressed, shared and thought about.

'Mrs Parker' and 'Jimmy' in this account are two fictitious characters, composite of similar teacher–student interactions.

The teacher

I'm Mrs Parker, 35 years old, happily married with two young children. And it was Monday.

The weekend had been busy. On Saturday, we had a birthday party for one of my children and we went out for dinner in the evening. On Sunday, we visited my parents for lunch. This was fine, but my youngest brother refused to join us, which upset my mother. We then did some shopping. By 9 o'clock I was exhausted. But marking and preparation had to be done for the week ahead.

By and large I had a good day on Monday. But at the end of it, things went wrong. I had a Year 7 class for English. They were restless and fidgety from the start. I thought I was well prepared and I tried to create as safe and well-structured an atmosphere as possible in the classroom.

Despite all my efforts, however, two boys would not stop giggling and playing about at the back of the class. They seemed to enjoy flicking bits of paper at each other. I told them to stop and attend to their work, but after a few moments, they carried on, just as before. I reprimanded them as straightforwardly as I could, but to no avail. They ignored me and, worse, one of the boys, Jimmy, the bigger and bulkier of the two, started laughing out loud and making farting noises, which got the whole class going.

I decided to separate them and bring one of them down to sit at the front, close to me. For a moment, I thought this might work. But much to my annoyance, he sat with his arms folded, smirking and staring at me, ignoring what he was supposed to be doing and continuing to make the farty noises right in front of me. I tried very hard to be patient and firm, but with no success. He then started to walk around the class 'accidentally' knocking off the paper work of the other children.

It is at that point that I lost it. I'd had enough. I shouted at him to behave and eventually I told him to leave the class and report to the year head. At first, he just grinned, but as he got up to go, he called me 'a fucking, stuck-up bitch' and a 'useless teacher'. His grin had gone and for a moment I felt scared of him.

After he had gone, I couldn't settle the class and I was left feeling furious but defeated. I had lost control of myself, I had excluded a child from my class and I had not managed to create the safe atmosphere I intended. Furthermore, I doubted whether I had properly covered the syllabus. I was 'a useless teacher' – just as Jimmy had said. I thought I should quit.

The student

I'm a student. I'm Jimmy, 12 years old and big for my age. I live with mum and dad, two older brothers and two younger sisters. And it was Monday.

Saturday had been boring and on Sunday I stayed in bed all morning. I had to stay in for lunch because my gran and uncle were coming over. All right, I suppose, but in the evening, things went mad. My dad got drunk and brought a couple of his mates over. Soon he and my mum were screaming at each other. My sisters were crying and my brother had a go at him, which ended up in a fight. The best I could do was to get out of the house. I found a couple of mates and just hung about until real late.

There are always rows at home. My dad drinks too much and he keeps on losing down the betting shop. He's got a nasty temper, takes it out on my mum and me. He's all right sometimes, especially when he's got some money in his pocket, but for most of the time, he's a pain in the neck and I don't like him. What really gets me, though, is that my mum lets him get away with it.

I don't really get her. Sometimes, she can be really nice and gives us treats and even cuddles. But she has always been sad, and this is getting worse. She drinks too much too, and on some days she can stay in bed all day and not lift a finger for anyone. My brother says she's got mental problems, whatever that means. But he tells me she has to take pills for it.

Anyway, back at school and I was sort of relieved not to be at home. School's all right. I've got a lot of mates there and we can have a laugh. But the teachers don't leave you alone. You can be just minding your own business, larking about and then bang, just like at home, some bloke is having a go at you. That sports teacher is the worst. Fat big bugger, full of himself, reminds me of my dad. Sod him.

And then there all these other teachers. I can't make them out most of the time. But on Monday, I got really pissed off. We've got these English lessons, all about verbs and things and books. Fair enough, but in walked this English teacher. We've had her before. Posh cow, fat arse. She took no notice of me. She's got her favourites and as far as I can see, couldn't care less about me and my mates. So I thought, if she's going to be that way, I wasn't going to be bothered to listen to her. So I decided to have just a little chat with my friend. We flicked a few bits of paper about and really we were just minding our own business.

The next thing I knew was that she was telling me to sit in the front of the class. That annoyed me but I put up with it. But she kept on having a go and then suddenly out of the blue, she just lost her rag and started yelling at me, calling me all sorts of names. I couldn't believe it. It was completely out of order. And then she told me to go to the year head. Well, that was it. I'd had enough. I told her she was a useless teacher and right stuck-up.

Not a good day. Good to be out of the house. But at the end of it all, I felt crap. Shouted at and pushed around, no one really taking any interest in me. So to hell with it. They are all like that. Just interested in themselves. Why bother? Who cares? I'll do what I want to do...

Teacher and student: the meeting

So here we are, at the end of an ordinary Monday in an ordinary school. Two worlds colliding, two people at odds with one another. Both, in their own ways, left feeling devalued, angry and wanting to give up. And the upshot? No cooperation, no enjoyment and no learning.

What on earth went wrong between these two people?

A whole range of factors might well have played a part – but common to them all in one way or another was perhaps the most pervasive, the emotional factor. That is to say, the experience of strong feelings that can so easily consume people's minds and have such a powerful impact on behaviour and attitude.

When we read of the impasse between 'Mrs Parker' and 'Jimmy', we are witnessing something very intense and irrational. There was a kind of 'madness' going on between the two of them in which neither could make full sense of themselves or the other. They were in the midst of an emotional muddle that was clouding their vision and judgement. Many perspectives on human behaviour can be drawn upon to make sense of this muddle, but two in particular need to be taken into account, one residing in psychoanalysis, the other in attachment theory – both contributing to a substantial body of knowledge that is built on extensive clinical insights and empirical research.

Psychoanalysis and attachment theory

Psychoanalysis refers to a body of theory drawn from a particular kind of clinical practice. It consists of a wide range of ideas and concepts that have emerged from the clinical experience and theoretical thinking of many psychoanalysts across the world since Freud began it all at the beginning of the 20th century (Freud 1910; see also Ellman 2010). These ideas and concepts have been attempts essentially to build an understanding of the complexity of human nature and behaviour. Psychoanalysis is viewed with suspicion by some who regard it as unscientific, even fanciful (Spence 1994). The fact that it highlights the existence of the unconscious – that is to say, that so much of what we do and think takes place outside the province of our conscious life and that we are moved and driven by forces of which we are not aware – does not add to its popularity (it being seen as an affront to our conscious rationality). Nevertheless, there is so much that it can offer to throw light on what goes on between people emotionally that it would be a pity if this were to be overlooked.

Like many other schools of thought it places great emphasis on the influence of infant and child experience on later life (Fonagy 2001). How well a child, or an adult in later life, can trust and care for other people, how well he or she can be curious and free to learn, how well he or she is able to cope with frustration and adversity – so much of this is determined by what has gone before.

Following on from this, psychoanalysis highlights the concept of 'transference' and 'counter-transference'.

Transference refers to how feelings and thoughts can be so readily 'transferred' from one person to another (Freud 1912, 1914; Horne and Lanyado 1999; Rycroft 1968). A child or an adolescent, for example, may behave towards a teacher in a similar way as he or she has behaved towards a parent in his or her past, or continues do so in the present. Basically, what transference means is that our early experiences can become revived, repeated and acted out in the ways we relate and behave with other people in the present. This is not to say that all our current relationships are affected in this way; far from it. But in particular circumstances and in some people (usually at times of stress), transference can play a particularly significant part. We become more inclined to relate to other people not as they actually are, but more as we imagine them to be, according to our past experience. For example, if a child's father was cruel and frightening when he or she was a child, it is likely that with certain men in authority, the child may well be inclined to perceive them in a similar way as the child experienced his or her father– and either defy them or flee from them.

The flip side of transference is 'counter-transference', which refers to the emotional response of the person who is in receipt of the impact of these transference expectations. So, if an adult in a position of authority is aggressively challenged by a male student like 'Jimmy' who, as a child experienced the kind of father that he did, then the adult may well react with indignation at being seen as someone other than who they feel that they are. The adult may thus become impatient, punitive or just walk away.

Attachment theory has evolved from the research and writings of many psychoanalytic theorists. Its founder, John Bowlby (1969, 1988), himself a psychoanalyst, re-emphasised in the 1950s and 1960s the importance of early childhood experience for the mental health of children and adults. His theories underwent extensive empirical scientific scrutiny from the 1960s onwards (see Ainsworth and Whiting 1969; Ainsworth *et al.* 1978: Main 1995), and it is now well accepted that the experience of security in childhood is key to the wellbeing and emotional development of children (Holmes 2010).

At the centre of Bowlby's theory is the concept of an 'internal working model', and this has been introduced by Heather Geddes in Chapter 2. Bowlby conceived of this as a fundamental structure in the mind, built up during the course of numerous infantile and childhood experiences in relationships with their parents. He saw how children 'internalise' the patterns of attachment that their parents create with them, and how this forms the basis of their personalities, their views of themselves and their perception of others. Juliet Hopkins, an experienced child psychotherapist, illustrates this most clearly:

> For example, if a child has experienced reliably responsive caregiving he will construct a working model of the self as competent and lovable, but if he has experienced much rebuff, he will construct a model of the self as unworthy of help and comfort. (Hopkins 2015, p.61)

The concept of an internal working model is not dissimilar to that of transference. What has been set as routine and familiar in the founding years of a human being's life finds a way of perpetuating itself in current relationships, colouring and flavouring the perception the child has of him or herself and the expectations of others.

Applications of theory in the classroom

So how can these theories be of any help to the teacher, Mrs Parker?

In recent years, there has been a growing interest in applying attachment theory to a greater understanding of school life. Heather Geddes (2006), Louise Bombèr (2007) and Marie Delaney (2008), for example, have written with great clarity about the tensions that can exist in the classroom, and have offered positive practical suggestions to help teachers better cope with the difficulties they encounter.

The psychoanalytic concepts of transference and counter-transference can be of considerable value in this regard.

If Mrs Parker, for example, could have figured out a bit more clearly what it was about Jimmy that distressed her so much, and if she could have extended herself as far as possible to imagine where Jimmy was coming from emotionally, then maybe there could have been a greater chance that what turned out to be so stressful could have been handled without the same degree of animosity and confusion. This is not to suggest that the conflict and tension between the two would have been 'cured' or that Jimmy would somehow have become transformed in his behaviour. It is likely, however, that greater flexibility would have been found to take the edge out of the tension between them – that is to say, cumulatively, bit by bit and over time, the moments of harshness and resentment might become less strident, thus allowing for a more cooperative learning experience to take place.

The teacher, Mrs Parker

We can only speculate what might have been behind all this for Mrs Parker. This is not to question her integrity or competence as a teacher, but in the context of her own life, it is important to wonder what it was about Jimmy that got under her skin. Who did he represent in her mind? For example, did he arouse in her similar feelings she had for her own younger brother? Was there something wild and delinquent in him that both excited and repelled her? Was there even something sexual in his general manner of taunting her, making her feel at times oddly uncomfortable?

Was there something in the way Jimmy made her feel so impotent that challenged the part of herself that needed to prove that she was, in fact, a much needed and valued human being?

In asking questions such as these, the purpose is not to undermine Mrs Parker in any way, but rather to explore and understand an experience that was, for that moment, intensely emotional and irrational. She, like all of us, is none other than a mortal human being with all kinds of strengths and sensibilities. It matters that she could make sense of what was, on reflection, an over-reaction to Jimmy. With understanding and self-awareness, there is always the possibility of doing things differently and hopefully more constructively.

The student, Jimmy

If we now turn to Jimmy, we can see more clearly what was driving him in his way of being in the classroom. From what he tells us, home was not a safe place. Above all, he lived with fear of his father and sadness in relation to his mother.

His father sounded violent, erratic and overbearing, while his mother, depressed. Simply in terms of his current life, Jimmy felt scared, neglected and angry. We can only speculate again on whether he had lived with these feelings all his life. Families do change and function differently according to changed circumstances. But too often they do not, and it may well have been the case that Jimmy had experienced considerable insecurity from early on, growing up with an overwhelmed mother in a turbulent and unpredictable family atmosphere.

With this behind him, it is not unlikely that his 'internal working model' was such that he believed himself to be unworthy and others to be uncaring and attacking. And so, in effect, he brought this into his current life in the classroom situation.

Such was the nature of his transference that he tended to anticipate being attacked by male authority figures and ignored by female teachers. So strong were these anticipations that he unwittingly acted in such a way as to bring about confirmation of his worst fears – to be angrily censured and excluded by the adults in school.

In a most extraordinary and unconscious way, he seemed ready to provoke the very destiny he dreaded – evoking such a strong counter-transference in Mrs Parker that she found herself responding so punitively to him, which was so out of character.

To be succinct, Mrs Parker was not seen by Jimmy for what she thought she actually was, but much more in terms of what he had made of her in his mind, based on his childhood experience.

'Hello'

One way of thinking about transference and the living of the internal working model in the school setting is to imagine how children say, in effect, 'hello' when they come into school – not just 'hello' in words, but much more broadly in their behaviour, demeanour and attitude (Wilson 2003). It is as if they present themselves as they believe themselves to be and as they anticipate what will happen.

Let us take the following example from a child, not unlike Jimmy, a girl, 13 years old, struggling with the emotional abuse meted out by her father.

Hello, my dad is horrible to me.

Sometimes he's nice, but then he puts me down and ignores me.

He laughs at me, at my clothes, and says I am rubbish.

I feel scared of him and humiliated.

I feel bad and stupid, and I feel guilty and confused.

All this must be my fault.

Now when I meet you, Mr Teacher, I expect you to laugh at me the same way that he does, because that is what happens, see.

I think you think I am rubbish.

And so, I might do something to get you to take the piss out of me, just as I expect.

But…

I don't like the way things are because it's not right.

So, I could just give in. Who cares? Let him (and you) say whatever. Not much I can do about it. I'll treat myself as useless, not eat, go dirty. Even run away, leave school, sleep rough, become a slag.

Or I could make a fuss. Turn the table on you.

Tell you to piss off. Not to get near me. Not to taunt me.

I might call you names, ridicule you in front of everyone.

I could do these things to make you feel as scared and as helpless as I do.

I could get my own back and make you feel as low and embarrassed as I do.

This way I could make you feel how awful I feel…

– and so, get to feel a bit more in control of my life.

There is so much sadness and anger in this 'hello' that it can be of no surprise that teachers are left fielding the full force of its intensity and anguish. They may find themselves experiencing a whole range of feelings – attacked, abused, ignored – as if they were the student him or herself, or indeed, attacking, abusing, ignoring, as if they were the parent. These feelings and reflections are profoundly disturbing and potentially undermining. They are not, for the most part, of the teacher's own making, but aroused through the pressure of their students' transference expectations onto them.

Final thoughts

This chapter has focused on one particular distressing encounter between a teacher and a student. Of course, in the large group context of the whole school, this kind of difficulty can only be amplified and complicated in a wide range of comparable situations. Schools are places in which people of all kinds and ages come together and say their 'hellos' to each other. All kinds of agendas are brought in – academic, vocational and social – and so, too, the emotional. Everyone brings to the party so much of their childhoods and family circumstances that affect their relationships with each other. Teachers and students alike carry the brunt of each other's wishes and fears, more pronounced in some relationships than in others. Their own personal vulnerabilities can so easily be augmented by the effects of each other's vulnerabilities.

Attention needs to be paid. Students need a range of supports, including counselling for the more troubled. And teachers need the time and the space to reflect on their experiences in the classroom. They need to find ways of keeping themselves aware and alert to what is going on in their relationships with their students. It is important that the confusing and disturbing feelings they are often left with from their students are shared through teacher support structures.

How practical it might be to provide the opportunities for this kind of teacher support to occur – for example, through work discussion groups, consultations or supervision – is not clear. Some schools may regard such support to be an indulgence and irrelevant to the teacher's task. After all, there is no tradition of supervision as part of working practice in schools as there is, for example, in the psychotherapy/counselling professions. Such an attitude, however, is misguided because teachers need to feel safe and free enough to explore and learn from their doubts and uncertainties about their work without fear of censure or accusation of incompetence. Indeed, Chapter 15 by Dave Roberts in this book makes a strong case for supervision for all staff in schools. The poor retention rates currently in the teaching profession testify to the importance of this need for teacher support, which is too often absent.

To end on a more positive note, it is as well to remember that not all children in a classroom prevail upon teachers in the same way as do children like Jimmy. Nor do most children feel prevailed upon by the teachers, as did Jimmy. The majority of children are less torn by their family experiences. They do not bring strife into the classroom. Instead, they are likely to bring positive expectations and good will, which, in turn, invites more good will. Here is a 14-year-old girl who has enjoyed throughout her life secure and loving attachment experiences with her parents.

Hello,
    I've been loved by my mum and dad.
    I've felt secure and I've known where I stood.
    I just feel good and valued.
    I expect you to like me, just like my parents love me.
    I like you and I am not afraid.
    I trust you and I want to learn from you.
    I want to be here in school and do well with you.

Too good to be true? Romantic? Silly? Maybe.

But not impossible nor, in fact, uncommon. This 'hello' makes its point. It simply matters that teachers and students feel appreciated and want to come to school to teach and learn together.

▨ REFLECTION POINTS ▨

1. What were your first responses to the conflict that arose between Mrs Parker and Jimmy? Did your response change as the chapter developed? If so, in what ways?

2. Have you ever experienced or are you currently experiencing conflict with a student that might be understood in relation to the concept of 'transference'? If so, how might you use this understanding to influence your way of relating to the student concerned?

3. Think about how your own life experience might affect your attitudes toward feelings for and responses to students who you teach (or have taught). What might you do to try to raise your own awareness of these effects?

Bibliography

Ainsworth, M.D.S. and Whiting, B.A. (1969) 'Attachment and Exploratory Behavior of One-Year-Olds in a Strange Situation.' In B.M. Foss (ed.) *Determinants of Infant Behaviour* (pp.113–136). London: Methuen.

Ainsworth, M.D.S., Blehar, M.C., Waters, E. and Wall, S. (1978) *Patterns of Attachment: A Psychological Study of the Strange Situation*. Hillsdale, NJ: Erlbaum.

Bombèr, L.M. (2007) *Inside I'm Hurting: Practical Strategies for Supporting Children with Attachment Difficulties in School*. Belper: Worth Publishing Ltd.

Bowlby, J. (1969) *Attachment and Loss. Volume 1: Attachment*. London: Hogarth Press and the Institute of Psychoanalysis.

Bowlby, J. (1988) *A Secure Base: Clinical Applications of Attachment Theory*. London: Routledge.

Delaney, M. (2008) *Teaching the Unteachable: Practical Ideas to Give Teachers Hope and Help When Behaviour Management Strategies Fail*. Belper: Worth Publishing Ltd.

Ellman, S.J. (2010) *When Theories Touch*. London: Karnac Books.

Fonagy, P. (2001) *Attachment Theory and Psychoanalysis*. London: Karnac Books.

Freud, S. (1910) *Five Lectures on Psychoanalysis*. Standard Edition 11 (pp.3–36).

Freud, S. (1912) *The Dynamics of Transference*. Standard Edition 12 (pp.99–108).

Freud, S. (1914) *Remembering, Repeating and Working Through*. Standard Edition 12 (pp.145–156).

Geddes, H. (2006) *Attachment in the Classroom: The Links Between Children's Early Experience, Emotional Well-being and Performance in School*. Belper: Worth Publishing Ltd.

Holmes, J. (2010) *Exploring in Security*. London: Routledge.

Hopkins, J. (2015) *An Independent Mind: Collected Papers of Juliet Hopkins*. Independent Psychoanalytic Approaches with Children and Adolescents Series. Hove: Routledge.

Horne, A. and Lanyado, M. (eds) (1999) *The Therapeutic Relationship and Process. Handbook of Child and Adolescent Psychotherapy*. London: Routledge.

Horne, A. and Lanyado, M. (eds) (2015) *An Independent Mind: Collected Papers of Juliet Hopkins*. Hove and New York: Routledge.

Main, M. (1995) 'Recent Studies in Attachment: Overview, with Selected Implications for Clinical Work.' In S. Goldberg, R. Muir and J. Kerr (eds) *Attachment Theory: Social, Developmental and Clinical Perspectives* (pp.407–474). Hillsdale, NJ: Analytic Press.

Rycroft, C. (1968) *A Critical Dictionary of Psychoanalysis*. London: Nelson.

Spence, D. (1994) *The Rhetorical Voice of Psychoanalysis*. Cambridge, MA: Harvard University Press.

Wilson, P. (2003) *Young Minds in Our Schools*. London: YoungMinds.

10

A Psychoanalytic Understanding of Change and Transition in Education

BIDDY YOUELL

This chapter aims to provide an inner world perspective on some of the seemingly ordinary transitions that children and young people have to negotiate as they make their way through the formal education system. There are the major points of transition that immediately come to mind: the move from home to nursery, from nursery to infant school and then on into primary school for a period of consolidation before secondary transfer. Some years later, a move to tertiary education or into the world of work will then occur. This chapter then goes on to look in more detail at these significant transition points while drawing attention to the myriad small changes that children and teachers have to manage in every school day.

School transitions

Each school day involves a timetable of different subjects, a variety of learning activities and teaching styles. Children move around from room to room and from group to group. In primary schools there is usually a consistent classroom base and a main class teacher, but the day is likely to involve time with other adults and class groups in the assembly hall, the library and the playground. In secondary school, there are many classrooms and also the science lab, the IT suite, the art room, the gymnasium and so on. Each place has a different function and each teacher a different set of expectations.

Some children appear to coast through, taking each change in their stride, whilst others struggle to cope and may act out their struggle in a variety of ways. Teachers usually get to know which children find change difficult. They begin to recognise the children who are different on a Friday afternoon or a Monday morning, the children who are thrown by a sudden absence of a friend or a familiar teacher, and those who need a lot of preparation for a change in activity in the classroom or a move from classroom to playground.

Schools have become much more sensitive to major transitions. There are usually plans in place for children to visit their new class, to meet their new teacher, and at secondary transfer, to spend time in their new school before the summer break. It is now generally understood that children need to be prepared for these transitions when possible. For example, they need to know in advance if a teacher is leaving and be given opportunities to say goodbye. If something upsetting or distressing happens suddenly, it is generally accepted that the children need opportunities to talk about their feelings and to share their thoughts.

Early experience of separation and starting school

Most children are anxious about their first day at school. Even those who are excited and hopeful will experience some anxiety as they cross the threshold for the first time. In those early days, teachers will be able to see which children come into school with enthusiasm and confidence and which children hang back and cling to their parent, as if separation is an unwelcome requirement of some malign force. They may also observe which parents are particularly anxious about leaving their child in the care of the school and how the child responds to the parent's concern. These dynamics are perhaps most in evidence as children make the first move away from their primary caregiver, but can resurface at major points of transition, perhaps most poignantly when a young person leaves home to pursue higher education or training. The move away from home at 18 years of age has much in common with that first separation, and certainly comes a close second in terms of what Alex Coren (1997) calls 'pressure on internal coherence'.

'Internal coherence' is what I would call, from my psychoanalytic perspective, an internal world populated by robust, flexible internal objects. Whether you share a psychoanalytic model or prefer an attachment theory approach, we are all agreed that transitions throughout life build on the experience of transitions between developmental phases in infancy and early childhood.

Birth and the early years

Psychoanalytic literature suggests that the experience of birth is the first, hugely significant transition from one state of being to another. Infants arrive with more or less ease into a world that is entirely strange to them. They are bombarded by sounds and sensations and do not have the apparatus to make sense of them. At this point, they are completely dependent on the people who greet them and care for them. They begin a journey through infancy and childhood that is a complex interaction between their natural endowment (personality and genetic inheritance) and their environment. From the moment of birth (and indeed, in utero) babies differ, and these differences cannot all be explained by the circumstances of their birth and what subsequently happens to them. Some are vigorous and protesting, others are passive and uncomplaining. It is not simply a matter of some parents being 'better' at parenting than others. Some babies allow themselves to be parented and some make it extremely difficult. The child who is fortunate enough to make a good 'fit' with his mother or primary caregiver in the early months is likely to be better able to manage his first experiences of separation and thereafter, to learn.

Wilfred Bion (1967) linked the capacity to learn with the experience of maternal containment. He described the way in which the mother (or caregiver) focuses on her baby, remains open to his unconscious communication and tries to take in and understand something of his experience in order to contain the anxiety or distress without becoming anxious or impatient herself. In the pre-verbal phase of life, the infant has hundreds of small experiences of a mother who is dependable and usually effective in relieving anxiety, discomfort and distress. Over time, the infant who is contained in this way comes to believe that the world is a benign place, full of interesting people and possibilities. We can see the way in which the teacher takes over something of this role when a child begins school. In reception classes, there are likely to be many children who call their teacher 'mummy'. This is not always just a slip up. Unconsciously, they may be seeking the kind of containing response they have become used to receiving from their parents. Later in their school careers (often at times of change and challenge such as on school trips), a slip of this kind causes embarrassment but comes from the same source, a desire to get back in touch with something familiar and secure (Youell 2006).

The baby who is not the first in the family may have parents who feel more confident about what they are doing. The baby may be less closely watched over and more may be expected of him in terms of adapting to new situations and a broader range of caregivers. For some babies this may be a completely manageable spur to development; for others it may leave them feeling that they do not have the degree of support they need. Characterological differences play a huge part here. It is interesting to see how, in nursery observations, it is possible to identify the children who have an older sibling who has already achieved the first transition from home to institution. It is often as if they are able to 'borrow' something of their sibling's confidence.

The experience of weaning (by which I mean the move from the intimate feeding relationship whether it be breast or bottle) is often identified as the prototype for later experiences of separation. After weaning may come greater and more prolonged separations, with mothers going out, introducing alternative caregivers into the home, returning to work, leaving their child with a child minder or in a nursery. If you watch a small toddler who has experienced a well-negotiated separation and who has been introduced to the world in careful stages, you will usually see him making more and more adventurous forays away from his mother to explore his surroundings. At first, he goes back often, for a cuddle or for verbal reassurance. As time goes on, he learns that she is still there on his return and he moves a little further away, perhaps looking back over his shoulder to check, but not needing to be in such close physical proximity. The child who has been led to believe that the world is a welcoming and fascinating place will be eager to explore it, so long as his secure base is there for him to return to.

This pattern does not really change as life and development move on. We all rely on a secure base to return to. Psychoanalytic thinking would suggest that the secure base, as one moves through childhood and towards adulthood, is increasingly an *internal* phenomenon. Experiences of containment and of well-managed separations are internalised, introjected in a way that provides the individual with a good internal object, a secure and flexible inner world.

These ordinary transitions are managed reasonably smoothly by most families in most circumstances. However, no transition can be achieved without a measure of anxiety, involving, as it does, both an ending and a beginning. There are gains and losses, hopes and fears.

A psychoanalytic theory of learning would suggest that anxiety is a necessary spur to learning. The anxiety that goes with the realisation that the world is, in fact, bigger than just the baby and the mother (or primary caregiver) is perhaps the greatest stimulus to development. The baby comes to notice the other people in his and his mother's life, to observe her comings and goings, to wait while she attends to something or somebody else. These minor 'separations' build the baby's confidence in the idea that the world has not come to an end and the mother will return; she has not gone away for ever when she is out of sight. The child psychoanalyst, Melanie Klein (1959), described this process in terms of a baby coming to understand that the mother who feeds and cares for him is one and the same as the mother who frustrates him by keeping him waiting, or who misunderstands what is troubling him when he cries. This is, she suggested, the beginning of being able to accept that the mother is a separate person. Klein sees it as the beginning of a capacity to feel concern for the other.

The kind of confidence-building experience described above equips most children with a capacity to cope to a greater or lesser extent with the demands of school. If the structure is sufficiently predictable, they will probably be able to relish new ideas and experiences. Psychoanalytic thinking is sometimes accused of dwelling on the negative, but it was Klein who, as early as 1930, identified what she described as the 'epistomophilic instinct', which refers to the individual's innate desire to find out about the world and one's place in it. This does not mean, however, that anxiety about change can be completely neutralised. Each ending and new beginning carries with it echoes of earlier endings and may stir up unwelcome memories and feelings.

If these incremental separations and manageable doses of anxiety are avoided by the baby, the mother or both, it is easy to see how starting school would be a traumatic experience, and how learning and development would be inhibited.

The child entering nursery or infant school is taking a first step into the outside world. For what feels like long periods of time, they are away from the familiar surroundings of home, and have to believe that they have not dropped out of the mind of their mother, who is at work or at home with other children. In school, they have to find a place amongst many others, sharing space, toys, equipment and most significantly, sharing the attention of the teacher and classroom helpers. The degree to which they are able to manage all this will depend on the individual and, of course, on the capacity of the school to respond sensitively.

External reality

I do not want to suggest that good early experience of nurturing relationships and careful transitions acts as a failsafe vaccination against future disturbance, but it is self-evident that such experiences are likely to increase the individual's chance of remaining stable through periods of stress. Nor do I underestimate the potentially devastating effects of real-life trauma, such as family breakdown, neglect, bereavement, illness, accident, dislocation etc. Where children, or indeed parents, have undergone traumatic separations, every new separation or change is likely to stir up unconscious memories and feelings associated with the traumatic loss. One only has to think of children in the care system who cannot really believe that their foster carers will be there at the end of the school day, or that the stranger at the door has not come to take them away. They are not usually able to verbalise these fears, but it is possible to see it in their non-verbal behaviour or attempts to distract themselves and others from what they do not want to face. The children of refugee or asylum-seeking parents live in a family context where the degree of loss and the challenge of adaptation to completely new circumstances are unimaginable for those of us who have not lived through such upheavals. For those children, it may be that school feels like a safe haven, a place of respite from the painful cocktail of fears and feelings at home. However, they are likely to be hypersensitive to the transitions that they are expected to negotiate during the school day, each one resonating in some way with feelings of uncertainty and powerlessness.

Secondary transfer

Having found their place in their first school and having moved up by stages to become the oldest and most experienced children, they are faced with secondary transfer, one of the points of vulnerability in a child's developmental journey. The relative anonymity of life in secondary school, the numbers, the noise, the complexity of the timetable and the constant changes of classroom and teacher all put pressure on the individual, and anxiety levels are high until the unfamiliar becomes familiar. Many 11-year-olds are articulate about how threatened they felt when starting secondary school. The fears they speak of are reminiscent of the experience of starting nursery. They fear getting lost, not finding the toilets, not being able to eat the lunch, having no friends, being bullied, being found to be stupid and so on.

The challenge of secondary education is exacerbated by the challenges of puberty and adolescence, and this process is rarely completed when the young person moves on again, whether it is into the world of work or into further study. In the later stages of adolescence, the adult world beckons and decisions have to be made about work, about higher education and about sexuality and couple relationships. The group life that has dominated in earlier adolescence gives way to some extent, and young people begin to think more seriously about their own futures and their own identity. The 'gap year' for adolescents going on to higher education is an interesting phenomenon. In fact, it is used in very different ways. For some it is a profoundly adolescent experience, a reward for the perceived privations of school life and study and an opportunity to be relatively irresponsible, adventurous and self-indulgent. For others it offers a taste of the adult world of work and wages before returning to student life.

Defences against anxiety

Observations of children at various ages reveal the ways in which they cope with the changing demands of the school day. There are the small but significant 'props' that some children cling to. These may be relational, such as friendships with peers or attachments to particular adults in the school. They may be minor obsessions, such as reliance on always sitting in the same place, having the same things in their packed lunch, or organising their pens and pencils in exactly the same way for each lesson. Children moving into secondary school often cope with the newness of everything by, for example, attaching themselves to somebody they already know, meeting up at break time with an older sibling, carrying a copy of their timetable and plan of the school buildings in their pocket, or hiding a favourite toy in their school bag – just as at the start of primary school some children cling to their bags that seem to represent all that is familiar and safe, whilst others do their best not to take off their coats or jackets. The outer layer is experienced as a protection, a 'second skin' (Bick 1968), a way of creating an illusion of being held together in the face of unwelcome anxiety. Most children feel reassured by routine and repetition, and are eventually able to let go of these external supports.

For others, the problem is not one of finding ways to adjust to new circumstances, but it is a much more deep-rooted problem, as suggested above. Changes and transitions stir up an unconscious, primitive anxiety about survival. Children and young people on the autistic spectrum are extreme examples of this. They need massive amounts of preparation for the smallest changes, and they live in fear of the unexpected, as if the end of the world really is just around the corner.

Misleading behaviour in the face of change

The behaviours described above can fairly easily be linked to anxiety about managing change. However, it is not always so clear, and patterns of behaviour can be very misleading. This is particularly so when the child himself is out of touch with the reason for his anxiety, and is acting in a way that is challenging to the teacher and disruptive to the class. It is then difficult to imagine that the problem might actually be that the child cannot manage the shifting context. I am thinking, for example, of children who become loud and over-excited on Friday afternoons. In 'golden time' they become competitive with their peers and full of complaints to the teacher about how unfair the teacher is being. They declare that they can't wait for the afternoon to end and the weekend to begin. In the face of this kind of onslaught, it is hard for the teacher to imagine that the opposite might be the case. While boasting about what he is going to do when he breaks free from school, the child may unconsciously be dreading the loss of structure and friendly support of his teacher.

This is just one example, but it serves to illustrate the way in which teachers have the opportunity to see what may be behind the behaviour and to respond in ways that help the child to feel that his anxiety and fears are understood. In this situation it would be easy to humiliate the child by suggesting that he is lying about his weekend plans. This would, of course, be cruel and counter-productive. However, paying him extra attention and helping him to choose an activity that he is good at and that usually calms him down may give him the message that he is in the teacher's mind. A reference to what is going to be happening in the following week may help him and others to feel reassured that the teacher is thinking of the future and will be there! I can remember one example of a child in Year 5 (aged 9) who, on a Friday afternoon, was winding up towards a fight with another boy when the teacher skilfully asked him whether he would be her special helper for the remaining half hour. She sent him with a message to the office, got him to carry piles of books to the library, and then played a brief game of snakes and ladders with him herself. Of course, she knew him well and was confident that he would not turn on her and say he wasn't a messenger and she should do her own jobs! Equally, he felt better because she was noticing the state he was in and was on his side in avoiding a negative ending to the week.

Sensitivity to times of transition may show itself in myriad ways. I am reminded of adolescents in a Pupil Referral Unit who could only manage the ending by avoiding it. Most left the provision early, claiming they had found jobs or were just too 'bored' to keep on attending until their official leaving date. Some carried on attending but picked fights with each other or with the staff and ended up being excluded. Once excluded, they could protect themselves from this loss by dismissing the Unit as 'rubbish' and certainly not to be missed.

Later transitions

The unconscious anxiety that can accompany times of change and transition does not miraculously disappear in adulthood. I was talking some time ago to a mature student who was coming to the end of a four-year postgraduate training course and who was feeling overcome by anxiety about the future. She was leaving a course she had loved and felt she was facing an abyss. Her words were, 'I can't see any continuity.' The connection between her student self and the rest of her professional life was temporarily severed in her mind. This was somebody with a significant career behind her and an enriched career ahead. She had a network of connections and knew how, when and why she would be in touch in the future. But in the moment, overwhelmed by feelings of loss, she lost touch with what she knew. She was describing a primitive internal experience of anxiety that interfered with her capacity for rational thought.

Teachers and times of transitions

Teachers are by no means immune to the anxiety that accompanies transitions of all kinds, ranging from the familiar, ordinary anxiety of moving from one part of the timetable to the next or from Sunday evenings into Monday mornings. The loss of a much enjoyed group at the end of the school year may be felt acutely and a new group be anticipated with dread. Teachers also have to contend with a constantly changing policy context, meeting new demands requiring constant revision of aspects of their practice. Just as with children and young people, total denial of anxiety is rarely helpful. Knowing that it exists and being able to recognise it and understand one's own defensive manoeuvres can make the work much more manageable.

The place and importance of rituals

We all have our own individual ways of managing the challenge that change presents. There are also some very well established, institutional ways of managing anxiety, or of managing the sadness that can accompany loss. There are the formal events such as Prize Giving, Founder's Day, leaver's assemblies etc. and parties often accompany ends of terms or departures of much loved teachers. These are important rituals but can sometimes spill over into more manic activity, an evasive response in which the sense of loss is quickly glossed over. The kind of drunken bonanza that for many students characterises Freshers' Week may be a celebration of new-found freedom, but it is also a way of anaesthetising oneself against feeling the loss of home and school…or fear of the future.

Denial of separation in the digital age

I mentioned above the kinds of difficulties that might be faced by children in school when they have not been helped to separate from their primary caregiver, and when each new transition feels like a re-enactment of that first cruel 'ripping apart'. I do not think I can conclude this chapter without recognising that the context in which this psychic work is done has changed enormously in the past two decades. With the advent of mobile phones, and more recently, social media of all kinds, it has become possible to remain 'in touch' anytime and anywhere at the touch of a button. Are we all less able to wait than once we were? Are we less able to manage our frustration if our computer network is down, our battery flat or our phone out of range? Email has led us to expect almost immediate responses – gone are the days of watching anxiously for the post, wondering whether we will receive a reply or whether our own letter ever reached the recipient. These doubts still exist, but it is usually resolved much more quickly, by a quick call, email or text.

We all sometimes use technology defensively, to avoid an internal experience of uncertainty or aloneness. Many of us, for example, reach for our phones to check for messages far more often than is necessary. A disagreement about a matter of fact may be resolved almost instantaneously, thanks to Google. Young people use electronic games to distract themselves, to pass time, to avoid becoming aware of feelings of fear or uncertainty. The defensive use of these channels of communication creates some difficulties. Rather like the notion of the 'too good mother' who anticipates her baby's every need and does not allow any experience of hunger or frustration, the digital age can create the illusion that you need never be alone.

I do not think we yet know the impact of modern technological advances on the internal work of separation. However, we can already see something of its impact on the school and college population. For some children and young people in school, particularly perhaps in secondary schools, the biggest challenge they face is how to manage their day without ready access to their phone or tablet. I have recently come across young people who react to the prohibition on phones in much the same way as a toddler might react to the removal of a dummy or the loss of a critically important toy. It is easy to see this as a stubborn refusal to comply with school rules, but for some individuals it may represent a much more deep-rooted sense of insecurity.

Final thoughts

Managing times of transition is an area of educational practice that has received increased attention in the past two decades. School institutions are now more aware of the need for preparation for major change and the likely difficulties that will arise when things happen in an unplanned way. There is understanding of the need for time and space to digest unexpected and traumatic changes. However, there is perhaps less understanding of the way in which some individuals struggle with even the most minor transitions, and the ways in which this struggle may link with their individual experience within their families.

▨ REFLECTION POINTS ▨

1. Consider your own experience of transitions (e.g. as a pupil in school, in university, as a newly qualified teacher). What were some of the factors that affected the success of the transition experience in one or more of these events?

2. Amongst the pupils you are working with (or have worked with), which one(s) stand out to you as having experienced difficulties with transitions? How do/did these difficulties manifest in terms of pupil behaviour?

3. What measures are in place in your school or classroom (or a school or classroom that you know) to facilitate successful transitions?

4. What could be done to improve support for pupil transitions in this setting?

Bibliography

Bick, E. (1968) 'The Experience of the Skin in Early Object Relations.' In E. Bott-Spillius (ed.) *Melanie Klein Today. Volume 1* (pp.187–191). London: Routledge.

Bion, W.R. (1967) 'A Theory of Thinking.' In W.R. Bion (ed.) *Second Thoughts: Selected Papers on Psychoanalysis.* London: Heinemann.

Coren, A. (1997) *A Psychodynamic Approach to Education.* London: Sheldon Press.

Klein, M. (1930) 'Symbol Formation and Ego Development.' In J. Mitchell (1986) *Selected Works of Melanie Klein.* London: Penguin.

Klein, M. (1959) 'Our Adult World and its Roots in Infancy.' In *The Writings of Melanie Klein, Volume 3*, 1975. London and New York: Routledge.

Youell, B. (2006) *The Learning Relationship: Psychoanalytic Thinking in Education.* London: Karnac Books, The Tavistock Clinic Series.

11

Supporting Children and Young People with Social, Emotional and Mental Health Difficulties

Working in a Multi-agency Team

KATHY EVANS AND ERICA PAVORD

This chapter explores the nature and importance of a multi-agency approach in education, and illustrates the value of psychodynamic perspectives to teachers and newly qualified teachers (NQTs). The first part of the chapter introduces current policy and guidance relating to multi-agency working in education, and provides an overview of some of the services available to teachers, children and families. Theoretical models of multi-agency working are introduced while the potential of and barriers to effective multi-agency working are discussed. The second half of the chapter uses a case study to illustrate some of the complexities of multi-agency working, and offers some practical ways to develop practice.

Multi-agency working is of vital importance for all children and young people who have a range of needs that cannot be met by one service alone. This might include children from vulnerable groups such as young carers, travellers, refugees and asylum-seekers, or looked-after children (LAC). Pupils with special educational needs (SEN) and pupils with social, emotional and mental health (SEMH) difficulties are particularly likely to be supported by other services. While it is important that all pupils are considered in the context of their wider experiences within families, communities and any other agencies that might be involved in their lives, note that there will be some pupils who are supported by a range of agencies outside of school, even though they are not experiencing any difficulties in school.

Current policy and guidance

It is recognised that there is a need for educational professionals to work effectively with other agencies (DfE 2014; Wolpert *et al.* 2013). The *Professional Standards for Qualified Teacher Status and Requirements for Initial Teacher Training* requires that new teachers should have 'a commitment to collaboration and co-operative working' (TDA 2008, p.5). Recent reviews of teacher education have emphasised the need to train teachers who are able to develop and sustain partnership work with other professionals (Donaldson 2011), and who are willing to work collaboratively with educational colleagues and other professionals (Furlong 2014). The Carter Review advises, 'trainees should be introduced to how to work with a range of colleagues and professionals, as well as parents and carers, to support children with SEND' (Carter 2015, p.10).

Every Child Matters (DfES 2004) recommended integrated working between a range of professionals in order to promote and protect positive outcomes for children and young people, and you will find that multi-agency working is essential with regard to safeguarding cases in your school. The Children Act 2004 states clearly that the primary responsibility for all organisations that work with children is to keep them safe. This underpins more recent guidance such as *Working Together to Safeguard Children*, which states unequivocally that:

> Whilst local authorities play a lead role, safeguarding children and protecting them from harm is everyone's responsibility. Everyone who comes into contact with children and families has a role to play. (DfE 2015, p.5)

The Munro Report (DfE 2011), which was commissioned in response to safeguarding failures, similarly highlighted the need for professionals to work together effectively in order to address safeguarding issues. The list of multi-agency services provided below is not exhaustive, and there will be regional differences in the nature and organisation of services. However, the beginning teacher should be aware of the following key agencies:

- *Child and Adolescent Mental Health Services (CAMHS):* A child or young person can be referred to CAMHS if there is a concern about their wellbeing or mental health. Specialist CAMHS are organised in different ways across the country and may be based in clinical or community settings. CAMHS workers usually consist of a multi-disciplinary team of psychiatrists, clinical psychologists, counselling psychologists, community psychiatric nurses, occupational therapists, counsellors, play therapists, family therapists and social workers. Some CAMHS professionals such as primary mental health workers might be attached to a cluster of schools.

- *Social Services:* A child or young person can be referred to Social Services if there is a concern about their wellbeing or their safety. When a child is referred to Social Services, a social worker, with their manager, will make a decision about the level of involvement required and feed this back to the referrer. They may decide that no further social care involvement is necessary, or that the case requires referral to another service. Sometimes they will decide that an assessment is required either under Section 17 or Section 47 of the Children Act 1989. A Section 17 assessment looks at whether the child is a child in need, whereas a Section 47 assessment looks at whether a child is at risk of significant harm.

- *Educational Psychology Service:* A child or young person can be referred to an educational psychologist if they are experiencing problems in learning and/or social-emotional functioning. An educational psychologist can provide direct support to the child, or consultation to the educational team in the child's educational setting, and would usually be involved in statutory assessments.

- *Educational Welfare Service:* A child or young person can be referred to the Educational Welfare Service if their attendance is poor. Educational welfare officers work predominantly with pupils and families to support regular school attendance. Very occasionally they may be involved in legal action being taken against parents who are deemed to be failing in their statutory responsibility to ensure their child's regular attendance at school.

- *Youth Offending Team:* A child or young person can be referred to the Youth Offending Team if they have committed an offence or if they are judged to be at risk of offending. Youth offending officers aim to prevent children and young people from offending and re-offending. They work with both individuals and groups of children and young people.

- *Police Service:* In recent years many schools have developed closer relationships with a local police officer or police community support officer (PCSO). The Safer School Partnerships scheme (DCSF *et al.* 2002) encouraged police officers to develop closer links with local clusters of schools.

- *Non-governmental organisations:* These are not-for-profit organisations such as Women's Aid or YoungMinds, which often hold charitable status or are supported through government, local authority or charitable grants, and that work in the community providing services to support vulnerable groups. Some might work directly with schools providing services like counselling or mentoring, whilst some might be involved in providing direct support for families.

Understanding multi-agency systems

Where safeguarding issues have been identified, there should be a standardised approach to the organisation of multi-agency working. However, the organisation of services for children who would benefit from a multi-agency response where there are no safeguarding concerns is different across local authorities. Traditionally in schools it has been the designated special educational needs coordinator (SENCO) who is the named professional charged with bringing together the different agencies but, depending on the setting, it can also be the class teacher, the headteacher, or other specialist staff who undertake this role (e.g. school counsellor, the pastoral head or pastoral care worker). Educational professionals have a responsibility to provide timely and detailed information to multi-agency meetings and to attend, where possible. In addition, they are expected to maintain good communication with relevant non-educational professionals, either formally or informally. A number of different roles, concepts and frameworks have been developed that support joint working, and educational professionals will encounter some or all of the frameworks set out below:

- *Team Around the Child (TAC)* (CWDC 2009). The TAC is a model of multi-agency service provision that brings together a range of different practitioners from across the children and young people's workforce to support an individual child or young person and their family. The members of the TAC develop and deliver a package of solution-focused support to meet the needs identified through the Common Assessment Framework (CAF).

- Within the multi-agency team, the *lead professional* (DCSF 2007; DfE 2015, p.14) will act as a single point of contact for the child and their family, and ensure that multi-agency services are coordinated and cohesive. The lead professional role could be undertaken by a general practitioner (GP), a family support worker, teacher, health visitor or SENCO. Decisions about who should be the lead professional should be taken on a case-by-case basis, and should be informed by the child and their family.

- *Information sharing* (DfE 2015:16). Multi-agency teams can work together more effectively to meet children and young people's needs through sharing information legally and professionally. Where different agencies have different thresholds for sharing information, developing a framework for information sharing and following guidance on when and how information can be shared is essential. Increasingly, information sharing is taking advantage of digital innovations.

- The *Common Assessment Framework (CAF)* (DfES 2006) is a standardised framework that enables professionals to assess children and young people's additional needs for earlier and more effective services, and to develop a common understanding of those needs and how to work together to meet them.

- An *Education, Health and Care (EHC) plan* (DfE 2014) is for children and young people aged up to 25 who need more support than is available through SEN support. EHC plans identify educational, health and social needs, and set out the additional support to meet those needs. A request can also be made by anyone who thinks an assessment may be necessary, including parents, teachers, health visitors and doctors. A young person can request an assessment themselves if they're aged 16–25.

- The *Personal Education Plan (PEP)* (DCSF 2014) provides a detailed record of what needs to happen for looked-after children (LAC) to enable them to fulfil their potential, and reflects any existing education plans, such as a statement of SEN, Individual Education Plan (IEP) or Provision Mapping. The PEP should reflect the importance of a personalised approach to learning, which secures good basic skills, stretches aspirations and builds life chances.

Models of multi-agency working

A number of writers have developed theoretical models that describe different forms of multi-agency working (Atkinson *et al.* 2002; Øvretveit 1993). Atkinson *et al.* (see Table 11.1) describe a range of organisational structures from decision-making groups to operational team delivery. Although it is generally argued that a higher level of multi-agency cohesion is more productive, there is no overt stated assumption in this work that the later models are necessarily more effective.

Table 11.1: Models of multi-agency working

Structure	Function
Decision-making groups	To provide a forum whereby professionals from different agencies can meet to discuss issues and make decisions
Consultation and training	For the professionals from one agency to enhance the expertise of those of another by providing consultation and/or training for them
Centre-based delivery	To gather a range of expertise together in one place in order to deliver a more coordinated and comprehensive service
Coordinated delivery	To draw together a number of agencies involved in the delivery of services so that a more coordinated and cohesive response to needs can be adopted
Operational team delivery	To enable professionals from different agencies to work together on a day-to-day basis and to form a cohesive multi-agency team that delivers services directly to clients

Source: Atkinson *et al.* (2002)

Local authorities have developed a variety of models of multi-agency working. Multi-agency meetings are often simply decision-making groups whereby information is shared and decisions taken. In some local authorities, teams such as Primary Mental Health Teams provide examples of a more coordinated or operational approach wherein practitioners from a number of different professional backgrounds are co-located in teams that are able to offer a more coordinated response. Increasingly, services are providing a more consultative service to schools where other professionals, such as educational psychologists or primary mental health workers, enhance the expertise of the educational professionals through consultation and/or training.

Atkinson *et al.* (2002) discuss the concept of the 'hybrid professional' who will have a range of professional skills derived from experience of diverse settings:

> …who has personal experience and knowledge of other agencies, including, importantly, these services' cultures, structures, discourse and priorities. (Atkinson *et al.* 2002, p.225)

Hybrid professionals are very well placed to engage in innovative multi-agency work (Sloper 2004). This said, there can sometimes be a perceived tension between 'specialist' and 'generalist' professionals, with generalists being seen to be inferior by specialists. The hybrid professional, however, would work with specialists in a multi-disciplinary setting and not replace the specialists. So, in the case of teachers, it is desirable that they develop a wider range of skills whilst recognising their own and other professionals' specialist knowledge and ways of working. For example, teachers and learning support assistants (LSAs) need to both recognise that their particular expertise is teaching and learning, and develop through consultation and training the ability to address a child's SEMH needs in the classroom.

A number of writers have explored the benefits of, and barriers to, multi-agency working (e.g. Farmakopoulou 2002; Milbourne, Macrae and Maguire 2003; Salmon 2004). Sloper (2004) carried out a systematic review of the literature relating to multi-agency working in children's services in the UK. He concluded that there are both practical challenges, relating to organisational issues, roles, budgets and information sharing, and ideological challenges emanating from different professional aims, expectations and cultures. Different professionals from different disciplines can have their own ways of working, their own terms of reference, different professional values, and specific traditions and boundaries that can prove challenging for teachers, especially as they are the ones who work with children on a daily basis. Difficulties can arise when different professions have conflicting expectations about each other's roles and ability to effect change. This can impact on the child and family who can be left feeling as if their needs have been sidelined in favour of ongoing professional conflicts. It is also recognised that multi-agency working often takes place against a background of constant reorganisation and associated frequent staff changes. Because ongoing professional relationships are seen to be key to effective multi-agency working, these circumstances can be seen to be highly problematic.

Understanding that all behaviour has meaning

A number of authors have applied various psychodynamic insights to multi-agency working (Conway 2009; Golding 2010; Granville and Langton 2002), and the next section uses a case study to explore some of the key psychodynamic concepts introduced in Chapters 9 and 10.

The term 'psychodynamic' originates in Freudian theory, and refers to all models of mind that are primarily concerned with unconscious processes (Howard 2006). Taking a psychodynamic approach offers us a way of understanding human relationships and behaviour in the context of our inner feelings, memories, beliefs and fantasies (Jacobs 1998).

In terms of multi-agency working, the psychodynamic perspective on behaviour would emphasise that all behaviour has meaning (Golding *et al.* 2016). Behaviour is often a communication of internal emotional states and can be related to previous negative experiences the child has had. When a child has had a lot of bad experiences and troubled relationships, particularly with close family members, the child comes to expect previous experiences to be repeated:

> Once an expectation is formed, it remains, and the world is experienced according to such preconceptions: children expecting to find the world terrifying will have a terrifying experience of the world. (Music 2011, p.44)

Children often act out their distress in a number of ways, and repeat the patterns of behaviour established from previous relationships in new relationships. Bowlby's concept of the 'internal working model' (1969), that was introduced in Chapter 2, suggests that mental models of how the world has worked in the past influence the way we think about how things will work in the future (Howe 2011, p.33).

In this section we will explore how these concepts can help practitioners make sense of complex cases and develop more robust multi-agency and intra-agency working.

Case study: Daniel

Daniel is currently in Year 4 (aged 8), in Mr Williams' class. In school Daniel is frequently disruptive and aggressive with peers and staff, and he has difficulty with friendships. Daniel has been assessed by an *educational psychologist* and identified as having special educational needs (SEN). He has an Individual Education Plan (IEP). He is supported in class by a *learning support assistant (LSA)*, Sarah, who has been working with Daniel now for almost a year, but will soon be moving on to take up another role within the school. The school has a mentoring programme for pupils who are at risk of disengagement, and Daniel has been working with a *learning mentor*, Simon, once a week in school time since he started Year 3. Daniel lives with his father, John, his mother, Louise, and his younger sister. John left the family home when Daniel was an infant, but has recently returned. John spends most of his time at home online gaming, and so Louise still provides most of the parenting. Louise has a history of anxiety. When Daniel was three, she was admitted suddenly to inpatient care and Daniel went to live with his maternal grandmother. Daniel's maternal grandmother has been very involved and often picks Daniel and his sister up from school, but she has recently been ill, and is consequently less able to support her daughter with the children. The family has ongoing occasional support from a *Mind support worker*. In the community Daniel is often unsupervised and has been spending time with a group of older boys. The local *police officer*, who has regular meetings with the school *SENCO*, has shared his concerns about Daniel. For the last two months the school have been increasingly concerned about Daniel's behaviour in school and the welfare of the children out of school, so a referral has been made to *Social Services*. The family has been assigned a *social worker* who is currently carrying out an assessment. Louise has found it difficult to accept the need for the involvement of a social worker, and has been talking to the class teacher and the LSA about her feelings. A multi-agency meeting has been called that will be held at school.

Daniel experiences Sarah's leaving for another role in the school as a huge loss, and his behaviour has deteriorated, particularly in relation to Simon, his learning mentor. This ending is echoed by the absence of his grandmother in his life out of school. It is likely that his expectations about the loss are also related to his earlier experience when his father disappeared from the family home and his mother was suddenly admitted to hospital.

Although staff changes and role changes are unavoidable, teaching staff can support Daniel by acknowledging his (and their own) feelings about people 'leaving', allowing Daniel sufficient time to process his feelings. It is important to find an individually appropriate way for Daniel and Sarah to mark her moving into a new role and 'leaving' Daniel. Simon, the learning mentor, could ensure that Daniel is able to say goodbye to Sarah by talking about the ending with him, acknowledging how difficult saying goodbye can be, and perhaps by helping him to mark the farewell with a card or letter. Teaching staff can share Sarah's leaving with the other members of the multi-agency team, as that is likely to help them understand Daniel's behaviour. Simon could reinforce the message the teaching staff were giving Daniel, and ensure that the boundaries around his work with Daniel (in relation to timing and length of engagement) were transparent.

Understanding controlling behaviour

From a psychodynamic perspective, children's early experiences and first relationships act as a blueprint for their subsequent interactions and relationships (Music 2011). If they have grown up in a situation where the adults have not had the resources to be able to understand their emotional needs, then often children will develop their own ways of managing their emotions and feeling safe within their relationships. If children have not felt able to trust the adults in their life to control their environment in a way that made them feel safe, then they may have developed patterns of controlling behaviour that make them feel safer.

Case study continued

This is shown in the classroom where Daniel feels safer if he controls relationships by creating tension, or a split between his teacher, Mr Williams and Sarah, his LSA. For example, Daniel tells Sarah that Mr Williams never helps him when she is not in the classroom, and then tells Mr Williams that Sarah has completed his work for him. When this creates tension between the two adults, Daniel feels safer because he has some control over the situation.

In situations like this, where children seem to know exactly what they are doing and enjoy creating conflict, it is important to understand that the motivation for the behaviour is grounded in a need to feel safe:

> Children do not split to be manipulative, although they are often accused of this, they do it to communicate and manage an internal and external world that they cannot control and cannot trust. (Conway 2009, p.22)

Communication and openness between professionals is essential. If good communication is maintained between the teacher and the LSA, then there is less opportunity for children to control relationships. A short debrief at the end of each day would ensure that all the adults in the team were aware of any issues that had arisen. Where possible it should be made apparent to Daniel that the adults that work with him are all communicating well.

Understanding 'splitting'

Early experience is always a mix of good and bad, frustration and satisfaction. Infant observation has shown us that the most common way for children to manage living in a world that is both good *and* bad is to split it into either good *or* bad in an attempt to keep it under control (Klein 1935). Children who have predominantly good experiences and nurturing relationships are more likely to be able to manage a world where people and relationships are both good and bad, for example, a parent who is both loving and strict (Conway 2009). They come to understand that most others are not good or bad, but good *and* bad and importantly, mostly good. Children who have predominantly bad experiences, particularly in childhood, are likely to continue to perceive others as either good or bad. To protect themselves they fall back on creating a black-and-white world of good people or bad people. In a multi-agency context this can be played out by the child, their family and sometimes by the professionals around them.

Case study continued

At the first multi-agency meeting Daniel's mother sits next to Sarah, the ('good') LSA, and refuses to acknowledge any of the contributions made by the ('bad') social worker. The LSA, who has worked hard over the years to build a relationship with Daniel, falls easily into this 'good' role, and Daniel's mother, Louise, reinforces this. In the meeting Sarah aligns herself alongside Louise, and challenges the social worker's concerns about the family, failing to mention the concerns that have been raised in school about Daniel in the community.

We can see how a split has been created between Sarah, the LSA and the social worker. Sarah feels vindicated as the one professional who really understands Daniel and his mother. The problem for Sarah is that if she engages positively with the social worker's concerns, she risks damaging the relationship she has worked so hard to build with Daniel.

> Professionals can find themselves convinced that this really is an awful foster carer/social worker/guardian/teacher, and that they really are the only one who understands, has got it right and so on. (Conway 2009, p.21)

It would be useful if both Sarah and the social worker could acknowledge that they hold different positions, and discuss the potential opportunities of and barriers to this. Sarah might continue to align herself with the mother, Louise, whilst developing her capacity to think about Daniel's safety. She could then be an effective link between Louise and the social worker, who would be able to continue with the assessment of the family's needs for feeling supported by the school and other professionals in the team.

Understanding projection

Projection describes a process whereby feelings that are too difficult to manage are projected onto another person (Freud 1988). So, for example, instead of feeling angry ourselves, we make someone else angry. Psychoanalytical theory suggests that early overwhelming experiences are often repeated or played out in this way in current relationships.

Case study continued

Daniel has had a difficult relationship with his father who has often been absent, hostile and rejecting. Daniel's feelings in relation to his father are a complex mix of shame, anger and loss. These unexpressed feelings can be overwhelming for Daniel, so they are frequently projected onto the class teacher, Mr Williams, through hostile and rejecting behaviour. Despite Mr Williams' attempts to engage Daniel and to show interest and kindness, the boy ignores these attempts, is challenging, volatile and abusive. Ultimately Mr Williams feels he is getting nowhere with Daniel, he is negative about him and often gives up trying to engage him, and is sometimes equally as rejecting and hostile.

This complex process can then be mirrored in Mr Williams' relationships with other professionals in Daniel's multi-agency system. Although he is an experienced teacher, he feels that no one understands or is prepared to listen to his concerns about Daniel's behaviour, and frequently ends the day with a high level of anger and frustration and feels very deskilled. Mr Williams believes that the multi-agency response to Daniel's needs has not engaged with his owns needs or the needs of the other children in the class, and is therefore unwilling to engage fully in multi-agency working.

Situations like these can have devastating results for children like Daniel who rely on the adults around them for their emotional wellbeing and safety. Often the professionals are unaware of the potential effects of interprofessional conflicts on children and their families. It is therefore essential that systems and practices are in place to raise awareness of processes that can occur, such as the potential for splitting and projection.

Final thoughts

Raising the awareness of professionals involved in multi-agency working can help them identify when communication is being affected. In situations like this, reflective practice (McGregor and Cartwright 2011) is an essential part of effective multi-agency working (Cheminais 2009). Reflecting on the tensions and conflict that can occur in work with children and families enables practitioners to approach situations with an attitude of curiosity and to develop a more flexible stance. This then helps them to modify their ways of working and relating. Reflective practitioners are encouraged, through personal and group reflection, to think not only about the outcomes of multi-agency meetings, but also about the processes of the meeting. In practice, a reflective approach would involve creating a thinking space with both families and professionals within the multi-agency team where it is normal practice to think about the different positions that people hold, and remain curious about the impact of different perspectives.

Mr Williams could, rather than reacting negatively to Daniel's behaviour, be curious about what it might be communicating and, with the support of the team, reflect on the impact the behaviour has on him. This could enable him both to work in partnership with Sarah and the multi-agency team, and also to feel more confident in his own practice. Mr Williams could then be a vital part of the team around Daniel, putting into place strategies that would support Daniel appropriately.

Where possible, professionals working with complex cases need timely access to individual and/or group clinical supervision to which the processes of multi-agency working can be brought. Here the consultative approach to multi-agency working can be useful where perhaps CAMHS support educational professionals in working effectively with complex children and families. Sometimes schools are able to provide supervision within the staff team, particularly for staff who predominantly work with pupils with SEMH difficulties.

Appropriate and innovative professional development is seen as one of the mechanisms for developing effective multi-agency working (Daniels et al. 2007). Creating opportunities for continuing professional development (CPD) across agencies potentially strengthens relationships and develops robust multi-agency practice (Cooper and Jacobs 2011).

The needs of children and young people must remain at the centre of professional dialogues. Everyone in the multi-agency team has a useful role to play, and where a range of different professional perspectives and skills contribute to effective joint working. Professional roles need to be understood and respected, and professional boundaries need to be clear, whilst allowing for individual flexibility and the adaptation and renegotiation of practice to best support the child.

▨ REFLECTION POINTS ▨

1. Please reflect on examples of multi-disciplinary working that you have observed in schools. Think about the positives and negatives of what you have observed.

2. If you have not observed examples of multi-disciplinary working, think about how such an approach might have helped in schools where you have had (or are currently having) experience.

3. How do you react to the psychodynamic approach?

4. Think about a pupil you know who presents with challenging behaviour and/or social, emotional or mental health problems, and consider how his/her manner of presentation might be understood through a psychodynamic lens.

Bibliography

Atkinson, M., Wilkin, A., Stott, A., Doherty, P. and Kinder, K. (2002) *Multi-Agency Working: A Detailed Study.* LGA Research Report 26. Slough: NFER.

Bowlby, J. (1969) *Attachment and Loss. Volume 1: Attachment.* London: Hogarth Press and The Institute of Psychoanalysis.

Carter, A. (2015) *Carter Review of Initial Teacher Training (ITT).* London: Department for Education.

Cheminais, R. (2009) *Effective Multi-agency Partnerships: Putting Every Child Matters into Practice.* London: Sage.

Conway, P. (2009) 'Falling between minds: The effects of unbearable experiences on multi-agency communication in the care system.' *Adoption & Fostering Journal 33*, 1, 18–29.

Cooper, P. and Jacobs, B. (2011) *From Inclusion to Engagement: Helping Students Engage with Schooling Through Policy and Practice.* Hoboken, NJ: Wiley.

CWDC (Children's Workforce Development Council) (2009) *The Team Around the Child (TAC) and the Lead Professional: A Guide for Managers.* Leeds: CWDC.

Daniels, H., Leadbetter, J., Warmington, P., Edwards, A., Martin, D., Popova, A., Apostolov, A., Middleton, D. and Brown, S. (2007) 'Learning in and for multi-agency working.' *Oxford Review of Education*, 33, 521–538.

DCFS (Department for Children, Schools and Families) (2007) *What Is a Lead Professional?* London: DCSF.

DCSF (2014) *Promoting the Educational Achievement of Looked After Children: Statutory Guidelines for Local Authorities.* London: DCSF.

DCFS, ACPO (Association of Chief Police Officers), YJB (Youth Justice Board) and Home Office (2002) *Safer School Partnerships: Guidance.* London.

DfE (Department for Education) (2011) *The Munro Review of Child Protection: Final Report.* London: DfE.

DfE (2014) *SEN and Disability Code of Practice: Statutory Guidance for Organisations Who Work with and Support Children and Young People with Special Educational Needs and Disabilities.* London: DfE.

DfE (2015) *Working Together to Safeguard Children: A Guide to Inter-agency Working to Safeguard and Promote the Welfare of Children.* London: DfE.

DfES (Department for Education and Skills) (2004) *Every Child Matters: Change for Children.* London: DfES.

DfES (2006) *The Common Assessment Framework for Children and Young People.* London: DfES.

Donaldson, G. (2011) *Teaching Scotland's Future: Report of a Review of Teacher Education in Scotland.* Edinburgh: Scottish Government.

Farmakopoulou, N. (2002) 'Using an integrated theoretical framework for understanding interagency collaboration in the special educational needs field.' *European Journal of Special Needs Education 17*, 1, 49–60.

Freud, S. (1988) *Case Histories II.* London: Penguin.

Furlong, J. (2014) *Teaching Tomorrow's Teachers.* Oxford: University of Oxford.

Golding, K. (2010) 'Multi-agency and specialist working to meet the mental health needs of children in care and adopted.' *Clinical Child Psychology and Psychiatry 15*, 4, 573–587.

Golding, K., Turner, M., Worrell, H., Roberts, J. and Cadman, A. (2016) *Observing Adolescents with Attachment Difficulties in Educational Settings.* London: Jessica Kingsley Publishers.

Granville, J. and Langton, P. (2002) 'Working across boundaries: Systemic and psychodynamic perspectives on multidisciplinary and inter-agency practice.' *Journal of Social Work Practice 16*, 1, 23–27.

Great Britain (2004) *The Children Act.* London: HMSO.

Howard, S. (2006) *Psychodynamic Counselling in a Nutshell.* London: Sage.

Howe, D. (2011) *Attachment Across the Life Course: A Brief Introduction.* Basingstoke: Palgrave Macmillan.

Jacobs, M. (1998) *The Presenting Past* (2nd edn). Milton Keynes: Open University Press.

Klein, M. (1935) *Love, Guilt and Reparation.* London: Hogarth Press and The Institute of Psychoanalysis.

McGregor, D. and Cartwright, L. (2011) *Developing Reflective Practice: A Guide for Beginning Teachers.* Maidenhead: Open University Press.

Milbourne, L., Macrae, S. and Maguire, M. (2003) 'Collaborative solutions or new policy problems: Exploring multi-agency partnerships in education and health work.' *Journal of Education Policy 18*, 1, 19–35.

Music, G. (2011) *Nurturing Natures: Attachment and Children's Emotional, Sociocultural, and Brain Development.* Hove: Psychology Press.

Øvretveit, J. (1993) *Co-ordinating Community Care: Multidisciplinary Teams and Care Management.* Buckingham: Open University Press.

Salmon, G. (2004) 'Multi-agency collaboration: The challenges for CAMHS.' *Child and Adolescent Mental Health 9*, 4, 156–161.

Sloper, P. 2004. 'Facilitators and barriers for coordinated multi-agency services.' *Childcare, Health and Development 30*, 6, 571–580.

TDA (2008) *Professional Standards for Qualified Teacher Status and Requirements for Initial Teacher Training.* London: TDA. Available at www.rbkc.gov.uk/pdf/qts-professional-standards-2008.pdf, accessed on 30 March 2017.

Wolpert, M., Humphrey, N., Belsky, J. and Deighton, J. (2013) 'Embedding mental health support in schools: Learning from the Targeted Mental Health in Schools (TaMHS) national evaluation.' *Emotional and Behavioural Difficulties 18*, 3, 270–283.

12

Emotional Development and Children in Care

The Virtual School Perspective

TONY CLIFFORD AND ANNE-MARIE MCBLAIN

Children in care (CiC), also known as looked-after children (LAC), are children who are in the care of their local authority. This may be with the agreement of their parents – for example, where a parent recognises that they are not coping – or because the local authority has intervened to remove the child because of neglect or abuse. In these circumstances, a temporary removal into care may lead to the granting of a full care order by a judge.

The role of the virtual school is to offer dedicated educational support to children in care within a particular local authority. This support may include additional tuition, help with school admission or exclusion issues, and close liaison with social care and health teams. Children who are looked after by their local authority are very likely to have unmet attachment needs arising from the circumstances that brought them into care. Research suggests that these experiences may also impact on their long-term mental health (ONS 2015) and their school performance (DfE 2016a). A small proportion of children in care may also experience further abuse while in the care system (Biehal 2014).

Unmet attachment needs will add to the challenges these children face in school and in the classroom. So what do 'unmet attachment needs' actually look like? Let us consider the case of 'Sam'.

Case study: Sam

At age 11 Sam lived in a family in which domestic violence was the norm. Both his parents had drug and alcohol issues, and his three older brothers had spent time in prison for GBH (grievous bodily harm). Sam spent a lot of time trying to protect his younger siblings from the worst effects of the chaos at home. Often he did not come to school or arrived late, tired, angry and distracted. He struggled with reading and writing, because he had missed lots of early learning. He didn't talk about what was going on, because he was terrified that if social care got involved, his family would be split up. In school he was described as 'sullen and uncooperative'. He was disruptive in the more academic lessons. His explosive temper led to regular exclusions and the threat of permanent exclusion.

When the primary school noticed severe bruising on a younger sibling during PE, social care was involved and Sam and the three younger children were taken into care. Sadly no foster placement could be found for all four. Sam had to live separately and 20 miles from the city because there were no local carers with vacancies. Sam also had to start a new school.

During the first week, Sam tried to text his siblings in class and a teacher told him that he would have to confiscate his phone. Sam became angry and threatened the teacher with violence. The headteacher put a five-day exclusion in place, but Sam ran out of school and went missing for 24 hours. The foster carers gave notice on the placement as they did not feel able to manage the level of behaviour and risk that caring for Sam entailed. Sam moved again, but this time to a children's home 50 miles away and had to start a new school – again.

This case study is collated from a number of children's stories – but take a moment to imagine yourself as Sam, walking into yet another new school, in a new city, having moved 'home' five days before. Remember that 10 per cent of children in care will have had three or more placement changes during one school year.

This chapter explains a little more about the particular challenges children in care face and the key people and actions that can help. The importance of multi-agency working, detailed in Chapter 11, is of particular relevance and importance when meeting the needs of children in care.

Two of the children whose stories contribute to the case study above have now gone on to achieve qualifications and have become settled and happy in their education through effective multi-agency working and excellent individual support. Despite adverse experiences, many children in care do amazingly well, showing both courage and resilience. But we need to be mindful that they will carry with them unmet attachment needs and experiences of trauma. This represents additional 'baggage' that many other children do not have to carry. Perhaps you could imagine a child navigating their way around your school while carrying a metaphorical, physical weight around with them – the emotional burden of neglect and abuse.

Virtual heads and designated teachers for children in care

There are a number of key people and statutory requirements designed to support the education of children in care.

Local authorities have a statutory duty to safeguard and promote the welfare of any child looked after by them. This includes a particular duty to promote the child's educational achievements and, in recognition of this, a decision was made in 2008 (by the then Department for Children, Schools and Families) to pilot the role of 'virtual school head' in a number of local authorities. The idea was that the virtual head would be a special, additional headteacher who would take on specific responsibility for the local authority's children in care, supporting and monitoring their education in whatever school or setting they were in. Virtual heads do not have a physical school, but the children in the care of their authority are their 'school roll' and the children for whom they are responsible. Following the success of the pilot, the Children and Families Act 2014 required every local authority in England to appoint a virtual head.

Virtual heads tend to see themselves as having three main roles. First, as an employee of the local authority they are a 'corporate parent' to children in care. Many would subscribe to the view that they must therefore always be prepared to ask themselves the question, 'Would this be good enough for my child?' Second, virtual heads are accountable for outcomes for their virtual school roll, in the same way that any headteacher would be for their own 'bricks and mortar' school. Finally, virtual heads need to ensure that strategies are working for their children, so they work closely with school support services, social care, health and other agencies.

In addition to the virtual head, the second role to be aware of is the designated teacher for children in care. From September 2009 all schools have been required under the Children and Young Persons Act 2008 to appoint a designated teacher to promote the educational achievement of children in care who are on the 'bricks and mortar' school roll. Naturally, the school's designated teacher should work closely with the local authority's virtual head.

Many children come into the care of the local authority because of neglect and abuse. You may come across the unspoken (or spoken) misconception that these are 'naughty' children. In fact, it is what has been done to the children that is the problem, rather than the children themselves. Social care will only make the very difficult decision to remove a child from their parents on the basis of there being a serious risk to the child. Sometimes this is with the consent of parents, who may recognise that they are not coping, but sometimes it is an emergency. In both cases it is traumatic. Children's responses to abuse and neglect and to being removed from their family will vary, but the classic survival responses of 'fight, flight or freeze', discussed at regular intervals in this book, will invariably be the result.

Key statistics

The number of looked-after children has increased steadily in recent years. There were 69,540 looked-after children in March 2015, an increase of 1 per cent compared to March 2014, and an increase of 6 per cent compared to March 2011 (DfE 2016b). These statistics include a rise in the number of 'unaccompanied asylum-seeking children'.

Long-term outcomes for children in care are a cause for concern. In 2007 a government report, *Care Matters: Time for Change* (DfES 2007), found that they were:

- 5 times more likely to move school in Years 10 and 11

- 8 times more likely to be permanently excluded from school

- 4 times more likely to have mental health problems

- 50 times more likely to go to prison

- 60 times more likely to become homeless

- 66 times more likely to have children who need public care.

As Sam's case study illustrates, the point at which a child is taken from their family is always an experience of great upheaval. Children who have been hurt or neglected by their families will often still love their families and want to stay with them, despite the negative consequences. The decision to take children into care is not taken lightly, and the process can be protracted and complex. There may have been a long build-up to the final decision that parents can no longer look after their children, or there may have been a significant event that precipitated the change almost overnight. Either way, emotional turmoil invariably follows such a decision, and this turmoil will be expressed by the children and young people in the home and in school. Once a child is placed in care, there will be ongoing discussions with parents (and often with the courts) about the longer-term care plan for the child. These plans involve a range of professionals and the care plans may change regularly before the crisis settles and the child stabilises.

Approximately 75 per cent of children in care will live with foster carers, and the remaining 25 per cent will live in a variety of residential settings (DfE 2016b). Although social care will work hard to find a permanent placement for a child, the reality is that care placements often break down. Twenty-three per cent of children will have one care placement change and 10 per cent three or more in one year, and many therefore will have to change school placements as well. The result for a child can be high degrees of uncertainty, stress and anxiety which, as previous chapters have highlighted, can interfere with concentration, emotional regulation and learning in the classroom.

REFLECTION POINTS

At this point, it may be worth imagining what these circumstances would feel like for you, as a beginning teacher.

Let us imagine that you start your newly qualified teacher (NQT) year and new term in a new school. You build relationships with your class and with the teachers, and you get to know the curriculum and your schemes of work. Excellent!

However, after a few weeks, the headteacher comes to find you and says that, unfortunately, this was only a temporary job, and you are now going to have to move on.

You move and the new head is initially delighted, saying that they see a great future for you! Unfortunately, you find your new classes extremely challenging, and you have some disastrous lessons. The disappointed head tells you that you will have to move.

You move and start again, and the same thing repeats again and again and again.

After a while, you stop unpacking your things; you are wary of building up new relationships; you don't trust what the headteachers say and you anticipate it all going wrong – and so perhaps it does.

This is the pattern for all too many looked-after children. A fresh start followed by failure that then repeats until the expectation is failure. So how can you work with your school and the wider network of support to ensure that failure is not the experience for children in care in your classroom?

To begin with, make sure, as part of your induction, you meet the designated teacher for children in care. Often this person is closely linked to safeguarding in the school. Find out from the designated teacher who your children in care are. Each child will have a Personal Education Plan or PEP, which is reviewed at least six-monthly. The PEP should contain information about all key contacts, the child's school history and achievement, their views about school and targets to support their learning and development. Every school can request Pupil Premium Plus funding from the virtual school to support looked-after children on their roll. For example, in Sam's case study, Pupil Premium funding might have been used to provide staff training with an educational psychologist (with a focus on meeting Sam's needs), additional literacy support and extra learning opportunities in a curriculum area in which Sam excelled, in order to build his self-esteem.

As a beginning teacher, it is important that you understand the PEP for every child in your care. If you can see that your child is struggling or not making progress, a review of the PEP is really helpful as it will bring together all the key people in the child's life to look at how best to work together to support the child. Supporting children in care is not something you will do on your own. It is important work that is undertaken collectively and with the support of a range of fellow professionals.

A note of caution – it is important that the child's voice is heard in the review, but find out how they feel about being taken out of lessons. Also, consider whether the discussion is *about them* – this should then not include them and should instead be a professional discussion – or *with them*, in which case the meeting should be small enough and safe enough for their voice to be heard.

When considering how you will meet the needs of a child in care in your classroom, it is vital that you respond to the child as an individual and not to their 'in-care' status. Many young people in care develop incredible resilience and self-sufficiency; they are motivated, skilled and determined despite their difficult experiences. First and foremost, these children and young people want and deserve our respect. For others, the experiences they are going through can be overwhelming, and we must work hard to establish the relationships from which trust and learning can emerge.

The Multi-Element Plan

In the case studies that follow you will see how the educational psychologist from the virtual school worked with schools in Stoke-on-Trent to develop better understanding and more effective responses to unmet attachment needs through a Multi-Element Plan (MEP) (LaVigna and Willis 1995).

When things get tough, a key strategy is to bring professionals and carers together, and with the support of an educational psychologist, to try to put together a picture of the child's strengths –there are always strengths – and challenges. We try to see the world from the child's point of view and then match our responses to this so we can help the child develop their own management strategies. This is very different from a simple 'rewards and sanctions' approach, and some people become anxious that a child-centred approach is in some way 'soft'. In our view, 'what is important is what is effective', and so the best way to enhance your authority in the classroom is to do what works rather than take a simplistic authoritarian approach, focused on your status.

The following case study illustrates how we developed a MEP, led by the educational psychologist who worked with the wider team. The team included the designated teacher, the form/class/subject teacher, relevant pastoral staff, the teaching assistant, carer and social worker, all of whom engaged in a structured problem-solving process to produce the MEP. The MEP process sets out to list a young person's strengths, protective factors, challenges, maintaining factors, skills to be developed and strategies to support this. A functional behaviour analysis is also undertaken as part of the MEP, and the MEP is then shared with the virtual head.

Case study: David

Woodlands Academy is a slightly larger than average secondary school. The large majority of students come from White British backgrounds, with a slightly smaller than average proportion coming from minority ethnic backgrounds. The proportion of students who speak English as an additional language is just above average, and a high proportion of students are known to be eligible for the Pupil Premium. The number of students with disabilities and those who have special educational needs (SEN) are well above average. The school meets the minimum levels expected for attainment and progress.

The school chose to do work with their staff team on the impact of unmet attachment needs and trauma because of the high proportion of students known to be eligible for the Pupil Premium and especially the high number of children in care. Both groups were taking a disproportionate amount of the pastoral and senior management team's time.

'David' was in Year 11 at Woodlands Academy and had previously attended five different primary schools. He arrived at Woodlands Academy in the September that he was in Year 7, when he was living with his father. Due to issues at home he had moved to live with his mother in October, and transferred to Riverside High School. As a consequence of violence against him perpetrated by his mother's then partner, he was taken into long-term care in December that year, and returned to Woodlands Academy. David was required to give evidence against his mother's partner in court. Whilst David had intermittent contact with his biological father, he had no contact with his mother who refused to see him.

During his time in care David was accused of drug use and theft from the mother of his foster carer, resulting in his carer allegedly hitting him, and he was moved to a new care home. This resulted in David losing the relationships he had built with the other foster children at the placement. He also lost contact with his siblings.

During David's transition into Woodlands Academy, persistent low-level behavioural issues were noted and he was described as a 'lovable rogue'. Staff at Woodlands Academy observed that in lessons he was easily distracted and seemed easily led and taken astray by others.

There were some key people around David at Woodlands Academy who helped him by supporting him through his transition to foster care and through the court case. A key worker was assigned in school who remained consistent throughout. Strategies such as 'meet and greet' and strategic withdrawal were implemented. There were regular meetings with social care and his foster carer while multi-agency working was solution-focused with a nurturing approach. A 'Pupil Passport' was generated through consultation with the educational psychologist and, in school, a looked-after child mentor kept David on their caseload for two years. David also received intensive form tutor support (even tutoring at the home was provided), as well as one-to-one support from the Specialist Education Support Team.

When he reached Year 11, David was unexpectedly given notice that his foster placement was ending two weeks before Christmas. Understandably this heightened his anxiety, and he experienced a sense of trepidation and the unknown. As a consequence there was a significant decline in his ability to cope in school, and this manifested itself as frequent displays of childish, attention-seeking behaviours such as pulling faces, flicking lights on and off and tantrums when he did not get his own way. His lack of respect for staff and their authority was apparent in the inappropriate things he said to them, such as asking if they had ever 'smoked weed' followed by attempts to minimise what he had said by turning it into a joke. Due to his refusal to engage with his work, David was underachieving at school. He often put his head on the desk and when asked what was wrong, said 'Nothing.'

David's relationship with his peers also deteriorated as he would not stop his annoying behaviours even when they requested that he did. He was also very easily led and consequently very vulnerable. David also started to engage in more risk-taking behaviours outside of school as he increasingly lost stability.

However, David was described to the educational psychologist by staff who knew him as 'someone who thinks of others', 'caring' and with a 'loving nature', and it was reported that he nurtured other foster children in his placement. David's sense of humour was noted along with his 'pleasant' and 'endearing' nature. It was reported that he had a great sense of humour and was 'always smiling' with his 'cheeky smile and blue eyes'.

A number of protective factors were also identified including his average ability (despite his underachievement due to reluctance to engage in his studies); his place at school; the support he received from one-to-one support staff; his care home placement; his talent for playing football; his love of cooking; his friends both in and out of school; and, despite his natural self-deprecation, his positive response to praise.

Working with the educational psychologist the team hypothesised that David's lack of contact with his mother whilst his siblings still had access to her was central to his problems. Having experienced repeated and extreme loss and rejection, David was terrified of leaving school and losing the people with whom he had formed attachments. Therefore key members of staff were identified with whom he had established some attachments. When he was placed on fixed-term exclusions he could not cope with being by himself and so, at times of distress and dysregulation, rather than excluding him he was given periods of 'time in' with these trusted adults who used calm, non-confrontational responses and empathy. David was educated in small groups where possible, and the number of people dealing with him directly was reduced and 'problem' lessons were avoided to reduce over-stimulation and threat.

David's refusal to engage with lessons and certain individuals was recognised as an unconscious attempt to avoid further loss of the attachments he had made (e.g. with staff and friends). By rejecting others first and shutting down his emotions, David was able protect himself from the overwhelming feelings precipitated by even more potential loss. An action plan was ready for when particular challenges arose, where the identified key people stepped in to support him. School and home created well-structured supportive environments where the rules and expectations for David's behaviour, learning and social relationships were clearly stated, taught, recognised and rewarded. These boundaries were made consistent between home and school, and thus all adults involved with him worked closely together to support David and each other. All transitions and endings were carefully planned, and sudden changes in routines were anticipated and avoided where possible. When unavoidable, warnings were provided, and the consequent difficulties for David were acknowledged.

It was noted that David had difficulty recognising, expressing and communicating his feelings. Therefore he was first helped to identify the nature and intensity of his emotions through the use of a 5-point scale, and he was then taught specific strategies to manage and cope with these feelings and responses. He was given access and permission to access a 'safe' specified area in school when he needed to and where he could feel emotionally contained.

In this area David could engage with activities and objects that helped him to self-regulate (e.g. word searches, card games, colouring, drawing, restful music and some calming computer games). Safety and/or calming routines were also developed for use with key staff when David was very distressed and could not self-regulate. These included relational and rhythmic activities and physical exercises (e.g. walking, breathing exercises, playing throw and catch with a ball). Permission cards were handed by David to staff to allow him to retreat quickly to this place when he needed to. He was also offered access to therapy.

Through discussion the team recognised that David had assumed a negative self-concept as a consequence of his mother's rejection, which was reinforced by the negative comments of his previous foster carer, and he tried to live up to this negative image through his inappropriate attention-seeking behaviours in order to maintain his credibility and gain a sense of acceptance and belonging from others, especially his peers. Therefore David was given opportunities to develop his skills, confidence and self-esteem with regard to friendships with his peers through sensitively facilitated support from his key workers who coached him and helped him practice these skills and reflect on his progress. In particular, this focused on group dynamics and how to initiate contact, make friends, discuss, exchange ideas and deal with conflicts. His strengths and achievements were also highlighted and emphasised by staff who gave him opportunities to demonstrate them to others.

In the absence of a protective parent figure and without the skills to articulate his fears, much of his childlike behaviour was a consequence of his unconscious regression to an earlier developmental stage where he used negative behaviours to elicit support, protection, attention, security and love from those he trusted the most. Therefore all staff who worked with him were made aware of the emotional, social and developmental level he was functioning at, and were encouraged to see past his inappropriate behaviour and recognise it as a developmental deficit rather than chosen behaviour. Staff were then asked to provide activities and experiences that matched this.

In order to manage his need for staff attention, David was also given 'teacher tokens' that he could 'bank' if staff were busy and couldn't give him attention immediately. He also used them to 'book' a pre-arranged time later on, if necessary. David was encouraged to work on emotion cards with younger children in the school to promote his self-esteem and understanding of his own emotions through teaching others.

David's teaching programme was sufficiently flexible to accommodate the variability in his performance from day to day, and included strategies to support his executive functions including a large proportion of practical hands-on learning where tasks were broken down into manageable steps, and a variety of ways to structure and organise his thinking were explored. These included templates, checklists, mind maps, key words, story boards, diagrams, use of a Dictaphone and IT packages with idea and concept maps to help him to structure his ideas. David was involved in the planning, decision-making and review of his learning throughout, not only in areas of concern, but also in areas of strength, setting his own targets to give him a more realistic and proactive view of himself as a learner.

David's requirement for constant praise, encouragement and reassurance reflected his drastically low self-confidence, self-esteem and self-efficacy. Therefore, wherever possible, staff made positive comments about David's achievements and behaviour. Furthermore, staff were made aware of the need to make the curriculum accessible to him by differentiating work programmes and ensuring a high level of positive feedback to maintain his motivation and involvement in learning, and there was close liaison between the SENCO and subject staff.

To further develop and improve his self-efficacy, self-confidence and independence as a learner, he was supported to develop 'metacognitive' strategies (to become aware of how he learned). Sometimes this involved talking with him explicitly about how he worked things out, how he remembered information, what helped him to learn in other situations, modelling the thinking through of tasks out loud, and encouragement to talk through how he did a task, stage by stage. David was also supported to develop self-help strategies, such as asking for repetition and clarification, self-repetition, allowing himself sufficient time to process information.

In order to further reduce David's anxiety and uncertainty regarding his future, a clear plan was made for his immediate future. A work-based learning programme was devised within Woodlands Academy that would enable David to remain at school and retain the attachments he had established with staff and peers as he moved into post-16 education. He was involved in a work experience programme over the Easter holidays to help him form contacts with staff who he would be working with on this programme.

This detailed case study illustrates a range of support strategies that schools can employ to support children in care who are struggling with the effects of trauma, rejection, unmet attachment needs and insecure placements.

The outcomes for David were that he was not permanently excluded from school. He retained vital attachment figures, both staff and peers, and remained in an environment that he knew and that knew and understood him. His anxiety levels were reduced and his confidence grew. He achieved some excellent GCSE grades and experienced a sense of achievement.

This worked because David's needs and challenges were recognised, understood and managed by those around him. He was taught how to recognise, understand and regulate his own emotions, and given space in which to do this. His developmental stage was also understood and supported.

Clear expectations, boundaries and plans for behaviour were made, which were consistently applied between home and school, and which anticipated difficulties and changes. A clear plan was made for his future that reduced his uncertainty and anxiety, while key relationships were maintained and new relationships were facilitated by trusted staff. In addition, all staff who worked directly with David were given a good level of support and helpful supervision.

Final thoughts

As a beginning teacher, an awareness of the emotional needs of children in care is vitally important. Many of these children will be hurt and demoralised by the experience of being placed in care, and this may be reflected in their attitudes to school, to learning and to you.

The school's designated teacher for children in care will be able to support you with information and guidance on best practice and effective support strategies in the classroom. In addition, the virtual head, social care teams and educational psychology teams will be there to support the PEPs that each child in care will have.

With care, understanding and high expectations, you can be part of a team that supports learners like David and Sam to succeed in your school.

▓ REFLECTION POINTS ▓

1. 'Good day, bad day': Think yourself into the mind of a child – this could be a child you've taught or know, or it could be Sam or David. Try writing their diary for a 'bad' school day. Use your five senses, notice everything – many children who have experienced trauma are hypervigilant.

2. Then imagine the same day, but this time consider how much the people they encounter know about attachment and how much the school itself has adapted to be aware of attachment and the impact of trauma.

3. Next time you are in school, spend a few minutes walking round as though you were this child. If you were this child's teacher, what would you do to help the child feel safe enough to learn successfully?

4. Try re-writing the 'bad' day and turn it into a good one through the support and responses of the staff.

Bibliography

Biehal, N. (2014) 'Maltreatment in foster care: A review of the evidence.' *Child Abuse Review* 23, 48–60.

Cairns, K. and Stanway, C. (2004) *Learn the Child: Helping Looked After Children to Learn – A Good Practice Guide for Social Workers, Carers and Teachers.* London: BAAF.

DfE (Department for Education) (2016a) *Mental Health and Behaviour in Schools.* London: DfE.

DfE (2016b) *Children Looked After in England Including Adoption: 2015 to 2016.* London. Available at www.gov.uk/government/statistics/children-looked-after-in-england-including-adoption-2015-to-2016, accessed on 20 March 2017.

DfES (Department for Education and Skills) (2007) *Care Matters: Time for Change.* London DfES.

Golding, K.S. (2008) *Nurturing Attachments – Supporting Children Who Are Fostered Or Adopted.* London: Jessica Kingsley Publishers.

LaVigna, G.W. and Willis, T.J. (1995) 'Challenging behavior: A model for breaking the barriers to social and community integration.' *IABA Newsletter 1*, 1, 1, 8–15.

ONS (Office for National Statistics) (2015) *Insights into Children's Mental Health and Well-being.* London: ONS.

13

Social Pedagogy in the Classroom
Supporting Children and Young People in Care

EMMA BLACK, MICHAEL BETTENCOURT
AND CLAIRE CAMERON

The hypothesis at the heart of this chapter is that you, the target reader of this book, have chosen to enter the teaching profession for a specific reason: you want to make a difference to the lives of the children and young people in your classroom.

As fellow professionals in the education sector, we recognise that demands such as implementing a high stakes accountability-driven curriculum can, without careful consideration, be to the detriment of supporting the emotional needs of the children and young people in your care. Drawing on the work of Cameron, Connelly and Jackson's (2015) *Educating Children and Young People in Care: Learning Placements and Caring Schools*, we argue that for children to thrive and flourish, the integration of care and education in daily life is key. We believe this is particularly pertinent to those children and young people who have experienced difficult childhoods. As such, it is these children who are the focus of this chapter. In an effort to support you in establishing and maintaining the synergy between care and education, we present the field of social pedagogy for your consideration.

Children and young people in care

As Chapter 12 has confirmed, the legal term for children and young people in care is 'looked-after children' (or LAC). These children and young people have been separated from their birth families – often for their own safety – and placed into the care of the local authority. They are considered one of the most vulnerable groups of children and young people in society, particularly when they first come into care. Most of these children and young people live in foster care and some live with extended family, while others are placed in residential children's homes. Many children and young people in care live in a state of flux, moving from placement to placement for reasons beyond their control. In contrast, however, a significant number are able to live in long-term placements, establish and maintain healthy relationships, perform well at school and describe feeling safe and happy.

Although children and young people in care are bound by a legal status,[1] they are not a homogenous group. That said, it is important to note that they usually share common traumatic experiences relating to separation, neglect, abuse and loss. Children and young people in care have often been subject to multiple forms of distressing events over a long period of time. Cairns (2013) explains that when placed in these situations, our bodies produce a toxic level of stress hormone (cortisol). This survival response has the power to influence our physical, psychological and social ways of functioning such as our ability to coordinate our body, focus on presented tasks, relate positively to ourselves and the world around us and to form relationships with others. Supporting children and young people through these difficulties is by no means an easy feat. We propose that *social pedagogy in the classroom* not only acts as a springboard to recovery for those who have experienced trauma, but also provides a context for establishing and maintaining the synergy between care and education for all children and young people in your classroom.

Social pedagogy in the classroom

In many continental European countries, social pedagogy is considered both a profession and a discipline (Bennett and Tayler 2006; Petrie *et al.* 2009). It can be traced back to the work of educational philosophers such as Rousseau, Pestalozzi and Frobel. It has influenced a range of children's services and organisations such as teacher education, youth work, early childhood education, community education and social work (Cameron *et al.* 2011a). In the UK, social pedagogy is becoming an increasingly familiar term in educational policy and

---

1   For a detailed analysis of legislation surrounding the education of children and young people in care, see Cameron *et al.* (2015, pp.24—42).

reform. Over 2000 care, education and related practitioners have attended social pedagogy short courses in the UK since 2009. Under the previous Labour government, Petrie *et al.* (2009) argued that the social pedagogic approach was well suited to English policy concerns relating to how society best served its children and young people. The recent changes made to the *Special Educational Needs and Disability (SEND) Code of Practice* (2015), which emphasises person-centred practice, have highlighted an ideal context for this plea, once again.

In practice, social pedagogy is considered a dynamic, humanistic approach to education that takes account of, but goes beyond, subject learning (Kyriacou *et al.* 2009). Humanism, as outlined in Chapter 1, focuses on developing human potential through relationships, wellbeing and happiness, holistic learning and empowerment (Eichsteller and Holthoff 2012). To demonstrate what this might look like in your classroom, we present some distinctive features of a social pedagogical approach below.

The classroom teacher as a social pedagogue

It would be a mistake to consider social pedagogy as reducible to a collection of techniques. Instead, it is helpful to consider it as an art form that connects the teacher to their fundamental values and beliefs. Cameron *et al.* (2011, pp.14–16) provide a helpful summary of a social pedagogical approach which, for the purposes of this chapter, have been rearranged to provide a useful insight into what it might look like in your classroom. Cameron *et al.* (2011) suggest that social pedagogues:

- Focus on the child as a whole person. They recognise that children are immersed in a complex relational system of support. They are aware that children and young people think, feel, have a physical, spiritual, social and creative existence, and that all of these characteristics continually interact in unison. Similarly they bring themselves as a whole person to their work.

- Constantly reflect on their practice. To overcome the challenging demands they are often confronted with, they draw on and apply theoretical understandings to their everyday practice (Petrie *et al.* 2009). They make decisions about moving forward according to the best interests of the children and young people in their care.

- Bring their hearts to their work as ethical and emotional beings. They are connected to their fundamental values and beliefs and are constantly aware of how these express themselves in the outer world (Eichsteller and Holthoff 2012). They are aware of how their own emotional reactions can affect their relationships and communications with children and others. Through their relationships with other people they show empathy and respect. They value, listen to and respond to the point of view of others, knowing that this will often be different from their own.

- Are both practical and creative. Simple activities that make up the many aspects of children's daily lives, such as preparing meals and snacks, or making music and building kites, are viewed as a medium for building safe trusting relationships (Petrie *et al.* 2006).

- Share their space. While they are together, children and adults are seen as inhabiting the same life space, not as existing in separate, hierarchical domains (Petrie *et al.* 2009).

- Value teamwork. They actively seek the contribution of other people in supporting children and young people. In doing so they form good working relationships with parents and carers, other professionals and members of the local community.

Now that we have briefly introduced you to social pedagogy and how this might influence you as a beginning teacher, our focus turns to how you can use this approach to establish and maintain the synergy between care and education in your classroom. We present to you what is often referred to as the 'head, heart and hands' triad of social pedagogical practice.

Exploring the head, heart and hands of your practice

The humanistic nature of social pedagogy is often encapsulated in the expression 'head, heart, hands' (Eichsteller and Holthoff 2012). This phrase was first coined by Johann Heinrich Pestalozzi, a Swiss educational reformer, in the late 18th century, to demonstrate how the whole person is involved in the art of teaching. Pestalozzi believed that the spirit of teaching came to light through the interaction of these three elements (Soertard 1994). From a social pedagogical perspective, the synergy of care and education in the classroom can be established and maintained through an art of 'being' with children as opposed to 'doing'. In this way, the focus of practice is directed toward:

- The values and beliefs you hold relating to education (Head).

- How you express these values and beliefs (Heart).

- Activities that form part of your everyday practice (Hands).

Exploring these elements in more detail provides a useful framework to explain how we believe the social pedagogical approach can support you to establish and maintain the synergy of care and education in your classroom.

Head: The values and beliefs you hold relating to education

In *Radical Education and the Common School*, Fielding and Moss (2010) explore the influential works of Loris Malaguzzi, founder of the Reggio Emilia approach, and his successor Carlina Rinaldi, a leading pedagogical thinker. Through this exploration, two fundamental questions relating to the values and beliefs you hold about education emerge: (1) What is your theory of learning? (2) What is your image of the child?

It is important to note the significance of these questions as your answers will inevitably shape and inform every aspect of your practice. The theory and image you hold will push you to behave in certain ways and influence your ability to understand and support children and young people in your class (Malaguzzi 1994). To support you with this we provide two opposing views for your consideration. These are presented to prompt reflection.

What is your theory of learning?

For some of you, education may be characterised by knowledge acquisition, league tables, performance and data recording. Here the role of the teacher is technical and focused on delivering the curriculum; learning is seen as a form of linear progression en route to a prescribed goal and caring or pastoral duties become the responsibility of specialists (Wetz 2009).

For others, education may be characterised by hypothesis testing, creativity and originality. Here learning is seen as 'something which shoots in all directions with no beginning and no end, but always in *between*, and with opening towards other directions and places' (Rinaldi 2006, p.8; original emphasis). In this manner the role of the teacher is as facilitator, and learning is seen as a process of co-construction (Fielding and Moss 2010).

What is your image of the child?

Some of you may view the child as a passive receiver of knowledge, an 'empty vessel' into which you must 'pour' knowledge. For others, children are considered to be 'rich in potential, strong, powerful, competent and most of all, connected to adults and other children' (Malaguzzi 1994, p.10).

Drawing on the work of Cameron *et al.* (2015), we believe it is necessary to adopt a view that considers learning to be a genuine, interactive and collaborative process. Building trusting and secure relationships is key to this process, particularly for children and young people in the care. To emphasise this point, Cameron *et al.* (2015) call on the work of Nel Noddings, an American feminist, educationalist and philosopher. Noddings (1992), like many others, argues that the academic objectives of schools cannot be met unless teachers provide students with a caring and supportive classroom environment. The emphasis on care in education is further reflected in the second element of the triad, the heart.

Heart: How you express your values and beliefs

Pestalozzi presents the 'heart' as a second element intrinsic to the everyday practice of the educator. This element cuts to the core of human relationships. It acts as a 'relational prompt' for the educator faced with the complexity of knowing how their daily interpersonal behaviour impacts on the development of children and young people in their classroom. People are viewed as relational participants in their own unique context. Their perception, awareness and consciousness are intertwined with their relationship with language, people and things (Heidegger 1996). Put simply, 'We are of the world, not merely in it' (Arendt 1971, p.22).

On entering a classroom, it does not take long to recognise this complex relational system at work. As the bell rings, the hustle and bustle of the school day begins. Individuals with their own unique history of experiences, thoughts and feelings come together to embrace a carefully planned schedule of events. Amongst this hive of activity children and adults share a multitude of interactions. It is the quality of these interactions that play a key role in children and young people's emotional development and educational progress.

Establishing and maintaining positive, encouraging and caring interactions can, at times, for a variety of reasons, be difficult for both children and adults alike. However, the importance of doing so is amplified through a growing body of literature exploring teacher–pupil relationships (e.g. Cemalcilar 2010; Furrer and Skinner 2003; Kennedy, Landor and Todd 2011; Schaps, Battistich and Solomon 2004). Findings suggest that the quality of this relationship influences not only the child's emotional and academic development, but also their sense of belonging to the wider school community. The psychological need to belong has long been recognised as one of our basic human needs (Maslow 1943). Baumeister and Leary (1995) argue that establishing and maintaining positive social connections is so important to human beings that it is a fundamental psychological motivation, determining what we think, feel and do.

Teven and McCroskey (1997) suggest that it is difficult for a teacher to care for every child or young person at all times, particularly when teaching large classes. They propose that although it is most favourable for teachers to truly care about their student, it is the perception of caring that is critical. 'If a teacher cares deeply, but does not communicate that attribute, he or she might as well not care at all' (Teven and McCroskey 1997, p.167). The emphasis on how to communicate in such a manner is further reflected in the third element of the triad, the hands.

Hands: Activities that form part of your everyday practice

The final element of the triad gives consideration to the 'hands'. This element concerns itself with how you demonstrate your practice. Due to the early experiences of children and young people in care, and the complexity of the difficulties they face as a result, they often need a bespoke relational approach to their education. The concept of an 'everyday expert' introduced by Cameron *et al.* (2015) is a helpful means to understanding what this might look like in the classroom. The 'everyday expert' fundamentally provides a model for what good parenting would provide. This can be achieved in the classroom through:

- Engaging in a 'common third' activity. The 'common third', a Danish concept central to social pedagogical practice, describes the act of engaging in an activity that connects both the adult and the child. An activity that creates mutual curiosity and provides an opportunity to plan, share ideas and enjoy the process of completing something together has the potential to become a 'common third' activity.

- Getting to know students, especially the 'hard to reach'. Listen to the children and young people speak to each other, the topics in which they choose to contribute; get to know their sense of humour, interests, passions and frustrations. Use this to support conversations with the child or young person. Official forums such as the school council may also provide a helpful platform for achieving this. Participation in forums can raise your awareness of the issues children and young people face.

- Encouraging and supporting children in care to access out-of-school learning. Participating in sports activities or clubs of interest provides an important platform for developing friendships and widening social networks. They also act as an important source of stability and consistency in the children's lives (Hollingworth 2012).

- Viewing education as a partnership (Prensky 2010). Plan learning opportunities that create a partnership between yourself and the child or young person or through a peer-to-peer partnership. Encourage children and young people to follow their passions. Allow them to research and find information through a variety of means, and share their thoughts and opinions using whatever technology is available to them.

- Making the world an exciting place to be. Use your personal experiences and connections to support and reinforce the children and young people's talents, hopes and aspirations. Open career pathways and make further education tangible.

- Valuing play. The benefits of play are not confined to the early years of development; joy and discovery can be at any age. Through play we learn how to refine concepts and test out theories, learn to regulate our emotions and interact with others. This is particularly relevant to those who may not have had this modelled in their formative years.

- Reflecting and questioning what challenging behaviour may be trying to communicate. Challenging behaviour can often leave both the child and the adult feeling frustrated, blameful and confused. As such, reflecting on the contributing factors to this behaviour and formulating a plan of support is important in maintaining the balance of care and education in the classroom.

The values and beliefs you hold relating to education influence the approach and execution of learning opportunities in your classroom. Similarly, what you plan for and demonstrate in your classroom can provide an interesting insight into the values and beliefs you hold relating to education. An explicit understanding of your position can help you immensely when faced with difficult, challenging or unfamiliar situations. Reflection is a method that seeks to support professionals in understanding situations with the intent of moving forward.

Reflecting as an essential part of everyday practice

There is a passing reference to reflection within the minimum requirements for trainee teachers working towards qualified teacher status (Teacher Standard four). This calls on trainees to 'reflect systematically on the effectiveness of lessons and approaches to learning' (DfE 2016). In order to establish and maintain the synergy between care and education within an accountability-driven curriculum, we believe the process of reflection warrants a standard of its own and should be underscored.

Critical reflection is regarded as a core part of a number of health and care professions such as nursing and psychology. Macfarlane *et al.* (2014), among others, argue that reflection is an essential part of practice integral to learning and development. Although it is often referred to as a key skill, we believe its real meaning and value is often misunderstood or lost, particularly in the context of the busy school.

Macfarlane *et al.* (2014) define reflection as:

- an ability to organise activities within your daily work

- a means of improving practice

- a way of connecting theory to practice.

It can be carried out on your own, within supervision, or as a team, and inevitably involves the cycle of experience–reflection–action (Cameron *et al.* 2015). There are many models and theoretical approaches to reflecting, such as Circles of Change (Macfarlane *et al.* 2014), Reflecting Teams (Hornstrup *et al.* 2008) and ThinkSpace (Swann and York 2011). A useful case study that highlights the impact of using a reflective approach to understand a complex case can be found in *Taking Action for Looked After Children in School: A Knowledge Exchange Programme* (Carroll and Cameron 2017).

The key to any model, according to Macfarlane *et al.* (2014), is to provide the professional with a scaffold or framework. To be most effective we believe the chosen model should provide the professional with the opportunity to examine issues beyond apparent constraints, construct new understandings and take action.

Reflection is valued as a way of making sense of what is going on in your classroom. As such, the 'Reflection Points' task at the end of this chapter provide you with the opportunity to reflect using the CLEAR model as presented by Hawkins and Shohet (2007).

Final thoughts

We are a miracle of complexity; billions of dynamic processes, both internal and external, are at play from the very beginning of our existence (Perry and Hambrick 2008). Our journey through life is both unique and malleable. We show the world our very own collection of strengths and vulnerabilities. While for many the journey through life is full of positive, healthy connections, others have been subject to very difficult experiences, particularly children and young people on the edge of or in care.

It is important to note that, for children and young people in care, it is often the care and commitment of an individual teacher that makes the critical difference to their development (Cameron *et al.* 2015). We propose that social pedagogy in the classroom provides an ideal context for you to demonstrate this commitment, and to manage the inevitable tensions that come with being a teacher.

REFLECTION POINTS

Take some time (approximately 40 minutes) to identify a positive change you would like to see for one of the children or young people in your care. Use the CLEAR (Hawkins and Shohet 2007) supervision model (see below) to reflect on the challenges you face. An example to guide you through this process is provided in the right-hand column. This can be completed in isolation or with the support of a colleague.

CLEAR supervision model	Example
Contract What outcome do you want for you, the student or the class? What do you want to focus on? What challenges are you facing?	I am on my second teaching placement and struggle with Kelsey, a particularly challenging student. I want to focus on behaviour management and want Kelsey to be able to conform to everyday expectations. Kelsey arrives late, is openly defiant, and seems determined to interrupt the flow of my class.
Listen Can you report what you see? Can you describe the emotions the situation evokes? How would others see the situation?	I know that Kelsey is in care and I have observed this behaviour in other contexts. I find Kelsey intimidating and difficult to deal with, the issues are low level, and she presents as beyond all of my strategies. Others might regard Kelsey as a hard-to-reach student and that I am a trainee who is bound to struggle with the complexity she presents.
Explore What does your intuition tell you about the situation? Are there any feelings you have not expressed? Can you think of different ways of tackling the situation?	I think there is something going on for Kelsey, and I'm not sure what her behaviour is trying to communicate. Perhaps she is fearful and that is why she appears angry and is intimidating. As a trainee I do not want to admit that I am struggling or that I am on edge when she is in the room. I need to share this with a colleague and consider how I can get alongside Kelsey.

CLEAR supervision model	Example
Action What is your objective? What are the pros and cons of each possible strategy? What is the first step you need to take?	I want to form a relationship with Kelsey so that this translates into fewer difficulties in the classroom. This might not work as she is so defiant and dismissive, but I've got nothing to lose. I need to find out more about her and take advice on how to approach her. I wonder what her interests are and what works for children in care.
Review What have you decided to do next? How did what you plan work out? What feedback did you receive? What have you learned? What worked well and what could have been better?	I have spoken to her form teacher and have a better understanding of her home life and what she is interested in. She has advised that I approach Kelsey as being developmentally younger. I am going to try to support her to join the school council. The designated teacher for looked-after children has commended my insight, and agrees that getting to know her in a different context will help me to see things from her perspective, create a sense of us working together, and could improve how she is in the classroom.

Read more widely around the CLEAR approach (see Hawkins and Shohet 2007) and try to employ the CLEAR approach to help resolve future difficulties.

Bibliography

Arendt, H. (1971) *The Life of the Mind*. London: Mariner Books.

Baumeister, R. and Leary, M. (1995) 'The need to belong: Desire for interpersonal attachments as a fundamental human motivation.' *Psychological Bulletin 117*, 3, 497.

Bennett, J. and Tayler, C. (2006) *Starting Strong II: Early Childhood Education and Care*. Paris: OECD.

Cairns, K. (2013) 'The Effects of Trauma on Children's Learning.' In S. Jackson (ed.) *Pathways through Education for Young People in Care: Ideas from Research and Practice*. London: BAAF Publications.

Cameron, C., Connelly, G. and Jackson, S. (2015) *Educating Children and Young People in Care: Learning Placements and Caring Schools*. London: Jessica Kingsley Publishers.

Cameron, C., Jackson, S., Hauari, H. and Hollingworth, K. (2011) *Young People from a Public Care Background: Pathways to Further and Higher Education in England. A Case Study*. London: Thomas Coram Research Unit.

Cameron, C., Petrie, P., Wigfall, V., Kleipoedszus, S. and Jasper, A. (2011a) *Final Report of the Social Pedagogy Pilot Programme: Development and Implementation*. Available at http://eprints.ioe.ac.uk/6767/1/Cameron2011Final(Report).pdf, accessed on 11 October 2016.

Carroll, C. and Cameron, C. (2017) *Taking Action for Looked After Children in School: A Knowledge Exchange Programme*. London: Institute of Education Press.

Cemalcilar, Z. (2010) 'Schools as socialisation contexts: Understanding the impact of school climate factors on students' sense of school belonging.' *Applied Psychology 59*, 2, 243–272.

DfE (Department for Education) (2016) *Teachers' Standards*. Available at www.gov.uk/government/uploads/system/uploads/attachment_data/file/283566/Teachers_standard_information.pdf, accessed on 30 March 2017.

Eichsteller, G. and Holthoff, S. (2012) 'The art of being a social pedagogue: Developing cultural change in children's homes in Essex.' *International Journal of Social Pedagogy 1*, 1, 30–46.

Fielding, M. and Moss, P. (2010) *Radical Education and the Common School: A Democratic Alternative.* London: Routledge.

Furrer, C. and Skinner, E. (2003) 'Sense of relatedness as a factor in children's academic engagement and performance.' *Journal of Educational Psychology 95*, 1, 148.

Hawkins, P. and Shohet, R. (2007) *Supervision in the Helping Professions.* Maidenhead: McGraw-Hill Education.

Heidegger, M. (1996) *Being and Time: A Translation of Sein und Zeit.* New York: SUNY Press.

Hollingworth, K. (2012) 'Participation in social, leisure and informal learning activities among care leavers in England: Positive outcomes for educational participation.' *Child & Family Social Work 17*, 4, 438–447.

Hornstrup, C. *et al.* (2008) *Team Coaching and Reflecting Teams.* Macmann Berg. Available at www.taosinstitute.net/Websites/taos/Images/ResourcesManuscripts/Hornstrup-Team_coaching_and_reflecting_teams.pdf, accessed on 11 October 2016.

Kennedy, H., Landor, M. and Todd, L. (2011) *Video Interaction Guidance: A Relationship-based Intervention to Promote Attunement, Empathy, and Wellbeing.* London: Jessica Kingsley Publishers.

Kyriacou, C., Ellingsen, I., Stephens, P. and Sundaram, V. (2009) 'Social pedagogy and the teacher: England and Norway compared.' *Pedagogy, Culture & Society 17*, 1, 75–87.

Macfarlane, K., Casley, M., Cartmel, J. and Smith, K. (2014) 'Understanding the "how": A model of practice for critical reflection for children's services practitioners.' *Journal of Playwork Practice 1*, 1, 47–59.

Malaguzzi, L. (1994) 'Your image of the child: Where teaching begins.' *Child Care Information Exchange*, 3, 52–61.

Maslow, A.H. (1943) 'A theory of human motivation.' *Psychological Review 50*, 4, 370.

Noddings, N. (1992) *The Challenge to Care in Schools: An Alternative Approach to Education.* New York: Teachers College Press.

Perry, B. and Hambrick, E. (2008) 'The neurosequential model of therapeutics.' *Reclaiming Children and Youth 17*, 3, 38.

Petrie, P., Boddy, J., Cameron, C., Simon, A. and Wigfall, V. (2006) *Working with Children in Residential Care: European Perspectives.* Buckingham: Open University Press.

Petrie, P., Boddy, J., Cameron, C., Heptinstall, E., McQuail, S., Simon, A. and Wigfall, V. (2009) *Pedagogy – A Holistic, Personal Approach to Work with Children and Young People, Across Services: European Models for Practice, Training, Education and Qualification.* Briefing Paper. London: Thomas Coram Research Unit.

Prensky, M. (2010) *Teaching Digital Natives: Partnering for Real Learning.* Newbury Park, CA: Corwin Press.

Rinaldi, C. (2006) *In Dialogue with Reggio Emilia: Listening, Researching and Learning.* Hove: Psychology Press.

Schaps, E., Battistich, V. and Solomon. (2004) 'Community in school as key to student growth: Findings from the Child Development Project.' In J.E. Zins, R. Weissberg and M.C. Wang (eds) *Building Academic Success on Social and Emotional Learning: What Does the Research Say* (pp.189–205). New York: Teachers College Press.

Soertard, M. (1994) 'Johann Heinrich Pestalozzi.' *Prospects – Quarterly Review of Education, Thinkers on Education 24*, 1–2, 297–310.

Swann, R.C. and York, A. (2011) 'ThinkSpace – The creation of a multi-agency consultation group for looked after children.' *Clinical Child Psychology and Psychiatry 16*, 1, 65–71.

Teven, J. and McCroskey, J. (1997) 'The relationship of perceived teacher caring with student learning and teacher evaluation.' *Communication Education 46*, 1, 1–9.

Wetz, J. (2009) *Urban Village Schools: Putting Relationships at the Heart of Secondary School Organisation and Design.* London: Calouste Gulbenkian Foundation.

14

Including Children with Disorganised Attachment in Mainstream Primary Schools

MAGGIE SWARBRICK

For some children who have been abused, neglected or placed in care, the inevitable behavioural responses to these experiences may then jeopardise their mainstream school placements. These behaviours may be said to reflect the disorganised (or disoriented) attachment profile, as described in Chapter 2. If outbursts of aggression, emotional lability, hypervigilance, extreme withdrawal or controlling behaviours are the natural manifestation of hurtful experiences, how, then, do schools include these children in their mainstream classrooms? This chapter draws on case studies and practical interventions undertaken in primary schools using the Treatment Foster Care Oregon (TFCO) programme.

Treatment Foster Care Oregon

Treatment Foster Care Oregon (TFCO) is an evidence-based programme that originated in Oregon, USA, to support children in care with behavioural difficulties who were at risk of breaking home and school placements (Chamberlain 2003). It was adopted as a fostering option by Oxfordshire County Council from 2008 to 2017, and the programme cares for a small number of children aged 3–11.

The aim of TFCO is to work with the whole child, in all areas of the child's experience, while adopting a structured approach to effect behavioural change. Individual foster carers are trained in the (behaviourist) social learning approach to care, and are supported 24 hours, 7 days a week. The foster carers are the 'therapists' for the children, who do not usually receive any additional therapeutic interventions. The children are supported in the community and the younger children attend the programme's therapeutic playgroup, where social skills are taught and practised.

An important feature of TFCO is that all children are supported in school by the programme's advisory teacher. The children are visited weekly at school, where explicit skills are taught 'in situ', and all school meetings, both formal and informal, are attended by the advisory teacher. This chapter draws on case notes from the work of the advisory teacher in TFCO, with illustrations from case studies.

The TFCO programme offers an example of a structured, relational approach to inclusion and can be seen as a behaviourist intervention, being informed by the behaviourist principles set out in Chapter 1. The programme's philosophy requires the child's behavioural needs to settle before any clinically therapeutic intervention can be undertaken successfully, and behaviour is modified through relationships – alongside rewards and consequences.

Work in this area of behaviour modification has tended to become polarised, with practitioners who follow a more deeply therapeutic approach calling into question whether rewards and consequences can have meaning when a child is traumatised. Indeed, there are authors in this book that question the efficacy of behaviourist approaches. Despite this, the TFCO is built unerringly on the social learning model of understanding behavioural change and asserts that, in practice, the most powerful therapy is achieved through positive behaviour management, support and care.

Disorganised attachment behaviours

In Chapter 2, Heather Geddes defined children with disorganised attachment as being 'the unpredictable, anxious and behaviourally challenging pupils' that we may encounter in our classrooms. Their behaviour tests all our resources, and the outcome is frequently school exclusion or referral to specialist settings. A clinical description for disorganised attachment is 'reactive attachment disorder', and this is recognised in the *Diagnostic and Statistical Manual of Mental Disorders, Fifth Edition* (DSM-5), a key publication in relation to psychiatric disorders.

While many children in school may have unmet attachment needs, very few experience this extreme form of insecure attachment. It is important to note that disorganised attachment is the only form of insecure attachment that should be referred to as a 'disorder'.

Research suggests that children experiencing disorganised attachment do badly in school at both primary secondary and tertiary levels (The Poverty Site no date), while 'scores for pro-Social behaviours at preschool and aggressive behaviours at first grade differ significantly for children who have secure and insecure attachment' (Seven 2010, p.353).

Disorganised children pose particular problems for schools 'exhibiting the highest levels of problematic behaviour related to learning' (Stacks and Oshio 2009, p.146).

The management of children showing disorganised attachment is likely to present the teacher and the school with unique challenges. Educating these children is primarily viewed, for teachers, as an issue of inclusion, not of therapy. However, we must not underestimate the therapeutic potential of belonging to a class and to a group of peers for these abused or neglected children for, to be part of a group and accepted as such is, in itself, a healing experience.

Including a child with severe social, emotional and attachment difficulties is the most problematic and complex aspect of inclusion that most teachers will meet in their careers. Children, whose needs centre on a search for security expressed, perhaps, as control through coercion or a chaotic and demanding presentation, do not fit easily into our current school system.

Playfulness, Acceptance, Curiosity and Empathy (PACE)

To develop key relationships in school, TFCO use PACE, the aptly grounded acronym referring to 'Playfulness, Acceptance, Curiosity and Empathy' (Hughes 2006, p.82). Hughes describes this as 'the attitude' for interacting with children with disorganised attachment, and it is suggested that the qualities of playfulness, acceptance, curiosity and empathy are central to the skill set for all adults working with these children. The PACE way of working seeks to affect change for the child in a connected and therapeutic way.

PACE was developed for the intimate work of re-parenting an adopted child, but it is also a helpful way of thinking about our work as teachers of children in schools.

Sousa and Rodrigues (2012) challenge professionals working with families to develop trusting, relational approaches while reinforcing small positive family achievements, and this family approach may also be mirrored in work with schools. Pecora (2013) has summed up, more emotively, a desire for all children to have 'someone who is crazy about them', and if this is experienced at school as well as at home, then the gains for the children are extensive and may be deeply realised.

For this level of connection to be achieved in institutional settings such as a school is, admittedly, ambitious, but not impossible. Witnessing a headteacher working with one of the programme's children in care, who had been excluded from class due to disruptive behaviour, exemplified this process. Instead of sitting him in silence, getting him to write a note of apology or enlisting him in manning the paper shredder, she instead did something different; in this case, she learned to play the recorder with him. This activity became a regular feature of his week (as he was so often removed from the class), and it developed into a timetabled activity for them both.

Why did this work where so many other interventions had failed? It worked because the headteacher was willing to adopt a relational view of the solution. She engaged in PACE and enabled the child to be socially acceptable by learning a skill with him and by giving him time and attention. Not every practitioner has the time or imagination to adopt this kind of intervention – but it works.

Case study: Rosa

In another case example from the TFCO programme using the PACE approach, 'Rosa' was beginning to show signs of 'attachment repair' in her school. She had devised a game with a little boy of jumping off the climbing frame into a pile of soft play mats and knocking them, and the child steadying them, over. This was a hugely enjoyable and exciting game. It involved taking turns with a group of four children, which soon grew to eight. There was quite a lot of waiting in line and behaving fairly. Children had to take the responsibility of stacking up the mats for the next child and willingly taking turns. Rosa managed this brilliantly with scaffolding from the advisory teacher. Rosa was playful and exuberant (if a little controlling) with the other children, and they clearly enjoyed each other's company. At the beginning of TFCO's work with Rosa, she had attempted to control children and adults continuously. She had frequently been removed from class and when at home with her family, she had been excluded from school aged four. Working with her to remain in class and play with other children is so important and is where the social learning and repair takes place. Removing her from this play (for example, into one-to-one situations) puts her at risk of developing shame and guilt, while working with her with PACE turned these interactions into a process of repair.

Case study: John

Working with every aspect of the child's experience and being aware of a child's history is central to the TFCO approach. In another case study, 'John' became very agitated in school following an incident where he was asked to put away a store catalogue. Lots of children had gathered around him and were involved in heated arguments about who was getting which toy for Christmas. John was ignoring requests from the teacher and became violent towards the other children. The advisory teacher sat with him and took the catalogue calmly from him. He tore at the pages and destroyed it. His face was full of tears and he said sorry, but then quickly, in an agitated voice, he said that she 'shouldn't have taken it from him'. She thanked him for saying sorry but he continued to complain, telling her that 'mummy lets him watch TV all the time – even when he was eating, but his foster carer turned the TV off and that wasn't fair because she watched TV when he had gone to bed'. Taking time to listen and giving John space to talk allowed school staff to see a fuller picture of the internal struggle that John was experiencing. To be heard, and to experience empathy, allowed John to feel fully part of the class, and allowed the other children to see him in this light too.

Shame and guilt

Hughes (2006) talks at some length about the development of shame and guilt in the toddler. This is of interest in clarifying some of the behaviours presented by some of our problematic children in school and in the case studies above. Hughes sees shame as a natural feeling in the toddler that is transformed by adults who are attuned and who are able to repair this feeling through PACE. This approach allows the child to learn 'the limits to self-expression, the need to integrate one's wishes with the desires of others and the necessity of considering the consequences of one own acts' (Hughes 2006, p.151). Children who are not led from shame to acceptance remain in a shameful and guilty state.

When Rosa crumbles, she rages. So, for example, not being at the front of the line when leaving class would cause a major incident which, on reflection, allowed us to think carefully about where this behaviour comes from. For Rosa, moving from being in charge to being one of the group was very difficult. She has not been able to trust adults in the past, so why should she trust them now? Managing these outbursts needs a strategy that conveys the important message, 'I can contain you and help you survive.' Rosa's internal chaos is not helpfully replicated by extreme responses.

The PACE approach described in these case studies illustrates how children with disorganised attachment can, over a period of up to six months, reflect on their behaviour, control their impulses, allow closeness, relinquish control and become children again. It took the six months duration of this study to achieve, and was more successful for some children than for others.

Social pedagogy

Social pedagogy, as outlined in Chapter 13, also has a great influence on the TFCO programme and is growing in influence as a way of affecting change for socially disadvantaged children.

Projects such as the Art Room (see www.theartroom.org.uk) exemplify this approach and support the social pedagogic view of school as being a 'shared living space', a place where all are entitled to live, work and learn together (Cameron *et al.* 2011). This approach can be helpful in steering willing schools to a holistic view of the inclusion of children with disorganised attachments. If social integration and repair of socially disadvantaged children is a goal, then to work in their social context (in these cases, the local school) seems to be a given. The work described in the case studies of Rosa and John mirrors the approach on which TFCO and social pedagogy is based.

Here the concept that children learn how to behave by experiencing people behaving in particular ways around them is central. For John, the understanding that he is most successful in taking on these messages outdoors and that here, he can play happily with four other children constructively and successfully, is reparative and positive. The concept of a 'shared living space' (Cameron *et al.* 2011) is powerful here, where a trained member of staff shows her presence through modelling working and playing alongside children using the 'head, heart and hands' approach (see Chapter 13). When this is done openly, thoughtfully and in full view of staff and children, this can be seen as a real catalyst for change.

Case study: Laura

Working within a Foundation class with 'Laura' (aged three), the advisory teacher had many opportunities to interact with the whole child and to become wholly involved. For example, playing in a boat outside the classroom, Laura was in charge and was able to use her skills as the oldest child in her birth family to organise the play. This behaviour is not simply 'bossy' – she is also concerned for their safety. As the oldest sister in the family she had to care for the younger brothers, and this responsibility is generalised in play at the moment. If, as an uninformed teacher, you were simply to chance upon this behaviour outside, rather than be fully involved in the play in an informed way, you may have come to a different and less insightful conclusion about her behaviour.

The gains that are achieved for society and individual children when we achieve inclusion in schools for children with disorganised attachment difficulties are significant. Perhaps it is particularly in the social pedagogy literature that practitioners, who are conscious of the multi-faceted way in which they work with vulnerable children, feel supported. This does not mean that these practitioners are the only ones who interact well with children or contribute to their 'upbringing' (Cameron *et al.* 2011, p.76), but it satisfies a professional need to be recognised as important and valued practitioners.

The work to repair the experiences of children with disorganised attachment must be inclusive. In the study undertaken there are examples of schools that have successfully kept children in the class and on the carpet with everyone, despite the difficulties posed. For children like Laura, the progress is manifest. When at home for the second time, she attended a school which, after four weeks, excluded her because of her chaotic behaviour. In foster care, however, her progress allowed her to achieve almost complete inclusion in class.

The teacher reported that Laura was able to sit for approximately the whole of carpet time and she could do this independently if a DVD was showing or if it was a singing session. Otherwise she still needed something in her hand, such as a clipboard. She was able to say complimentary things to other children, which was real progress for her. Occasionally she continued to be very loud!! But in these statements from school, you see a gradual, growing inclusive attitude, reaping its rewards.

Whether we can change attachment patterns is a key question for the study in Oxfordshire, and evidence suggests that over time and with PACE approaches, repair in behaviours that characterise disorganised attachment behaviour may be witnessed.

Children in care

Children in care, or looked-after children, come with their own set of difficulties that limit progress, and these have been explored in Chapter 12. The fact that they are the most vulnerable children in society only serves to compound their educational difficulties (DfE 2009). Children are often moved to a new school following removal from their birth family, which immediately sets them at a disadvantage. The new school may struggle to cope with the complex needs that the children have, and may have even been 'instructed' by the local authority to take the child, despite the school being at capacity. There may be a need to buy in more specialist support in terms of educational psychology and social, emotional and behavioural support, which has a real cost to the school in our world of traded services.

Children in care enter the new school with a strong likelihood that they will cause difficulties for the class teacher, in terms of social, emotional, behavioural and learning needs. For the headteacher, there may be extra demands in terms of budget, external scrutiny and additional paperwork. The new arrival is likely to bring the school's average SATs results down, and may yet increase the number of exclusions recorded by the school. Nothing substantial is provided to the school to alleviate this, and the Pupil Premium payment may be seen as a token of good will, at best.

The child in the TFCO programme may already have experienced a number of placement moves – either within the family or within the care system. John, for example, had experienced three prior placements by the age of four. The children may also have experienced a number of failed returns home.

Developing a reflective approach to your teaching

Working in a reflective way contributes to a pedagogy that can be passed on and celebrated, creating a body of knowledge that is sadly missing in the UK in terms of how to best interact with socially challenging children. For the child with disorganised attachment to enjoy lessons and have friends we need not 'shout more loudly', but we do need to reflect more deeply. We also need to develop creative inclusive practices. Indeed, the fundamental educational questions around 'What is childhood?' and 'How is difference tolerated in society?' may be answered in the lived experience of truly inclusive education.

Managing a traumatised child with disorganised attachment can be very challenging, and it is important to have a person who will give you, the beginning teacher, structured time to discuss the issues at a supportive level. The importance of staff supervision is considered in detail in Chapter 15 that follows, but staff need to understand that the ability to reflect thoughtfully as a teacher is crucial.

The transference of the pain of emotional abuse from the traumatised child onto an adult's shoulders in school is hard to bear, and can leave the adult feeling vulnerable and deskilled. Professional supervision helps to identify this, and enables staff in school to 'admit to it' and manage the interactions in a way that contributes to the healing of the child, without demoralising the teacher.

The reflective approach through professional supervision is an aspect that elevates the work above support, as simply defined. There are examples in the study where wondering, hypothesising and experimenting are suggested tools for progress. For Rosa, especially early on in the placement, much reflection and wondering took place with important and far-reaching questions being raised, such as, 'Does Rosa know what it is to be a child?'

Supervision of teachers may seem to be a 'luxury', but perhaps it is a 'luxury' that we need in order to develop our work for the most vulnerable children. This may well be more cost-effective than many other expenses incurred by schools that include staff retention, absence, stress and ill health.

Final thoughts

As beginning teachers, the time spent working with and supporting children with disorganised attachment in your classroom will be thrilling, challenging, demanding and intensely rewarding. If you can develop trusting relationships with children who have had the very worst start in life, then you will be making a very significant contribution to that child, their families and their communities. Inclusion, engagement and repair will lead in small steps to emotional development and resilience, under your guidance.

It can be predicted that children with disorganised attachment behaviour will need more than the average foster care and school provision in order to experience real change and head off any long-term issues. By working in the way described in this TFCO programme, teachers are able to be part of the process of real preventative change. In summary, they do this by:

- being mindful of the PACE approach: Playfulness, Acceptance, Curiosity and Empathy (Hughes 2006, p.82)

- taking time to be with children: in conversation, at play, in work

- being prepared to play at developmentally younger levels than one would expect, and playing in this way again and again

- keeping the child in class with their peers

- talking about their experience with a thoughtful and supportive mentor or supervisor and recognising the importance of their everyday teaching interactions.

It is in this way that class teachers become empowered and therapeutic practitioners.

REFLECTION POINTS

1. What are your key understandings about how disorganised attachment presents in the classroom?

2. How would you approach planning a series of lessons to include a child in care with disorganised attachment?

3. Who would you need to contact in advance, as part of this planning process?

4. In what way might this challenge also prove to be a very rewarding experience for you?

Bibliography

Allen, G. (2011) *Early Intervention: Smart Investment, Massive Savings*. London: HM Government.

APA (American Psychiatric Association) (2013) *Diagnostic and Statistical Manual of Mental Disorders, 5th Edition (DSM-5)*. Arlington, VA: American Psychiatric Association.

ATTACH team (Achieving Therapeutic Attachments for Children). Available at http://oxme.info/cms/life/attach-team, accessed on 21 August 2016.

Bandura, A. (1977) *Social Learning Theory*. Upper Saddle River, NJ: Prentice-Hall.

Cameron, C., Petrie, P., Wigfall, V., Kleipoedszus, S. and Jasper, A. (2011) *Final Report of the Social Pedagogy Pilot Programme: Development and Implementation*. London: Thomas Coram Research Unit, Institute of Education, University of London. Available at http://eprints.ioe.ac.uk/6767/1/Cameron2011Final(Report).pdf, accessed on 16 February 2012.

Chamberlain, P. (2003) 'The Oregon Multidimensional Treatment Foster Care Model: Features, Outcomes, and Progress in Dissemination.' In S. Schoenwald and S. Henggeler (eds) 'Moving evidence-based treatments from the laboratory into clinical practice.' *Cognitive and Behavioral Practice 10*, 4, 303–312.

DfE (Department for Education) (2009) *Improving the Attainment of Looked After Children in Primary Schools. Guidance for Schools*. Available at www.gov.uk/government/publications/improving-the-attainment-of-looked-after-children-in-primary-schools-guidance-for-schools, accessed on 21 August 2016.

DfE (2012) *Education of Looked After Children: Frequently Asked Questions*. Available at www.education.gov.uk/childrenandyoungpeople/families/childrenincare/a0066445/education-of-looked-after-children-frequently-asked-questions#faq9, originally accessed on 16 February 2012. Now archived at http://webarchive.nationalarchives.gov.uk/20130123124929/http://www.education.gov.uk/childrenandyoungpeople/families/childrenincare/a0066445/education-of-looked-after-children-frequently-asked-questions, accessed on 22 August 2016.

DfE (no date) *Social and Emotional Aspects of Learning (SEAL): Improving Behaviour, Improving Learning*. Available at http://webarchive.nationalarchives.gov.uk/20110809101133/nsonline.org.uk/node/87009, accessed on 21 August 2016.

Ecclestone, K. (2007) 'Resisting images of the "diminished self": The implications of emotional wellbeing and emotional engagement in education policy.' *Journal of Education Policy 22*, 4, 455.

Hughes, D. (2006) *Building the Bonds of Attachment. Awakening Love in Deeply Troubled Children*. Oxford: Aronson.

O'Brien, J. (2016) *Don't Send Him in Tomorrow: Shining a Light on the Marginalised, Disenfranchised and Forgotten Children of Today's Schools*. Bancyfelin: Independent Thinking Press.

O'Neill, L., Gueunette, F. and Kitchenham, A. (2010) '"Am I safe here and do you like me?" Understanding complex trauma and attachment disruption in the classroom.' *British Journal of Special Education 37*, 4, 193.

Morgan, R. (2011) *Younger Children's Views: A Report by the Children's Rights Director for England*. http://dera.ioe.ac.uk/2591, accessed on 21 August 2016.

Pecora, P. (2013) Contribution to a seminar at the Rees Centre, Oxford, 21 February.

Poverty Site (no date) 'Looked-after children.' Available at www.poverty.org.uk/29/index.shtml, accessed on 21 August 2016.

Schwartz, E. and Davis, A. (2006) 'Reactive attachment disorder: implications for school readiness and school functioning.' *Psychology in the Schools 43*, 4, 476.

Seven, S. (2010) 'Attachment and social behaviors in the period of transition from preschool to first grade.' *Social Behaviour and Personality 38*, 3, 347.

Sousa, L. and Rodrigues, S. (2012) 'The collaborative professional: Towards empowering vulnerable families.' *Journal of Social Work Practice 26*, 4, 411.

Stacks, A. and Oshio, T. (2009) 'Disorganised attachment and social skills as indicators of Head Start children's school readiness.' *Attachment and Human Development 11*, 2, 143.

TFCO (Treatment Foster Care Oregon) (no date) Available at www.tfcoregon.com, accessed on 21 August 2016.

von Ryzin, M. (2010) 'Secondary school advisors as mentors and secondary attachment figures.' *Journal of Community Psychology 28*, 2, 13.

15

The Importance of Professional Supervision for All Staff in Schools

DAVE ROBERTS

The emotional wellbeing of school staff is vital when striving to meet the needs of children with social, emotional and attachment difficulties. An important means of supporting staff and promoting staff resilience is the use of professional staff supervision. Ensuring the regular supervision of staff is an accepted key indicator of best practice in health, social care, counselling and therapy environments – but in schools, staff supervision is uncommon. Indeed, the word 'supervision' is often given negative connotations in educational settings, or felt to be inappropriate or irrelevant.

The supervision referred to in this chapter is a protected, regular and disciplined space for a staff member or group of staff to meet with a line manager or peers in which they reflect on work-based situations in an atmosphere of professional trust and support. Supervision is not the same as a professional development review, where targets are discussed with the line manager. During supervision meetings, staff will candidly review their own practice and reflect on how they reacted in certain situations. The emphasis of supervision is on what staff might learn from this experience, and how this critical reflection and analysis might improve their professional practice.

In a culture that is all too often driven by data, this chapter seeks to argue the case for developing reflective supervision as an essential tool for establishing best practice and ensuring the emotional wellbeing of staff across the education sector. Through introducing supervision we can recognise the emotional impact upon staff working alongside all children, but especially those who experience social, emotional and attachment difficulties. All too often, the children who have experienced adverse life events develop a range of complex needs that can have a negative impact on their own learning and the learning of others. Through the use of supervision, it is argued that staff can become more attuned and ultimately more able to meet the wide range of needs of these children.

The use of supervision is contextualised in this chapter with a review of the work of the Mulberry Bush School in Oxfordshire (see www.mulberrybush.org.uk). Supervision is defined and a model of working described that can lead to wide-reaching benefits in schools, including reduced staff stress, reduced staff absence and increased team working – all of which can lead to improved outcomes for children.

The model is illustrated with vignettes based in primary, secondary and special schools that have adopted supervision structures.

With teaching staff facing increased pressure to support children with social, emotional and attachment difficulties in the classroom, structures are required that support the emotional wellbeing of teaching staff. Such structures exist across other sectors and can easily be developed in schools to support staff, not just newly qualified, but experienced staff as well.

This chapter sets out to explore the meaning and role of supervision within schools, recognising the benefits of a safe, structured space. A framework for supervision is outlined, drawing on the experiences of the Mulberry Bush School.

Background and context

The internationally recognised Mulberry Bush School is a therapeutic, residential, special school providing education and care for primary-aged children who have experienced severe early years trauma, resulting in them experiencing, and exhibiting, significant emotional, behavioural and attachment difficulties.

The school's model of intervention is underpinned by a close synthesis of disciplines, notably:

- attachment theory

- child psychotherapy

- key concepts of the therapeutic community, planned environment, milieu therapy models, including:

- the use of a group, not just living in a group, but the full use of it

- systemic thinking recognising the child as a part of a system, not in isolation

- psychodynamic thinking to help understand behaviour as a communication (Diamond 2013).

Throughout its work, the Mulberry Bush School aims to effectively understand, educate and treat children who display challenging and disturbing behaviours, whilst being reflective practitioners, highly attuned to the communication and needs of the children. Through understanding their verbal and non-verbal communications, the work and environment are adapted to better meet their needs. The school provides an environment in which they feel safe, understood and able to engage in learning, socially, emotionally and academically. This is emotionally challenging work for the staff team who receive high-quality supervision to support them to make sense of the children's needs, recognise the impact upon themselves, and develop ways of working that safely meet the children's needs.

The school environment has developed throughout the 70-year history, and currently consists of three clearly defined task areas:

- *Education:* the education model is focused on the emotional need and stage of each child, rather than chronological year groups. The aim is to match each child's educational experience to the child's emotional and academic abilities.

- *Group living:* this is where the residential therapy is delivered by highly trained staff using groups to enable children to make sense of the feelings associated with living alongside others and to function as part of a social group.

- *Therapies and networks:* this is a multidisciplinary team composed of therapists, family practitioners and a school nurse. Its aim is to help look after the therapeutic needs of the children and their families, and to facilitate collaborative working with the child's network and other professionals.

These task areas are carefully integrated to provide the therapeutic milieu, working together to provide an integrated and holistic environment that is organised to maximise the emotional growth of each child (Diamond 2013). At the heart of the school's model is the 'treatment team', a multidisciplinary group of staff able to proactively hold the child and family in mind at all times, rather than being crisis-led.

Recognising that the models of working can be replicated in other settings, the school has developed an outreach model. This focuses on working with staff teams to make sense of the behaviour children present, seeing 'behaviour as a communication' of an unmet need, and how these can be responded to. By working with staff teams, rather than individual children, more sustainable and thoughtful therapeutic approaches are being developed, all underpinned by supervision.

What is the impact on staff of working with children with social, emotional and attachment difficulties?

Naturally, the central concern of this book is on approaches to working with children who are experiencing social, emotional and attachment difficulties, with a clear focus on understanding and meeting the needs of these children. But it is equally important to consider the impact that working alongside these children can have on both teaching and non-teaching staff. It is not possible to meet the emotional needs of children unless the emotional needs of staff are first acknowledged and met. To do this it is necessary to employ a form of structured, professional staff supervision.

Have you ever felt relaxed and calm in school and then, within a few minutes of working alongside a child, felt completely overwhelmed and at breaking point? The likelihood is that all education professionals have experienced this many times in the setting of a special school, but these challenges are now occurring more frequently in mainstream settings too. Children with a variety of special educational needs (SEN) are being included in mainstream settings, and the majority of mainstream staff are now expected to teach, support and manage children with social, emotional and attachment difficulties.

For these children their defence systems are well used to dealing with unbearable feelings. The most classic defence system is the 'fight or flight' response, with children challenging, often physically, those around them or removing themselves from the classroom/learning environment. However, for many of these children, another defence mechanism is unconsciously engaged, and that involves projecting their unbearable feelings onto someone else. This 'someone else' is often the teacher, or teaching assistant, who ends up with feelings that, put simply, 'are not theirs'. Following this projection by the child, staff can go home feeling full of these negative feelings or overwhelmed and pushed towards collapse – often feeling alone in managing these situations. But staff should not be left alone to deal with this barrage of raw emotions, and regular staff supervision can help ensure that they are not.

Supervision and education

In recent years the field of social work has been under intense scrutiny with high-profile reports and serious case reviews looking at a range of issues, including child protection and professional communication. Lord Laming, in his 2003 report into the death of Victoria Climbié, highlighted that, 'Effective supervision is the cornerstone of safe social work practice. There is no substitute for it. In particular, the need for such supervision cannot be met by what were referred to as "corridor conversations" between managers and staff' (2003, p.211).

It is clear that the word 'supervision' is met with confusion by many in the education system. This is an interesting perception when you consider that in the fields of health, social work and counselling there is a requirement that staff are supervised and use this space to reflect on themselves as practitioners, to explore the complexities of their work, and to explore difficulties and find new ways of approaching issues. Given that education professionals are required to work with severe social and emotional issues, it could be argued that the impact that this has on their emotional and physical wellbeing, and subsequently the impact on their ability to sustain their roles and support the learning of children (Reid and Soan 2015), is being worryingly ignored.

For many in education there is scepticism around the role of staff supervision in schools. For example, during a recent training workshop looking at the role of supervision in schools, it was striking that only 2 out of approximately 40 education professionals responded positively when asked if they felt they were supervised. The rest were confused by what 'supervision' meant and thankful that they didn't have to endure yet more monitoring (as this was how they perceived supervision to be). By the end of the workshop, and having explored the true meaning and role of supervision, this number had risen from 2 out of 40 to 8 out of 40, which still represented a very low figure. During the training, there was widespread apprehension that introducing supervision would mean an overbearing sense of being observed, monitored and placed under further scrutiny. One colleague's perception was that 'I only get supervised when I'm not doing a good enough job', which perhaps links to the feeling teachers express of being 'measured' rather than 'valued', or 'surveyed' rather than 'supported' (Westergaard and Bainbridge 2014). This raises the question of where empathy and trust sit within the culture of our schools, and across our education system.

Further evidence of the confusion about supervision was apparent at a recent National Union of Teachers (NUT) conference that gave an opportunity for education staff to review their use and understanding of supervision in their schools. There was a marked response from the floor that supervision was something that was not relevant in their settings. An exploration of this revealed that many headteachers, special educational needs coordinators (SENCOs) and teachers felt supervision was strongly linked to staff competency, and that it would not be required in their schools as they did not have staff competency issues. Only a minority spoke about receiving supervision and how positive this was for their practice, all of whom, it was noted, worked within special schools. Thus it is apparent that not only is there an issue of supervision not being widely available, but that there is a lack of recognition and understanding of the need for supervision in developing best practice. We need to recognise that not only is staff supervision crucial in retaining staff and promoting staff resilience, but it should lead to the needs of children in the classroom being met more effectively. However, this raises an important issue of organisational ethos and the potential clash between supporting staff and improving outcomes, which needs careful negotiating within any school setting. Where the ethos is geared towards supporting staff and promoting their resilience, then schools are likely to see children's needs being more clearly met, but where the ethos is too heavily outcome-focused, then staff will not feel supported, leading to the needs of the children not being effectively met.

What is meant by 'supervision'?

Although many definitions for supervision exist, that given by Inskipp and Proctor (1993) seems particularly helpful:

> Supervision is a working alliance between two professionals where supervisees offer an account of their work, reflect on it, receive

feedback and receive guidance if appropriate. The object of this alliance is to enable the worker to gain in ethical competency, confidence and creativity to give the best possible services to clients. (Inskipp and Proctor 1993, p.313)

Clearly supervision involves a number of functions, which can be understood to include the need to attend to the development of best practice, the management of best practice and the emotional and psychological effects of the work, outlined by Inskipp and Proctor (1993) as 'formative, normative and restorative'.

Many authors have defined supervision for a range of professions, including social work, health and counselling (see Harris and Brockbank 2011; Hawkins and Shohet 2012; Morrison 2005), but there is no evidence of supervision being defined in an educational context. The ideas of Hawkins and Shohet (2012) match closely those of Inskipp and Proctor (2001) and, although primarily written for social care settings, they are easily transferable to education. For Hawkins and Shohet, supervisors should hold a 'helicopter ability' to look with objective distance at individuals and issues without taking the position of the line manager, the expert or what many experience as the 'judge and jury'!

But underpinning the range of definitions is the development of good practice through exploring staff's experiences and developing their learning and practice for the future. As such, supervision should be viewed as a professional learning opportunity, an opportunity to make sense of the emotional challenges arising from the practitioner's work, but should never be seen as a luxury! It should sit at the heart of education, linking practice, research and training in a structured and formal professional process (see Figure 15.1).

Many people in education meet with their line manager on a regular basis and reflect on their work and plan for the future, so how does supervision differ from line management? The key difference is the development of a working alliance, or relationship, based on open and honest communication, which is often hard to achieve when staff meet with the person who sets their salary or targets or with whom they are working on competency issues. This raises an important question of who the supervision is for – for the supervisee to develop and grow, or for a line manager to manage? For the model to be effective, this issue needs to be addressed at the outset and documented through organisational policy, becoming a thoughtful part of the culture as well as directly addressed in the supervision contract.

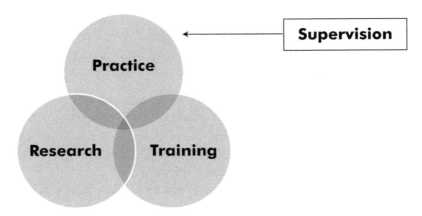

Figure 15.1: Supervision links practice, research and training

In short, supervision should be introduced to schools as a means of deepening and broadening the knowledge, reflective capacity and skills of their staff teams. To be effective it needs to be embedded within the culture, documented through school policies showing a real commitment to 'this is what we do and why', and not be allowed to become an informal structure or staff member dependent.

Staff supervision at the Mulberry Bush School

> Experience on its own, however, is not enough. It needs to be allied to reflection – time and attention given to mulling over the experience and learning from it. This is often best achieved in conversation with others, in supervision. (Munro 2011, p.87)

Within the Mulberry Bush a model of supervision has been developed that sits at the core of the work. The school's policy identifies that supervision and performance support are fundamental to the provision of a high-quality service, and this requires staff, at all levels, to not only be committed to professional and personal development, but to be aware of how their work supports the school's strategic development, annual development plans and, of course, improving outcomes for children and families.

The model places a strong emphasis on self-reflection and self-evaluation, and is delivered through individual supervision, at least half-termly, and group supervision, normally every two to three weeks.

Whilst the model is not a perfect fit for all roles, or all individuals, it is embedded throughout the organisation and viewed as the school's core support and development structure for all levels. Supervision sessions are structured throughout the year so all staff can feel they have an upcoming protected space to think through their work, to look at what is working well, but also to look at difficulties, and for the practitioner to be supported to find ways forward. In this sense it is a proactive space, not a purely reactive meeting to address difficulties that places emphasis on developing the practitioner's skills.

Like many organisations, the Mulberry Bush does not have the luxury of external supervisors for all staff, and most staff would feel that they are supervised by someone who holds a management position above them. It has been important to acknowledge the inherent tension between staff freely reflecting upon their work and feeling they are being managed, which has been overcome, in part, by the development of a culture of reflection. By this it is meant a commitment from the school to enabling staff to self-reflect throughout their work, and not exclusively within the supervision structure. It must be recognised that the identification of such tensions is a joint responsibility, as highlighted below, and needs discussion between supervisor and supervisee and more widely across schools. Tensions such as these have been further addressed through clear policy guidance and training, for supervisors and supervisees, to enable clarity and consistency across the Mulberry Bush, an organisation with almost a hundred employees. However, in addition to the need for clear policy guidance and training, what has been developed is an organisational culture that places supervision at its core.

Case study 1: Jane

Arriving for supervision, Jane had identified three areas she wished to explore: (1) why she had no preparation; (2) what boundaries to hold with one of the children who always ran out of class when she said 'no'; and (3) could they have a rota for supporting Michael (a pupil) when he could not be alongside the class, as it always falls to her?

Her supervisor, James, noted this on her electronic supervision record, which both have constant access to, but also added, to Jane's discomfort, 'How is Jane feeling?', her relationship with

Michael, and the role she took/was given within the class team. James asked Jane where she would like to start, and unsurprisingly she wanted to start with the items she had identified, all of which were areas she was unhappy about or felt unable to 'sort out'.

Through supervision Jane was encouraged to reflect on her role in the team and where this might come from. James questioned why all of her supervision issues were practical examples that needed 'fixing'. He asked her a series of reflective questions, 'If these three issues were resolved, what would you be bringing to supervision?', 'What do you feel and do when the children leave you feeling out of control?' and 'What is the impact of Michael on you?'

Initially Jane was cross with James, who she felt was avoiding her issues, but through reflection, she was able to identify that when she felt stressed, which a number of the children currently left her feeling, she needed to 'take control' and make things right or better. Her struggles related to having to work, and live, in the messy area created by the children – the place she identified as making her feel overwhelmed by being unable to make things right for the children. She recognised that Michael left her feeling sad, vulnerable and unable to do her job, and that her response was to try and take control rather than be left with these feelings. James encouraged Jane to reflect on how others may be left feeling when working with Michael, leading Jane to recognise that taking these issues and feelings to her class team would not only enable them to be in touch with how she felt, but also give an insight into how others, including Michael, may feel.

During the following supervision Jane chose to return to these issues having had time to reflect and digest their conversation. She identified that she had felt cross with James for raising uncomfortable feelings, but in hindsight, she could see the longer-term benefits and how she now felt more in touch with Michael's state of mind and his impact on others, including herself. She was able to recognise that she had been fearful of raising how she felt, as she may be perceived as weak or unable to do her job. She was reassured that actually part of her work was to make sense of these feelings, enabling her to make sense of the children's feelings and difficulties which, in turn, would enable them to feel safer and be able to learn.

How can staff supervision impact on learning?

With all the requirements placed upon schools, and the constant need to evidence that interventions impact positively on progress and attainment, it can be easy to see supervision as a luxury and not a priority. There is sometimes an anxiety that supervision equates to therapy, and it is common for supervisors to have been met with the defensive response of 'If I'd wanted therapy, I'd have had it'. There is clearly a therapeutic benefit to good supervision – it should enable staff to develop their emotional understanding of themselves and the impact of the work on them. However, it is important to recognise that staff may deny these feelings, perhaps for fear that opening up in supervision may produce an avalanche of stress and anxiety that is bottled up, and which may pour out uncontrollably. But perhaps this denial may link to the increasing numbers of staff leaving the profession.

A well-implemented model of supervision that is seen as a means to reduce stress, connect staff teams and promote staff resilience will ultimately have a positive impact upon learning.

Benefits of staff supervision for the individual and the school

Supervision structures in education should be seen as a tool for managing staff stress levels and reducing absence, something that should please all school business managers! Using reflective supervision provides an opportunity for staff to explore and understand their stresses and anxieties whilst developing a deeper understanding of children's needs. The development of a culture of emotional wellbeing and support reduces the impact of these stresses, burnout and ultimately staff absence/turnover. It is common for senior leadership teams to experience this management of staff stress as enabling them to feel more emotionally available to the wider school.

Reid and Soan (2015) identified a number of areas of professional development as a result of supervision structures. These included staff becoming more reflective, finding their own solutions, enhanced strategic thinking across schools alongside the development of 'good' practice.

Further benefits noted with the Mulberry Bush include:

- developing clarity of roles and tasks across the organisation

- better use of time

- enabling confident, competent, creative and independent decision-making, leading to improved job satisfaction

- helping staff build clear plans that seek to enable positive change for children and families

- relationships that help staff feel valued, supported and motivated

- improved staff emotional resilience and self-awareness

- the development of a learning culture within the organisation.

One local secondary head teacher told us, 'By developing a culture of supervision my staff are able to ask themselves, "Do I need to ask this now or can it wait until supervision?". This improved insight to their own emotional functioning has helped lead to a significant reduction in my time being spent on troubleshooting.'

Benefits of staff supervision for children

The overall increased emotional wellbeing of staff leads to improved stability and outcomes for the children. It is clear that there is a strong correlation between staff stress/anxiety levels and the ability of children, particularly those regarded as vulnerable, to engage in the learning process. This is most often seen with children who struggle to remain in the classroom where teachers are anxious about behavioural issues and the wider impact on the class. Reflective supervision is shown to develop more consistent relationships with children (Wonnacott 2013) as well as improved outcomes (Morrison 2009). Many schools have recognised the need to supervise staff working with vulnerable children, and have used their Pupil Premium as a proactive way to fund this as a proven intervention.

Case study 2: James

James had been headteacher of a small rural primary school when he had been introduced to a model of supervision by a member of his governing body. This wasn't a line management process, but drew on one of the school governor's skills of supervising staff in a stressful special school environment. The governor shared a model of reflective practice that had, in the special school, proven to be challenging of staff, yet enabling of their development and improved outcomes for the children. James had initially been unsure of the benefits of supervision, but was willing to trial it. Earlier this year I interviewed James about his experience and he spoke positively about the personal benefits supporting him to make sense of the day-to-day stresses within his school. However, although he clearly valued the personal benefits, he spoke enthusiastically about the wider benefits to his staff team and subsequently to the children. James clearly felt less stressed, leading to him being more available to support his staff team. He described the change in the staff team, evidenced by an improved atmosphere in the staffroom, who were more able to recognise their feelings, identify which were related to specific children, and develop a greater understanding of the needs of these children. This, in turn, had led to increased time in the classroom for these children with increased levels of progress, which had led to a less stressful environment for the children and adults alike.

It is clear that the development of a culture where staff are more self-aware of their own feelings, and understand how these are impacted by certain children, supports a culture of awareness that leads to far greater insight into the needs of the children, and an increased ability to meet these needs.

Supervision models and school policy

In recent years there has been a slowly increasing number of schools and colleges introducing reflective supervision to their settings.

Each supervisee and supervisor should develop a supervision contract/agreement to establish how they will work together, to ensure there is a shared understanding of the term 'supervision' and what this entails. There needs to be a shared belief in the collaborative nature with emphasis, as already highlighted, on the role of the supervisee being an active participant. There are likely to be anxieties about confidentiality and the boundaries that need to be discussed and clearly set out as well as detailing the practical aspects of where supervision will occur, the frequency and duration, and the process for review and managing concerns, from either party.

Within the sessions there should be a shared understanding of positive challenge, that things may not always be comfortable and that at times there may be disagreements. Supervision is not about remaining in your comfort zone but about development; again, the focus should be to view supervision as part of professional continuing professional development (CPD). It is helpful to view this as a parallel process to the children's learning.

Case study 3: Jess

When I last spoke with Jess, she proudly and energetically told me her story of developing a culture of supervision in the medium-sized primary school of which she is head. It was interesting to note that she had started her career not in school education, but in children centres. Here she had been introduced to the concept of supervision for staff working alongside vulnerable children and families, and had seen first hand the level of emotional pressure placed upon staff and the benefits of individual supervision. When she moved to being a primary head, she immediately set out to replicate the model, starting with identifying an external supervisor to help her design a model for the school. She met with her external supervisor every six weeks, and used the space to make sense of the stresses of running a small academy school with a high number of vulnerable pupils who exhibited a wide range of behavioural difficulties that were leading to a high level of staff stress and absence.

Having established a model of supervision, all members of the senior leadership team were trained in being supervised and, at a later date, being supervisors. Jess would supervise the ten senior members of the school every third week, who, in turn, would use a group supervision model to support the remaining 40 staff on a fortnightly basis. When asked how she knew the model was effective, she gave an example of a recent visitor to the school who had commented how calm and settled things appeared to be, and how uninterrupted Jess was in her office. At first it was assumed staff were told not to interrupt her, but it transpired that a culture of personal responsibility was developing across the school whereby staff were able to take difficulties into their supervision spaces on a regular basis. This left Jess more able to focus on the strategic development of the school rather than the firefighting she had previously experienced.

When asked how she funded the model in terms of time and finance, she quickly highlighted the savings in both time and money that the school had made – reduced cover required for absence, and better results for vulnerable children. The school had chosen to use its Pupil Premium money to develop supervision as an intervention that would support the most vulnerable children, with clearly positive results.

A number of schools have developed group supervision models that still require the setting of a contract/agreement but require more time to ensure a shared understanding across the group. Consideration also needs to be given early on to potential changes in the group – where will a new member of staff or student fit in? Is the group static or flexible, and how does this impact the members' anxiety levels?

Final thoughts

Supervision can help us recognise the impact of the work on ourselves whilst supporting us to develop as practitioners and increase outcomes for children.

Using the Mulberry Bush School as a framework, this chapter has emphasised that the introduction of supervision is not an overnight cure that can be parachuted into schools without thought, but the development of a culture of reflection that can have wide-ranging benefits for children, staff and schools. Supervision should not be seen as a luxury, or something that works in other schools, but as a vital tool that should be developing within all schools. Clearly there will be challenges ahead, but these can be managed effectively through good quality support and supervision.

Given the increased number of children with social, emotional and attachment difficulties, supporting the emotional wellbeing of staff through supervision can only be a significant step forward.

> I'd never heard of supervision in schools; it was only when talking to a colleague about how overwhelmed I felt that I was introduced to the idea of being supervised. Since my headteacher implemented supervision, it's been a life saver, no matter how stressful things get, I know I have a safe space to talk things through and make sense of my work. I can't imagine working without supervision. (Newly qualified primary teacher)

▨ REFLECTION POINTS ▨

1. Which aspects of teaching have you found to be stressful thus far?

2. What sort of support have you received in relation to stress?

3. To what extent do you think that supervision might be desirable, from your point of view?

4. How might this benefit your own teaching and the learning of your students?

Bibliography

Diamond, J. (2013) 'The Mulberry Bush School and UK therapeutic community practice for children and young people.' *Therapeutic Communities: The International Journal of Therapeutic Communities 34*, 4, 132–140.

Harris, M. and Brockbank, A. (2011) *An Integrative Approach to Therapy and Supervision: A Practical Guide for Counsellors and Psychotherapists.* London: Jessica Kingsley Publishers.

Hawkins, P. and Shohet, R. (2012) *Supervision in the Helping Professions* (4th edn). Maidenhead: Open University Press.

Inskipp, F. and Proctor, B. (1993) *The Art, Craft And Tasks Of Counselling Supervision, Part 1. Making the Most of Supervisors.* Twickenham: Cascade Publications.

Inskipp, F. and Proctor, B. (2001) *Making the Most of Supervision. Part 1.* Twickenham: Cascade Publications.

Laming, L. (2003) *The Victoria Climbié Inquiry, Report of an Inquiry by Lord Laming: Presented to Parliament by the Secretary of State for Health and the Secretary of State for the Home Department by Command of Her Majesty.* London: The Stationery Office.

Morrison, T. (2005) *Staff Supervision in Social Care: Making a Real Difference for Staff and Service Users* (3rd edn). Hove: Pavilion.

Morrison, T. (2009) *Trainers Manual: CWDC Training for the Supervisors of Newly Qualified Social Workers.* Leeds: CWDC.

Munro, E. (2011) *The Munro Review of Child Protection: Final Report, a Child-centred System.* London: The Stationery Office.

Reid, H. and Soan, S. (2015) *Supervision – A Business and Community Service for Colleagues in Schools. Delivering Supervision to Senior Leaders/SENCOs in Schools.* Canterbury: Christ Church University.

Westergaard, J. and Bainbridge, A. (2014) *Supporting Teachers in their Role: Making the Case for Formal Supervision in the Workplace.* Available at www.consider-ed.org.uk/supporting-teachers-in-their-role-making-the-case-for-formal-supervision-in-the-workplace, accessed on 3 September 2016.

Wonnacott, J. (2013) 'Supervision: A Luxury or Critical to Good Practice in Times of Austerity?' Child Protection in a Time of Austerity Conference, Bournemouth University National Centre for Post Qualifying Social Work.

16

Emotional Development and Approaches to Classroom Management

JON REID

As a beginning teacher, it is important that you link your classroom management approach to the social and emotional development of the children in your class. While the Department for Education (DfE) makes a range of recommendations regarding classroom management, behaviour and discipline (e.g. DfE 2012, 2016), this must be viewed through a critical lens. There are alternatives to the behaviourist DfE rhetoric, and these alternatives take into consideration the socio-emotional and attachment needs of the children in your classroom.

Influential organisations, both nationally and internationally, recognise the importance of positive social and emotional development as the basis for happy and engaging lives (NICE 2008, 2013; WHO 2012). Policy guidance within the UK also recognises the role that teachers play in supporting social and emotional health, wellbeing and resilience (DfE 2016a; Public Health England 2015). However, government guidance on behaviour and discipline in schools often ignores or negates this important area, stating instead that all schools must have a behaviour policy that aims to:

- promote good behaviour, self-discipline and respect

- prevent bullying

- ensure that pupils complete assigned work and

- regulate the conduct of pupils.

DfE (2016, p.4)

As a beginning teacher, you may be encouraged to access a range of 'tip texts' (Slee 2015) such as those prepared by DfE advisors including Charlie Taylor (DfE 2010) or Tom Bennett (2011), who provide 'top tips' for teachers with regards to classroom management:

1. Set out your behaviour expectations from the moment you meet the students.

2. Have a seating plan.

3. Know the students' names.

4. If they break the rules, they have to pay the penalty.

5. Follow up: If at first you don't succeed, keep it up. If students try to avoid your first sanction, then escalate, and involve other parties higher up the food chain.

6. Don't walk alone: You can't do it all by yourself; you exist in a structure, a hierarchy of adults and authority that can all be wielded for your purposes.

7. Get the parents involved.

8. Don't freak out.

9. Be prepared.

10. Be the teacher, not their chum.

While these top tips provide a useful introduction to the management of pupil behaviour in schools, they can also be a dangerous over-simplification of the series of complex social interactions that make up every hour of the school day. In reality, the school community and each individual classroom is a multi-layered and multi-dimensional social space that is invigorating, challenging and dynamic. In this space, moods will fluctuate, learning will go well, mistakes will be made, arguments may break out and rules will be transgressed. There will be laughter, enjoyment, negotiation and compromises.

This is the stuff of the school. Classrooms are nuanced, human and complex, meaning that effective classroom management will require more than a spurious collection of 'top tips'.

Classroom management and a critical review of current guidance

For Emmer and Stough (2001, p.103), 'classroom management' is defined as the 'actions taken by the teacher to establish order, engage students, or elicit their cooperation'. Hart incorporates the phrase 'classroom behaviour management' to refer to 'an attempt to control or alter other people's behaviour through, for example, increasing motivation, engagement or compliance' (2010, p.354), while Korpershoek *et al.* (2016) use the phrase 'Classroom Management Skills' in their definition, stating that:

> Classroom management is about creating inviting and appealing environments for student learning. Classroom Management Skills are tools that the teachers can use to help create such an environment, ranging from activities to improve teacher–student relationships to rules to regulate student behaviour. (2016, p.3)

For the majority of schools in the UK, classroom management approaches are based, for the most part, on a system of rewards and sanctions or punishments (Oxley 2015). These types of approach are endorsed by DfE guidance (2016), which states that:

> Schools should have in place a range of options and rewards to reinforce and praise good behaviour, and clear sanctions for those who do not comply with the school's behaviour policy. (DfE 2016, p.8)

Such approaches are underpinned by behavioural strategies that aim to increase desirable behaviour using rewards (reinforcement), and to decrease undesirable behaviour using sanctions (extinction) (Hart 2010, p.356). Typically schools use a wide range of rewards (such as praise, points, stickers, certificates, letters or a phone call home) to recognise and reinforce positive behaviours. These may relate to positive engagement in learning, positive interactions with others, or overcoming a personal challenge.

At the same time, teachers are encouraged in their classroom management to utilise a variety of consequences, sanctions and punishments as indicated in recent policy guidance, which confirms the 'powers' members of staff have to 'discipline pupils' (DfE 2016, p.3), and which recognises that 'sanctions should be implemented consistently and fairly in line with the behaviour policy'. A hierarchy of consequences, sanctions and punishments are provided in the policy that range from a verbal reprimand through to a temporary or permanent exclusion (DfE 2016, p.8).

As a beginning teacher, it is important to consider the DfE guidance critically, and be mindful of the concerns that have been raised both internationally and nationally regarding the current focus on these behaviourist approaches (Johnson 2016; Oxley 2015; Slee 2015; Sullivan 2016). Selected examples of such concerns recognise that:

- behaviourist approaches are usually applied by teachers as a way of controlling pupil behaviour, which denies the individual personal responsibility or agency for their behaviour (MacAllister 2014)

- behaviourist approaches can, in certain circumstances, reduce intrinsic or continued motivation to engage in a task (Hart 2010)

- an over-reliance on competition for rewards leads to a surface approach to learning where pupils are motivated to maximise their rewards at the expense of investing time and effort in their learning (Galloway *et al.* 1998)

- children and young people are sometimes very aware of issues relating to 'fairness' and will be resentful and oppositional if they perceive inconsistency in the distribution of rewards (Ingram 2012)

- consequences, sanctions and punishments when applied as 'reactive' strategies to a behaviour of concern are less effective in changing behaviour than proactive strategies that involve pre-empting potential difficulties by carefully considering appropriate approaches, strategies and interventions in recognition of the individual or group characteristics of a class (Korpershoek *et al.* 2016)

- teachers who utilise classroom management approaches disproportionately based on punishment, where behaviour is seen by the class teacher as a personal challenge, intentional or under the pupil's control, miss opportunities to understand the 'causes' of such behaviour (Weare 2015).

As a classroom teacher it is therefore important to interpret policy guidance carefully, and to appreciate that while rewarding specific behaviours may be effective in positively influencing behaviour (Oxley 2015), it is also well recognised that 'exclusionary and punitive approaches…have limited value' (Osher *et al.* 2010, p.48), and that punishment is rarely an efficient way of modifying an undesired behaviour (Apter 2014, p.3). It is also important to recognise that most effective teachers will tend to adopt a theoretically eclectic approach to classroom management (see Chapter 2). Within such an approach behaviourist methods can be very useful in establishing basic ground rules and teacher expectations so that pupils know clearly what a particular teacher's behavioural expectations are. That said, in a diverse and inclusive classroom, the teacher's knowledge of and relationships with individual students enable more individualised approaches that may involve occasional departures from set rules when appropriate. In this sense the teacher's ability to be consistently fair and to take into account specific pupil characteristics and circumstances will take precedence over the over-zealous robotic adherence to rules.

The emotionally 'vulnerable' in your classroom

When critically considering the wide variety of classroom management approaches that are applied in schools, it is important to recognise that the pupils in your class will differ with regards to their social and emotional development and will, therefore, have differing social and emotional needs.

So, while it is suggested that the majority of pupils will respond appropriately to whole-school behaviour management approaches (Oxley 2015), it is important to recognise that such approaches may not be effective for a significant minority of pupils who may experience a range of vulnerabilities. These learners may require differentiated and alternative approaches to behaviour management (Woods 2008).

Having an awareness of the potential childhood vulnerabilities that may follow multiple health, social and educational difficulties (see DH 2012) will support you as you prepare to meet the social and emotional needs of all the learners in your class.

The DfE publication, *Mental Health and Behaviour in Schools* (2016a), recognises that some children and young people experience multiple vulnerabilities that may include a child with special educational needs or disabilities (SEND), a child experiencing family adversity, or a child living in an area of deprivation (Brown, Khan and Parsonage 2012).

In addition, a range of life events can compound the emotional vulnerability of children and young people, which might include:

- *Loss or separation*, resulting from death, parental separation, divorce, hospitalisation, loss of friendships (especially in adolescence), family conflict or breakdown that results in the child having to live elsewhere, being taken into care or adopted.

- *Life changes*, such as the birth of a sibling, moving house or changing schools or during transition from primary to secondary school, or secondary school to sixth form.

- *Traumatic events*, such as abuse, domestic violence, bullying, violence, accidents, injuries or natural disaster.

DfE (2016a, p.10)

Your professional knowledge of social and emotional development and an appreciation of these potential childhood 'vulnerabilities' will support you in differentiating your approaches to classroom management.

Enhancing the social and emotional skills of your learners

Clarke *et al.* (2015) have undertaken an in-depth review of evidence on the effectiveness of school-based programmes that aim to enhance the development of social and emotional skills during childhood and adolescence. They identify the following common characteristics of effective school-based programmes that involve:

- focusing on teaching skills, in particular, cognitive, affective and behavioural skills and competencies

- using competence enhancement and empowering approaches

- using interactive teaching methods including role-play, games and group work to teach skills

- having well-defined goals and using a coordinated set of activities to achieve objectives

- providing explicit teacher guidelines through teacher training and programme manuals.

Clarke et al. (2015, p.7)

Additionally, McNeil, Reeder and Rich (2012, p.17) have identified a 'consistent core set of social and emotional capabilities' that are of value to children and young people with regards to both internal outcomes (e.g. happiness, self-esteem and confidence) and external outcomes (e.g. educational achievement and good health). When determining how best to support the children and young people in your classroom, it is useful to consider approaches, interventions or strategies that support the development of the following capabilities:

- *Managing feelings:* reviewing, self-awareness, reflecting, self-regulating, self-accepting.

- *Communication:* explaining, expressing, presenting, listening, questioning, using different ways of communicating.

- *Confidence and agency:* self-reliance, self-esteem, self-efficacy, self-belief, ability to shape your own life and the world around you.

- *Planning and problem-solving:* navigating resources, organising, setting and achieving goals, decision-making, researching, analysing, critical thinking, questioning and challenging, evaluating risks, reliability.

- *Relationships and leadership:* motivating others, valuing and contributing to team working, negotiating, establishing positive relationships, interpreting others, managing conflicts, empathising.

- *Creativity:* imagining alternative ways of doing things, applying learning in new contexts, enterprising, innovating, remaining open to new ideas.

- *Resilience and determination:* self-discipline, self-management, self-motivation, concentrating, having a sense of purpose, persistent, self-controlled.

McNeil et al. (2012, p.17)

Whole-class approaches that recognise social and emotional development

Concerns have been raised about reduced opportunities within the curriculum to support the development of social and emotional skills due to a narrowing of the curriculum, a focus on literacy and numeracy, an intense scrutiny of school performances and school comparison measures. However, there are a number of initiatives that provide guidance, resources and activities aimed at supporting the social and emotional development of children and young people.

One way in which schools can deliver a curriculum with a focus on social and emotional development is through Personal, Social, Health and Economic (PSHE) education. Although PSHE is currently a non-statutory (or compulsory) subject, the DfE states that 'all schools should make provision for PSHE, drawing on good practice' (DfE 2016b, p.5), and that 'schools have the flexibility to create their own PSHE curriculum and many use this to focus on developing children's resilience, confidence and ability to learn' (DfE 2016a, p.20).

This guidance provides you with a justification to *create your own curriculum* in response to the social and emotional needs of the children and young people in your class, and therefore to strategically plan flexible opportunities at whole class, small group and individual levels.

The PSHE Association is one example of an organisation that is associated with and recommended by the DfE. They have produced a series of useful resources, activities and guidance for children and young people from Key Stage 1 to Key Stage 4 with a focus on emotional wellbeing and mental health (see www.pshe-association.org.uk).

Other whole school, class or group approaches involve those with a specific focus on social and emotional learning (SEL). According to the Education Endowment Foundation (EEF), SEL interventions aim to 'improve attainment by improving social and emotional dimensions of learning' (EEF 2016), and can be grouped into the following broad categories:

- *universal programmes* that generally take place in the classroom

- more *specialised programmes* that are targeted at students with particular social or emotional problems and

- *school-level approaches* to developing a positive school ethos that also aim to support greater engagement in learning.

The EEF suggest that 'SEL interventions almost always improve emotional or attitudinal outcomes' and have an 'identifiable and significant impact on attitudes to learning, social relationships in school, and attainment itself' (2016).

In the UK the Social and Emotional Aspects of Learning (SEAL) programme is an example of one such SEL intervention. The SEAL materials include whole school, whole class and small group activities for children and young people from Key Stage 1 to Key Stage 4 with a focus on personal and social development, emotional literacy, emotional intelligence, and social, emotional and behavioural skills (DfES 2005).

The SEAL resources for primary schools are organised around seven whole-school themes (new beginnings, getting on and falling out, say no to bullying, going for goals, good to be me, relationships, and changes), and include staff development activities and ideas for assemblies. The materials also include whole class activities, cross-curricular links to other relevant subject areas and suggested activities for families to do together. These themes are explored in all class groups on a yearly cycle.

Recent evaluations of the SEAL initiative highlight the importance of adopting a whole-school, embedded and well-coordinated approach to its implementation (Weare 2015). Where this has been achieved, Hallam (2009) reports positive impacts of the SEAL programme with regards to 'the introduction of the language of emotion into schools, increased awareness of difficult emotions and the provision of ways and materials to consider them, and the facilitation of the development of staff social and emotional skills' (2009 p.329). Such increased awareness led to changes in staff behaviour that related to a better understanding of pupil behaviour and increased confidence in staff interactions with pupils, which encouraged staff to consider pupil behaviour in a more thoughtful way (Hallam 2009). The research also identified that both staff and pupils reported improvements in behaviour.

More recently Banerjee, Weare and Farr (2014) found that the effective implementation of the SEAL initiative supported pupils' consolidation of learning by 'promoting more positive motivation and goal-setting, self-awareness of progress, and collaborative group-working skills' (2014, p.733).

The materials to develop SEAL in your setting can be found at www.sealcommunity.org.

Restorative practices in education

An alternative to a system that is built on sanctions and punishment is one that seeks to repair harm that has been done. Research confirms that relationships 'provide the keystone to effective classroom management' (Jennings and Greenberg 2009, p.500), and that high-quality relationships in schools are 'a central factor in the child's successful development, not only in relation to academic achievement, but also in the development of positive social skills, social adjustment and future' (Mental Health Foundation 2016, p.13). One approach that recognises the importance of relationships within a school community is the restorative practice (RP) approach, which is 'a relational approach to school life grounded in beliefs about equality, dignity, and the potential of all people' (New Zealand Ministry of Education 2015, p.4).

The principle of RP is that we are all human and that we all make mistakes. Rather than blame and punish, it is argued that all incidents and conflicts in school should be understood in terms of harm done, and that repairing the harm done should be the priority so that relationships are preserved (and resentment does not fester). Through a structured meeting, the child who has caused harm is invited to meet with the person harmed. One or two neutral staff members facilitate this. A structured script allows each to speak openly and honestly about their experience in turn. At the conclusion of the meeting agreement is reached on how the harm done can be repaired. Expressing emotions, listening to the perspective of others and being heard are all central to this ancient and healing process.

In the UK, the DfE recognises RP approaches as being effective in tackling issues such as bullying in schools, through 'developing a restorative ethos and culture that supports the development of social and emotional skills and the adult modelling of positive relationships and communication' (DfE 2011, p.31). RP offers another alternative way of thinking about classroom management and behaviour, reflecting a structured, whole-school approach that relates to the ethos and culture of a school community. It has been found that having adopted a RP approach, schools find 'that relationships are stronger and learning is more effective, and so there is less need to resort to sanctions and punishments to try to "manage" behaviour' (Hendry, Hopkins and Steele 2012, p.1).

Solution-focused approaches

The National Society for the Prevention of Cruelty to Children (NSPCC) suggest that solution-focused therapy provides opportunities for adults to work together with a child or young person to 'move towards what is wanted instead of trying to move away from an unwanted problem' (NSPCC 2014, p.4). From a solution-focused perspective, it is understood that children and young people have the skills and resources needed to resolve their own difficulties. It is the role of the adult to empower the children to take control and to find the solution that works from within themselves.

Daki and Savage (2010) provide an example of a child who may exhibit behaviours that challenge in a particular context who is asked to describe instances where those specific behaviours of concern are absent. The child is then asked to explain why, in this specific circumstance, they were able to 'manage' their own behaviour, thus providing an insight into the their competence in resolving these difficulties independently.

This approach to classroom management recognises that children and young people are 'experts' on their problems and will have a strong desire to change their behaviour. The approach promotes a collaborative relationship, where the teacher encourages the child or young person to 'construct a vision of a problem free future', and then support them in achieving that goal through small, measurable steps (Daki and Savage 2010, p.311).

Compassion-focused approaches

The final and perhaps most important consideration with regards to behaviour management and developing an understanding of social and emotional development is an awareness of the theory and processes involved in compassion-focused interventions. According to Welford and Langmead (2015), the compassion-focused therapeutic approach, which was developed initially in the UK by Professor Paul Gilbert, is a way to understand emotional regulation and basic social motivation systems by drawing on social, neurophysiological and evolutionary theory, especially attachment theory (Welford and Langmead 2015).

A key feature of a compassion-focused intervention is the recognition that a 'compassionate understanding of ourselves and others can lead to a greater sense of connection with oneself, others and the community and collective motivation to improve and achieve greater things' (Welford and Langmead 2015, p.73). The aim of any compassion-focused intervention is to support the child or young person to replace 'self-criticism' with 'self-kindness' through experiences of 'social safeness, acceptance and being cared for' (Gilbert 2009, p.202). Gilbert provides guidance with regards to specific attributes and skills to support compassionate-focused interventions that include:

- *Care for wellbeing:* Harnessing the motivation to be caring for the purpose of alleviating distress and facilitating flourishing and development.

- *Sensitivity:* Being emotionally engaged with stories and moved by the feelings and distress of others.

- *Distress tolerance:* Being able to contain, stay with and tolerate complex and high levels of emotion, rather than avoid, fearfully divert from, close down, contradict, invalidate or deny them.

- *Non-judgement:* Not condemning, criticising, shaming or rejecting.

- *Empathy:* Working to understand the meanings, functions and origins of another person's inner world so that one can see it from their point of view.

Gilbert (2009, pp.202–203)

As a beginning teacher, classroom activities that are compassion-focused might include opportunities for children to create feelings of warmth, kindness and support. You might create opportunities that promote *compassionate attention* where children remember times when they were kind to others or others were kind to them. *Compassionate reasoning* involves supporting a child or young person to experience kind, supportive and helpful thoughts as opposed to self-critical thinking, while *compassionate behaviour* is focused on alleviating distress and facilitating development and growth through stimulating 'positive affect processing' and understanding of others. *Compassionate imagery* would involve an activity where a child or young person is encouraged to 'create and explore their image of their "ideal" of compassion' (Gilbert 2009, p.204). This might include what their ideal 'compassionate other' might look like, their facial expressions, their voice tones etc. Or there may be a preference for non-human image of the 'compassionate other' such as an animal, a tree or a memorable place such as a river, woodland or mountain (Gilbert 2009).

Compassion-focused approaches understand that the behaviour and the emotional responses of children and young people may, at times, seem inappropriate in the context of a classroom or school – but they have a reason and serve a purpose (for the learners). Rather than punish, this approach seeks to understand what is being communicated by the behaviour and to address this in a supportive and collaborative way.

Final thoughts

This chapter aimed to explore how a knowledge and understanding of the social and emotional development of children and young people might inform the development of your own classroom management approaches. In this process, the chapter has provided some definitions of 'classroom management' and reviewed DfE guidance on how classrooms might be managed.

By critically interpreting previous, current and future policy initiatives with regards to pupil behaviour and classroom management, particularly those that involve warnings, sanctions, consequences and punishments, you will continue to develop your own individual philosophy with regard to classroom management. By carefully assessing the social and emotional development needs of the individual pupils within your class you will be able to use your professional judgement to justify the strategies and interventions that you employ.

With regard to recognising, promoting and encouraging the social and emotional wellbeing of your pupils, your differentiated approaches to classroom management will help ensure that the children in your class experience empowerment, recognition, respect and most importantly, feelings of connectedness and belonging. It is hoped that the classroom management approaches, strategies and interventions that you adopt in your classroom will include those that:

- focus specifically on social and emotional learning

- explore positive human values such as responsibility, respect, fairness and kindness (Hawkes 2016)

- recognise the importance of building and maintaining positive relationships across the school community and

- empower children and young people to focus on solutions rather than problems.

By understanding the reasons for and functions of behaviour in the classroom and by modelling empathy, warmth and support, you will encourage feelings of 'social safeness, acceptance and being cared for' (Gilbert 2009, p.202). Perhaps the most important feature of any classroom management approach with regard to supporting the social and emotional development of the children and young people in your class is compassion.

REFLECTION POINTS

1. Consider the range of 'classroom management' approaches that you have been introduced to through national and whole-school school 'behaviour' policies or that you have observed in various school settings. How do these approaches reflect those described here in this chapter?

2. Imagine a child or young person who frequently engages in low-level disruption or behaviours that may challenge. How might you interpret these behaviours in recognition of their unmet social and emotional needs?

3. How might you then differentiate your responses to these behaviours?

4. Which combination of the 'classroom management' approaches discussed in this chapter might be most appropriate to support this pupil's ongoing social and emotional development?

Bibliography

Apter, B. (2014) *Behaviour Change: School Attendance, Exclusion and Persistent Absence.* London: British Psychological Society: Promoting Excellence in Psychology.

Banerjee, R., Weare, K. and Farr, W. (2014) 'Working with "Social and Emotional Aspects of Learning" (SEAL): Associations with school ethos, pupil social experiences, attendance, and attainment.' *British Educational Research Journal 40*, 718–742.

Bennett, T. (2011) *Tom Bennett's Top Ten Behaviour Tips.* Available at www.tes.com/teaching-resource/tom-bennett-s-top-ten-behaviour-tips-6081343, accessed on 30 May 2016.

Brown, E.R., Khan, L. and Parsonage, M. (2012) *A Chance to Change: Delivering Effective Parenting Programmes to Transform Lives.* London: Centre for Mental Health.

Clarke, A.M., Morreale, S., Field, C.A., Hussein, Y. and Barry, M.M. (2015) *What Works in Enhancing Social and Emotional Skills Development During Childhood and Adolescence? A Review of the Evidence on the Effectiveness of School-based and Out-of-school Programmes in the UK.* Galway: National University of Ireland: World Health Organization Collaborating Centre for Health Promotion Research.

Daki, J. and Savage, R.S. (2010) 'Solution-focused brief therapy: Impacts on academic and emotional difficulties.' *The Journal of Educational Research 103*, 309–326.

DfE (Department for Education) (2010) *Getting the Simple Things Right: Charlie Taylor's Behaviour Checklists.* London: DfE.

DfE (2011) *The Use and Effectiveness of Anti-bullying Strategies in Schools.* London: DfE. Research Report DFE-RR098.

DfE (2012) *Ensuring Good Behaviour in Schools. A Summary for Headteachers, Governing Bodies, Teachers, Parents and Pupils.* London: DfE. Reference DFE-00027-2012.

DfE (2016) *Behaviour and Discipline in Schools: Advice for Headteachers and School Staff.* London: DfE. Reference DFE-00023-201.

DfE (2016a) *Mental Health and Behaviour in Schools.* London: DfE. Reference DFE-00435-2014.

DfE (2016b) *Statutory Guidance: National Curriculum in England: Framework for Key Stages 1 to 4.* London: DfE. Reference DFE-00177-2013.

DfES (Department for Education and Skills) (2005) *Excellence and Enjoyment: Social and Emotional Aspects of Learning Guidance.* London: DfE. Reference DfES 1378-2005.

DH (Department of Health) (2012) *Future in Mind: Promoting, Protecting and Improving our Children and Young People's Mental Health and Wellbeing.* NHS England Publication Gateway Reference 02939.

EEF (Education Endowment Foundation) (2016) *Social and Emotional Learning.* Available at https://educationendowmentfoundation.org.uk/resources/teaching-learning-toolkit/social-and-emotional-learning/, accessed on 25 November 2016.

Emmer, E.T. and Stough, L.M. (2001) 'Classroom management: A critical part of educational psychology, with implications for teacher education.' *Educational Psychologist 36*, 2, 103–112.

Galloway, D., Rogers, C., Armstrong, D., Leo, E. and Jackson, C. (1998) 'Ways of Understanding Motivation.' In H. Daniels and A. Edwards (eds) *The Routledge Falmer Reader in Psychology of Education* (pp.87–105). Abingdon: Routledge.

Gilbert, P. (2009) 'Introducing compassion-focused therapy.' *Advances in Psychiatric Treatment 15*, 199–208.

Hallam, S. (2009) 'An evaluation of the Social and Emotional Aspects of Learning (SEAL) programme: Promoting positive behaviour, effective learning and well-being in primary school children.' *Oxford Review of Education 35*, 3, 313–330.

Hamston, J., Weston, J., Wajsenberg, J. and Brown, D. (2010) *Giving Voice to the Impacts of Values Education: The Final Report of the Values in Action Schools Project.* Carlton, VIC: Commonwealth of Australia.

Hart, R. (2010) 'Classroom behaviour management: Educational psychologists' views on effective practice.' *Emotional and Behavioural Difficulties 15*, 4, 353–337.

Hawkes, N. (2016) *The Value of Values: The Definitive Guide to the Impact and the Inner Workings of Values in Education, Business and Society.* Bucks: Values-Based Education.

Hendry, R., Hopkins, B. and Steele, B (2012) *Restorative Approaches in Schools in the UK.* Cambridge: University of Cambridge, Economic and Social Research Council. Available at www.educ.cam.ac.uk/research/projects/restorativeapproaches/RA-in-the-UK.pdf, accessed on 25 November 2016.

Ingram, R. (2012) 'The educational meets the evolutionary.' *The Psychologist 25*, 3, 246–248.

Jennings, P.A. and Greenberg, M.T. (2009) 'The prosocial classroom: Teacher social and emotional competence in relation to student and classroom outcomes.' *Review of Educational Research 79*, 491–525.

Johnson, B. (2016) 'Daring to Disagree About School "Discipline": An Australian Case Study of a Media-Led Backlash.' In A. Sullivan, B. Johnson and B. Lucas (eds) *Challenging Dominant Views on Student Behaviour at School Answering Back* (pp.15–26). Singapore: Springer.

Korpershoek, H., Harms, T., de Boer, H., van Kuijk, M. and Doolaard, S. (2016) 'A meta-analysis of the effects of classroom management strategies and classroom management programs on students' academic, behavioral, emotional, and motivational outcomes.' *Review of Educational Research XX*, X, 1–38.

Lovat, T. and Hawkes, N. (2013) 'Values education: A pedagogical imperative for student wellbeing.' *Educational Research International 2*, 2, 1–6.

Lovat, T., Toomey, R., Dally, K. and Clement, N. (2009) *Project to Test and Measure the Impact of Values Education on Student Effects and School Ambience: Final Report for Australian Government Department of Education, Employment and Workplace Relations.* Newcastle, Australia: The University of Newcastle.

MacAllister, J. (2014) 'Why discipline needs to be reclaimed as an educational concept.' *Educational Studies 40*, 4, 438–451.

McNeil, B., Reeder, N. and Rich, J. (2012) *A Framework of Outcomes for Young People.* London: The Young Foundation.

Mental Health Foundation (2016) *Relationships in the 21st Century: The Forgotten Foundation of Mental Health and Wellbeing.* London: Mental Health Foundation.

New Zealand Ministry of Education (2015) *Positive Behaviour for Learning: Restorative Practice Kete: Book One Introduction.* New Zealand Ministry of Education.

NICE (National Institute for Health and Care Excellence) (2008) *Social and Emotional Wellbeing in Primary Education: Public Health Guideline.* Manchester: NICE.

NICE (2013) *Social and Emotional Wellbeing for Children and Young People: NICE Local Government Briefings.* Manchester: NICE.

NSPCC (2014) *Solution-focused Practice: A Toolkit for Working with Children and Young People.*

Osher, D., Bear, G., Sprague, J.R. and Doyle, W. (2010) 'How can we improve school discipline?' *Educational Researcher 39*, 1, 48–58.

Oxley, L. (2015) 'Do schools need lessons on motivation?' *The Psychologist 29*, 9, 722–772.

Public Health England (2015) *Promoting Children and Young People's Emotional Health and Wellbeing: A Whole School and College Approach.* London.

Slee, R. (2015) 'Beyond a psychology of student behaviour.' *Emotional and Behavioural Difficulties 20*, 1, 3–19.

Sullivan, A. (2016) 'Schools' tough approach to bad behaviour isn't working – and may escalate problems.' *The Conversation.*

Values-Based Education (2016) *What Are Values?* Available at www.valuesbasededucation.com/vbe.values.html, accessed on 25 November 2016.

Weare, K. (2015) *What Works in Promoting Social and Emotional Well-being and Responding to Mental Health Problems in Schools? Advice for Schools and Framework Document.* National Children's Bureau. Partnership for Well-being and Mental Health in Schools.

Welford, M. and Langmead, K. (2015) 'Compassion-based initiatives in educational settings.' *Educational & Child Psychology 32*, 1, 71–80.

WHO (World Health Organization) (2012) *Risks to Mental Health: An Overview of Vulnerabilities and Risk Factors. Background Paper by WHO Secretariat for the Development of a Comprehensive Mental Health Action Plan.* Geneva: WHO, Department of Mental Health and Substance Abuse.

Woods, R. (2008) 'When rewards and sanctions fail: A case study of a primary school rule-breaker.' *International Journal of Qualitative Studies in Education 21*, 2, 181–196.

17

Disruptive Behaviour and Unsolved Problems

POPPY NASH

All learning has an emotional base.

Plato

The aim of this chapter is to explore the relevance of attachment theory for understanding disruptive behaviour at school. What can this theory tell us about what is going on in the classroom?

Attention is first paid to examining the important contribution attachment theory can make not just to an understanding of behaviour, but also in how to best support the most troubled pupils in our schools today. In particular, this chapter looks at how teacher attitudes and perceptions of disruptive behaviour in the classroom can have a profound effect on the pupil's educational progress. The chapter then provides some good news regarding what school staff can do to engage troubled pupils by offering them a positive way forward and creating a supportive school community.

Much continues to be written about the merits of embedding an effective school behaviour policy in primary and secondary schools (e.g. Taylor 2012). A key feature of this approach is the assumption that a pupil is *choosing* to engage in disruptive behaviour. But what if pupils are not always in control of their behaviour and not always choosing to be disruptive? A growing range of literature indicates that disruptive behaviour in the most troubled and disruptive pupils may be associated with a trauma/fear response triggered by some form of attachment difficulty (e.g. Bombèr 2007; Geddes 2006). Where a deep-seated emotional response is triggered by something in the school environment, the pupil may not be able to control their behaviour, and therefore, cannot be said to be 'choosing' to act in the way that they are.

As Heather Geddes highlighted in Chapter 2, a useful framework for understanding the dynamics of disruptive behaviour at school is attachment theory, as proposed by Bowlby (1969). Because of its onus on the significance of early relationships, attachment theory continues to play a central role in clinical interventions, especially those offered by psychotherapy. If we wish to understand what is going on in the classroom, we need to consider this theory with respect to what it can contribute to teacher–student relationships. There is now a growing interest in the implications and application of attachment theory to education, most notably Geddes' (2006) *Attachment in the Classroom*, Bombèr's (2007) *Inside I'm Hurting*, Perry *et al.*'s (2009) *Teenagers and Attachment* and more recently, Bombèr and Hughes' (2013) *Settling Troubled Pupils to Learn: Why Relationships Matter in School*. These are key resources for the beginning teacher, and are highly recommended.

Attachment theory and understanding disruptive behaviour at school

The following section develops the key ideas first introduced by Heather Geddes in Chapter 2, and asks how attachment theory can enhance our understanding of disruptive behaviour in the classroom. In doing so, attention is given to how the distinct attachment styles of secure, insecure-avoidant, insecure-ambivalent and insecure-disorganised present in terms of pupil behaviours. By recognising the characteristics of these patterns, school staff are able to address the particular emotional needs being expressed by the individuals concerned.

In addition, reference is made to Geddes' concept of the learning triangle (Geddes 2006), which offers a valuable means of understanding the relationship between teacher, pupil and task in every learning situation at school. Since attachment difficulties are fundamentally concerned with how the individual relates to other people, the learning triangle provides an insight into how and why relationships between the pupil, teacher and learning opportunities can be especially challenging in the school environment. Please note that each of the following sections begins with the voice of the pupil.

Secure attachment style

> Adults are reliable and helpful. I know that I can trust them to look out for me to meet my needs. I find it easy to trust you and others. I am ok if you are with me or busy doing other things. You find me relatively easy to relate to. (quoted in Bombèr 2007, p.27)

Key characteristics:

- Student has learned through early experiences with primary caregiver(s) that they are okay, adults are okay and the world is okay in general.

- Student is able to take risks required by learning and so will usually reach their academic potential at school. They are generally able to cope with school, in terms of both academic and social challenges (such as resolving conflict and making and keeping friendships).

The links between attachment and learning can be made more explicit by referring to the learning triangle of secure attachment behaviour (Geddes 2006, p.59). As Geddes indicates, '…the balance of this relationship reflects a fluid dynamic between engagement and support with the teacher, and involvement in the task.'

Avoidant attachment style

> Adults are rejecting or intrusive. So when I meet you I will avoid and ignore you, and look after myself. I won't be asking you for help no matter what I face. Love? Care? Why would I trust you? You have no idea what I need. (quoted in Bombèr 2007, p.30)

Key characteristics:

- Student actively tries to meet needs on their own, due to a depressed or abusive caregiver who has been unable to respond to those needs.

- Student may present as very self-sufficient and may be difficult to connect with emotionally.

- Student can therefore be easily overlooked or 'forgotten' in class, and 'suffer in silence'. Difficulties may arise in coping with both academic and social challenges at school (such as resolving conflict and making and keeping friendships).

With respect to the learning triangle, Geddes (2006) explains that in the case of avoidant attachment, the student actively avoids any relationships with the teacher. Instead, they focus their attention on the task/lesson in hand.

Ambivalent attachment style

Adults are unpredictable. I have to draw attention to myself to get you to notice me and to make sure I get my needs met... I can't rely on you working out what I need and when. Sometimes you will feel like I'm in your face, but you've got to understand that I can't bear to be ignored – that terrifies me. (quoted in Bombèr 2007, p.33)

Key characteristics:

- Student attempts to get adult's attention by whatever means, so extensive attention-seeking behaviour at school.

- Behind constant chattering and interrupting lies student's extreme anxiety that they won't be noticed, so, for example, they may be disruptive in class.

- Student is so preoccupied with their relationship with their teacher, they have little energy left for learning. Therefore, difficulties may arise in coping with both academic and social challenges at school (such as resolving conflict and making and keeping friendships).

The implications for the learning triangle for this pattern of insecure attachment differ distinctly from the previous pattern, in that '...this pattern reflects the tension between the pupil and adult at the expense of the task' (Geddes 2006, p.97).

Disorganised attachment style

> Adults are either frightening…or frightened…most of the time. I don't know whether to approach you or to run away from you. I feel confused by you and others. I'm bad… Why should I trust you? But then I need you sometimes. I need to stay in control – ready. Who knows what will happen next? (quoted in Bombèr 2007, p.35)

Key characteristics:

- These students are often hardest to relate to in school, as their behaviour is often erratic and unpredictable and may lead to permanent school exclusion. Indeed, unpredictability is a particularly challenging aspect of this attachment style.

- Student expects the worst as they can't imagine anyone wishing to take a genuine interest in them, least of all teachers.

- Student tries to control everything as they can't risk being vulnerable in any way, as this triggers a sense of helplessness and acute anxiety.

- Student is so preoccupied with needing to survive that they can find it very hard to settle in lessons and relax into relationships with staff and peers at school. Therefore, difficulties may arise in coping with both academic and social challenges at school (such as resolving conflict and making and keeping friendships).

The student with a disorganised/disoriented insecure attachment pattern can pose the greatest challenge for those wishing to support them at school, as evidenced by the lack of any meaningful relationships between pupils, teacher and task in the learning triangle.

Clearly, there is much that a supportive, inclusive school can provide in terms of understanding and nurturing students experiencing any of these forms of attachment pattern. For many insecurely attached children and young people (whether at nursery, primary or secondary school), their school community may be the first experience they have had of a 'secure base'. By acknowledging this possibility, school staff can build on the many positive and psychologically significant features of the school environment.

Table 17.1 indicates the many ways in which primary and secondary school communities can become a secure base for students, and how this can be reinforced by school staff.

Table 17.1: Characteristics of 'school as a secure base'

For pupils this would reflect…	For school staff this would reflect…
Respect for all pupils no matter what their skills and difficulties	Strong leadership which listens to all staff and can be relied upon for consistent, available support
A building that is safe and adequately supervised	Respect for physical comfort of staff – well-kept staffroom as a symbolic secure base!
Sensitivity to meaning of communications implied by behaviour – empathy	A capacity to reflect on difficulties when they arise, rather than react in an unthinking way
Predictable, reliable routines	Mutual support and collaboration across whole staff group
A fast response to absence – noticing absent pupil	A common language and framework for understanding pupils' behaviour
Consistent rules and expectations framed around keeping pupils, staff and building safe	A regular forum for review of difficulties in a reliable and supportive group
Familiar long-term relationships – pupil feels 'known'	A school which can become a surrogate 'secure base' that contains anxiety surrounding learning
Modelling of good relationships between adults	A school that is able to provide compensatory relationships and experiences to pupils, whose capacities to learn have been impaired by adverse emotional and social experiences
Informed reflection about incidents rather than reactivity	
A system of disciplinary procedures which is fair to all – and non-abusive	

Source: Adapted from Geddes (2006, p.140)

In exploring the relevance of attachment theory for understanding disruptive behaviour at school, it is important to acknowledge its value in understanding the dynamics in all relationships in the school community. Riley (2011) discusses the relevance of the theory to classroom and staffroom relationships, in helping to identify why some teachers may encounter more disruption in their classes than others. The nature of teacher–student relationships also depend upon the secure or insecure attachments experienced by the teachers themselves.

In understanding the student's perspective and behaviour at school (at whatever age), it may be helpful at this stage to remind ourselves of the mindset that the student brings with them into the school environment. We need to ask, where does their negative self-talk come from?

If a child in the early years of their development is repeatedly told by those around them that they are useless, hopeless, undeserving and so on, the child is likely to internalise these messages and believe that they are true. Babies and young children at this stage accept all that is said to them as true since they know no different. Over time, these internalised messages shape the young child's 'internal working model' that includes their self-perception, self-esteem and sense of self. By the time the child reaches school, they already have a negative view of themselves and expect that others (school staff and peers) will do so too. Such negativity can have an increasingly damaging impact upon the child's school education, perhaps most evidently at secondary school.

The teacher's perception of disruptive behaviour in school

In view of what we know about the challenges experienced by children and young people with attachment difficulties, it clearly matters how teachers perceive disruptive behaviour at school.

Nash, Schlösser and Scarr (2016) undertook a research study to investigate teachers' views on disruptive behaviour at school. They sent a postal questionnaire to 548 primary and secondary schools across England. A total of 21 (8.4 per cent) and 69 (23.8 per cent) of the questionnaires were completed and returned from respective primary and secondary school headteachers.

For the purposes of this chapter, attention is turned to the responses to two particular questions on the questionnaire, which reflect a school's understanding of disruptive behaviour in the most troubled and most vulnerable students. The findings from this relatively small-scale study throw light on the perception of disruptive students in our secondary schools. They indicate the need to raise staff awareness of the psychological/psychodynamic implications of disruptive behaviour, and the need for staff training on the relevance of attachment theory for schools, in managing disruptive behaviour more effectively. Needless to say, the perception of disruptive behaviour directly relates to how a school addresses and supports the students concerned.

1. To what extent do primary and secondary school teachers think that pupils can control their disruptive behaviour at school?

2. To what extent are teachers aware that a pupil's disruptive behaviour is a means of communicating emotional distress (notably anxiety, anger, shame or fear)?

The questionnaire responses to each of these key questions are now considered in turn, followed by a discussion of the implications of the findings for schools.

To what extent do primary and secondary school teachers think that pupils can control their disruptive behaviour at school?

The rationale for asking this question is the assertion that if staff believe that pupils can control their disruptive behaviour, pupils warrant discipline or 'punishment' for choosing to behave in this way. However, those familiar with the attachment theory perspective understand that the most troubled pupils cannot always control their behaviour, and may clearly not be choosing to behave in disruptive ways at school. The findings show that a sizeable majority of both primary and secondary schools in Nash *et al.*'s study (2016) thought that pupils were 'mostly' or 'totally' in control their behaviour (85.7 per cent, $n=18$, and 89.9 per cent, $n=62$ respectively). Only a small minority of schools (14.3 per cent, $n=3$, and 10.1 per cent, $n=7$ for primary and secondary schools respectively) indicated that pupils had 'some' or 'no' control over their disruptive behaviour. These findings have far-reaching implications in reflecting the need to raise staff awareness of how attachment difficulties may affect pupils' behaviour at school.

To what extent are teachers aware that a pupil's disruptive behaviour is a means of communicating emotional distress (notably anxiety, anger, shame or fear)?

The purpose of including the second question in the questionnaire was to discover the extent to which schools are aware of the fundamental relationship between disruptive behaviour and emotional distress. To gather this information, schools were asked to indicate how far they agreed/disagreed that disruptive behaviour was attributable to 12 different factors. The findings show general agreement across all primary and secondary schools, that five of the factors are related to disruptive behaviour, namely, low engagement with learning, learning difficulties, social and emotional difficulties, troubled home environment, and difficulties with friendships/peer relationships. However, a different picture emerges when schools were asked about the more psychological/psychodynamic factors in relation to disruptive behaviour, as shown in Table 17.2 (Nash *et al.* 2016, p.10).

Table 17.2: Possible factors related to disruptive behaviour at school

Possible factor	Total (valid %) Secondary schools (n=69)	Total (valid %) Primary schools (n=21)
Deep-seated anxiety		
Agree	67.7	85.7
Disagree	32.4	14.3
Total	100.1	100.0
Feel shame/fear		
Agree	60.8	71.4
Disagree	39.1	28.6
Total	99.9	100.0
Feel misunderstood		
Agree	60.9	57.2
Disagree	39.1	42.9
Total	100.0	100.0
Feel not liked		
Agree	60.9	66.6
Disagree	39.1	33.3
Total	100.0	99.9
Behaviour communicates distress		
Agree	73.2	90.5
Disagree	*26.8*	*9.5*
Total	100.0	100.0

As Table 17.2 shows, there is a discernible difference in the findings for primary and secondary schools regarding the contributory factors of disruptive behaviour. For example, it appears that a large majority of the participating primary schools was aware of the association between deep-seated anxiety and disruptive behaviour (85.7 per cent agreed; 14.3 per cent disagreed), whereas this majority was reduced for secondary schools (67.7 per cent agreed; 32.4 per cent disagreed). The level of disagreement shown by schools is concerning, since high levels of anxiety can be strongly equated with insecure attachments.

Another notable difference between primary and secondary school participants is evident in their responses to the association between behaviour as communicating distress and disruptive behaviour (90.5 per cent and 73.2 per cent agreed in primary and secondary schools respectively). As discussed earlier, disruptive behaviour needs to be seen as a means of communicating emotional distress in the most troubled students, if they are to receive the appropriate support. In view of this, the findings shown in Table 17.2 generally suggest that primary schools are more familiar than secondary schools with the basic tenets of attachment theory. One explanation for this might be the fact that primary school staff tend to be more emotionally engaged with their pupils compared with the subject-focused nature of secondary school teaching. These findings have clear implications regarding priorities for staff training.

The intimations of the research findings are clear, that there is an urgent need to raise awareness in schools about the relevance of attachment theory to schools and the psychological underpinnings of disruptive behaviour. Indeed, it can come as no surprise that the incidence of disruptive behaviour and behaviour-related permanent school exclusions persist where there is only a focus on the sanctions and reward systems of behaviour management in schools – that is, where pupils are considered to be deliberately choosing to be disruptive and fully in control of their behaviour, they will continue to be disciplined and 'punished' for their actions. In such instances, key questions need to be asked about the long-term effectiveness of this approach, and whether it is actually exacerbating the situation by antagonising further already anxious and distressed students.

Having analysed the questionnaire findings, Nash and Schlösser (2015) were subsequently invited to work closely with a secondary school in the north of England, on developing materials for whole-school staff training. The aim of the one-day training was to enhance staff awareness of the psychological implications of disruptive behaviour, with particular reference to the relevance of attachment theory. Later evaluation of the training day showed that 76.1 per cent (*n*=51) of participating staff reported that their ideas about disruptive behaviour had changed as a result of attending the one-day training on attachment.

In summary, the research undertaken by Nash and colleagues (Nash and Schlösser 2015; Nash *et al.* 2016) advocates a framework for managing disruptive behaviour in school, whereby sanctions and rewards behaviour management strategies are used in conjunction with a more collaborative, problem-solving approach. Particular mention must be made here of the Collaborative and Proactive Solutions (CPS) approach developed by clinical psychologist Dr Ross Greene (see www.livesinthebalance.org). This approach sees disruptive behaviour as expressing an emotional need, which requires a reflective and compassionate proactive response from school staff, rather than a reactive and punitive one. It highlights the need for collaboration between staff and students in reaching an agreed course of action, built on mutual respect, creative problem-solving and the use of conciliatory language.

Collaborative and Proactive Solutions

In explaining the CPS model, Greene (2016) states that challenging children may be '…challenging because they're lacking the skills to not be challenging' (2016, p.5). That is, their challenging behaviour reflects a developmental delay, with respect to the fact that they do not yet possess the skills to manage their emotions and regulate their behaviour. Another way of understanding this concept is Greene's assertion that '…if the kid *could* do well, he *would* do well, and that if he's not doing well, he must be lacking the skills to do well' (2016, p.5). All too often challenging and disruptive behaviour continues at school, precisely because attention is paid to the by-products of the underlying problems (the behaviour), rather than the problems themselves (the lagging skills). Therefore, it is the responsibility of those educating the children or young people to identify the barriers, the unsolved problems and the unmet needs.

In addressing exactly how school staff can most effectively support disruptive students at school (of whatever age), Greene (2016, p.24) highlights that the two most essential roles are:

1. To work out 'what skills the student is lacking and the expectations he/she is having difficulty meeting' (unmet expectations = unsolved problems).

2. To 'start solving those problems', but to do so both 'collaboratively and proactively'. This approach actively seeks the engagement and ideas of the individual concerned, in thinking creatively about how to solve problems affecting the child's life at school.

Thus, creatively solving problems becomes a joint activity with the student, rather than something 'done' to them. There is clearly a fundamental distinction between problem-solving that is proactive and that which is reactive, as they convey very different messages to the students concerned. As one teacher puts it: 'You're letting kids know they're an important part of the team' (quoted in Greene 2016, p.174), while another teacher highlights the difference this approach can make in supporting pupils:

> …in the old days, when we'd get together to meet about a kid, all the people who worked with the kid in the school would get together to talk about everything we knew about the kid and then brainstorm solutions… Now we know someone was missing from the problem-solving process: the student. Now we only really talk about lagging skills and unsolved problems in our meetings, because we can't come up with solutions without knowing the kid's concerns and without involving the kid in the solution. (quoted in Greene 2016, p.61)

It is possible to work proactively with disruptive students, because if we can identify why and when the challenging behaviour is occurring in school, it is possible to predict when that behaviour is most likely going to occur in future. By identifying the student's lagging skills (or the 'why?') and the associated unsolved problems (or the 'when?'), vital progress can be made in understanding the situation from the student's perspective.

Greene has developed the Assessment of Lagging Skills and Unsolved Problems (ALSUP) for the purpose of highlighting key information in this process (Greene 2016, p.31). The blank ALSUP Form and Guide can be freely downloaded by going to www.livesinthebalance.org/LostandFound.

Final thoughts

Delaney (2012, p.122) captures the essence of the current challenge for those concerned with the welfare of troubled pupils. She suggests that it may be the 'lack of shared knowledge about each other's professions that can lead to unhelpful assumptions'. There is a growing realisation that educational psychotherapy in particular has an enormous contribution to make in enabling schools to better understand the 'meaning' of disruptive and challenging behaviour. There is also an increasing recognition that secondary school communities have a vital role to play in 'second chance learning' (Bombèr 2007, p.47), and Greene's CPS provides an intervention focused upon addressing the unsolved problems of those students disrupting our classrooms. There is an urgent need to develop a shared knowledge, based on a mutual respect and understanding, around what challenging behaviour in the most disruptive and troubled individuals is telling us.

REFLECTION POINTS

1. How is disruptive behaviour traditionally understood and managed in schools?

2. Why might some students struggle to manage their own behaviour?

3. Can you envisage a situation in class where a student is no longer capable of 'choosing' how they behave?

4. How might staff respond to a student who is emotionally overwhelmed and incapable of 'choosing'?

Bibliography

Ainsworth, M.D., Blehar, M.C., Waters, E. and Wall, S. (1978) *Patterns of Attachment: Assessed in the Strange Situation and at Home.* Hillsdale, NJ: Erlbaum.

Bebbington, E. (2008) *Stop Wasting My Time! Case Studies of Pupils with Attachment Issues in Schools with Special Reference to Looked After and Adopted Children.* Stirling: PACS (Post Adoption Central Support).

Bombèr, L.M. (2007) *Inside I'm Hurting: Practical Strategies for Supporting Children with Attachment Difficulties in Schools.* Belper: Worth Publishing Ltd.

Bombèr, L.M. and Hughes. D. (2013) *Settling Troubled Pupils to Learn: Why Relationships Matter in School.* Belper: Worth Publishing Ltd.

Bowlby, J. (1969) *Attachment and Loss. Volume 1: Attachment.* London: Hogarth Press and the Institute of Psychoanalysis.

Delaney, M. (2012) 'What Can Educational Psychotherapy Teach Teachers?' In H. High (ed.) *Why Can't I Help this Child to Learn? Understanding Emotional Barriers to Learning* (pp.121–136). London: Karnac.

Fernet, C., Guay, F., Senécal, C. and Austin, S. (2012) 'Predicting intraindividual changes in teacher burnout: The role of perceived school environment and motivational factors.' *Teaching and Teacher Education 28*, 4, 514–525.

Geddes, H. (2006) *Attachment in the Classroom: The Links Between Children's Early Experience, Emotional Well-being and Performance in School: A Practical Guide for Schools.* Belper: Worth Publishing Ltd.

Gerhardt, S. (2004) *Why Love Matters: How Affection Shapes a Baby's Brain.* Abingdon: Taylor & Francis.

Geving, A. (2007) 'Identifying the types of student and teacher behaviours associated with teacher stress.' *Teaching and Teacher Education 23*, 5, 624–640.

Greene, R.W. (2014) *Lost at School: Why Our Kids with Behavioral Challenges Are Falling Through the Cracks and How We Can Help Them.* New York: Scribner Book Co.

Greene, R.W. (2016) *Lost and Found: Helping Behaviorally Challenging Students (And, While You're At It, All the Others).* San Francisco, CA: Jossey-Bass.

Howe, D. (2005) *Attachment Theory for Social Work Practice.* Basingstoke: Palgrave.

Kyriacou, C. (2009) *Effective Teaching Skills: Theory and Practice* (3rd edn). Cheltenham: Nelson Thornes.

Ladnier, R.D. and Massanari, A.E. (2000) 'Treating ADHD as Attachment Deficit Hyperactivity Disorder.' In T.M. Levy (ed.) *Handbook of Attachment Interventions* (pp.27–65). London: Academic Press.

Marshall, N. (2014) *The Teacher's Introduction to Attachment. Practical Essentials for Teachers, Carers and School Support Staff.* London: Jessica Kingsley Publishers.

McCrory, E., De Brito, S.A. and Viding, E. (2010) 'Research review: The neurobiology and genetics of maltreatment and adversity.' *Journal of Child Psychology and Psychiatry 51*, 10, 1079–1095.

Nash, P. and Schlösser, A. (2015) 'Working with schools in identifying and overcoming emotional barriers to learning.' *Educational Studies 41*, 1–2, 143–155.

Nash, P., Schlösser, A. and Scarr, T. (2016) 'Teachers' perceptions of disruptive behaviour in schools: A psychological perspective.' *Emotional and Behavioural Difficulties 21*, 2, 167–180.

Perry, A. (ed.) (2009) *Teenagers and Attachment: Helping Adolescents Engage with Life and Learning.* Belper: Worth Publishing Ltd.

Riley, P. (2011) *Attachment Theory and the Teacher–Student Relationship. A Practical Guide for Teachers, Teacher Educators and School Leaders.* Abingdon: Routledge.

Sunderland, M. (2009) 'Foreword.' In A. Perry (ed.) *Teenagers and Attachment: Helping Adolescents Engage with Life and Learning.* Belper: Worth Publishing Ltd.

Taylor, C. (2012) Behaviour checklists. Available at https://www.gov.uk/government/uploads/system/uploads/attachment_data/file/571640/Getting_the_simple_things_right_Charlie_Taylor_s_behaviour_checklists.pdf

Wilson, V. (2002) *Feeling the Strain: An Overview of the Literature on Teachers' Stress.* Glasgow: University of Glasgow, Scottish Council for Research in Education.

18

Classroom Behaviour
Finding What Works for You

JOHN VISSER

The behaviour of children is one of the most talked about issues in the media and in political life, with pundits, some of them in education, often harking back to some golden age when children all sat quietly and did exactly as they were told all the time. If such a time ever existed it isn't recorded in any of the literature about schools and schooling. Then, as now, there was a search for the 'fool-proof scheme of the management of behaviour' that will work in all situations and circumstances, if faithfully followed. My experience as a teacher in a wide range of schools is that this pursuit of a 'one size fits all' approach is futile (Royer 2001). It may be stating the obvious, but schools, curriculums, teachers, children, families and carers all differ and make for very different atmospheres and environments within which learning takes place.

For the beginning teacher to read that there is not a single answer to the age-old issue of managing classroom behaviour may be disconcerting, but this chapter argues that a set of unifying, core principles around behaviour management do exist. This underlying set of core factors are present in all effective classroom approaches and have been passed down from one generation of pedagogues to the next. These are the *eternal verities* of effective classroom practice.

What works and why?

The term *eternal verities* resonates with a personal quest for an underlying set of unifying principles within all approaches to meeting the educational needs of pupils with social, emotional and mental health (SEMH) needs. Is there a set of principles that are seldom enunciated, associated with good practice, which, to quote Whelan

(1998), are the field's 'memory banks', subliminally passed on to each succeeding generation of teachers?

My quest has its origins in my early development as a teacher. I faced contradictions, as I perceived them, between the various approaches put forward as ways of meeting these pupils' behavioural and learning needs. Some of the approaches seemed to me to be diametrically opposed to each other. As a young teacher struggling to do what was right for the pupils in my charge, which should I choose? What could ensure that the approach chosen would work? And as a provider of professional development for teachers and others working with 'challenging' children, what approaches should I espouse? What advice could be given to examine the likely success of any given policy shift, any 'new' initiative or change in provision?

As part of my professional development I took a year off to gain a Master's in Education. The course provided me with the opportunity to visit a number of schools, among them one that espoused a behavioural approach and one that had a psychodynamic basis for its work (see Chapter 1). Both were perceived at that time as schools of good practice. In one setting I felt more comfortable than in the other, but it was evident that they were both successful in meeting the needs of pupils. Were there common underlying factors/principles/beliefs that accounted for this success? Are there *eternal verities* that are part of all successful approaches? The DNA of approaches? Just as cells within the human body perform different functions but contain the same DNA, are there *eternal verities* to be found in all effective interventions to meet the needs of children and young people with SEMH needs?

What is an 'eternal verity'?

'Verities' are truths that are apparent in the web and weave of methodologies that effectively promote learning and engagement in the classroom. As factors within the teacher–pupil relationship, they create the context in which nearly all children and young people behave in conducive ways that support their learning. They are eternal in as much as they are necessary for the proficiency of all approaches to teaching – regardless of the time frame in which the approaches are developed and applied. *Eternal verities* provide the strongest links between different approaches and the achievement of successful learning outcomes. As such, they carry values and beliefs about the human condition and the quality of life to which we, and our students, are entitled. They are rarely made explicit, often emerging implicitly from the literature, discussion and research. They are observable but their quantification is seldom helpful and their measurement is not linear. Having more or less of them is not so much the issue as their quality and presence within an approach. The *eternal verities* sustain teachers and other professionals in times of stress, and from them, all good practice flows.

The list that follows is not presented as a definitive one. It is idiosyncratic, and this list of *eternal verities* has drawn on three sources. The first is my experience as a teacher in a variety of settings, from the classroom to researcher and provider of staff development programmes, and from parent to foster parent. The second is from my involvement with education in a number of research and consultancy projects. The third comes from a review of the literature, which describes the various understandings and perspectives of the broad range of emotional and behavioural difficulties that children encounter.

Amongst these I have drawn particularly on the work of Ayers, Clarke and Murray (2000), Bowlby (1969, 1973), Cooper (2001), Cooper, Jacobs and Martin (2009), Elton (1989), ERIC (1997), Greenhalgh (1994), Kauffman (2001), Laslett *et al.* (1998), Maslow (1943, 1954), Porter (2000), Steer (2005, 2009) and Whelan (1998). These writers offer the reader a comprehensive view of the variety of approaches to understanding behaviour and its relationship to learning, and thus provide a basis for seeking possible *eternal verities*.

This list of verities is offered as a 'litmus test' against which any particular approach to behavioural issues in teaching and learning can be held. When examining suggestions as to how one should go about managing behaviour in a learning context, ask to what extent, if at all, each of the verities that follow is to be found in the strategy suggested.

It is the contention of this chapter that interventions, strategies and approaches that support the stated *eternal verities* (below) will be successful. Where teachers blindly follow a given strategy or approach without first examining the link to these 'verities', then I contend there is a much smaller chance of success in meeting, in the longer term, the socio-emotional and learning needs of the children in the classroom.

The eight *eternal verities* of effective classroom practice

1. Behaviour can change: emotional needs can be met

2. Intervention is second to prevention

3. Instructional reactions

4. Transparency in communications

5. Empathy and equity

6. Boundaries and challenge

7. Building positive relationships

8. Humour

1. Behaviour can change: emotional needs can be met

Having a belief in the ability of even the most troubled and disengaged child to change and develop into a positive and resourceful adult (albeit with a great deal of support) sustains most teachers when employing a range of approaches in the classroom. This belief is one of the *eternal verities*, where behaviour is perceived by proficient, dedicated staff as being capable of development and change.

Whether the presenting behaviour is viewed as being learned behaviour, biologically driven, or the result of internal, psychological conflicts, this *eternal verity* views the learner as being capable of altering their actions. There is an understanding that to be human is not to be at the mercy of instincts or genetic predispositions, and that the learner can attain control over the actions and emotional challenges that have caused their emotional and behavioural difficulties.

This belief in the possibility of change provides staff with the ability to continue to work with these children and young people when so often they appear to reject their attempts to meet their needs.

Dedication, commitment and going 'the extra mile' is central to this eternal verity (Cole, Visser and Upton 1998), for, as Rodway points out:

> However much a child may wound his own self-esteem (s/he) cannot change the esteem in which (the teachers should) hold him. (Rodway 1993, p.379)

2. Intervention is second to prevention

When behaviour becomes a challenge for a teacher it generally leads to an identification process where the cause of the challenge is sought. Once causality is 'established' a solution is sought. The challenges are identified before the approaches are developed. The interventions seek to meet the challenge presented by the identified difficulties. Publicising the success of the intervention inevitably leads to the identification of 'fault lines' within the child's environment, be that the school, home or community. Prevention strategies are then put forward to correct the 'fault line'.

This verity suggests that we should plan ahead and ensure that the faults lines do not occur in the first instance. All effective approaches underscore the proverb: 'Prevention is better than cure'.

A second aspect of this verity is to be aware of possible precursors to behaviour that could escalate into being a challenge. For example, noting the manner in which pupils enter school or a classroom can give an early indication of possible issues with individuals.

Maslow (1943, 1954) offers a model of the hierarchy of human needs which, if not met, can lead on to difficulties. These are a useful listing of what may be 'missing or inadequate' in an individual's life. As teachers we may not be able to fill all of these 'gaps', but we can come up with interventions that mitigate their effects, in particular, how the children and young people we teach feel about themselves as learners.

3. Instructional reactions

Children and young people with behaviours that teachers find difficult to manage do not always understand the relationship between their behaviour and the reaction that those behaviours have caused. Few children set out with malice aforethought to be the disturbed and disturbing characters that many of them develop into. When they do, it is to achieve some gratification or status that protects their self-esteem. Effective approaches in the classroom recognise this to be the case and will work to actively teach the relationship between cause and effect. With empathy and understanding, staff will instruct the learners in how different reactions can be achieved through their behaviour, which will then meet their emotional needs. Just telling pupils off or issuing sanctions for inappropriate behaviours has little effect, except, perhaps, to persuade the child not to get caught next time! Teachers using strategies that give the child clear reasons as to why a behaviour is inappropriate, together with alternative ways to respond positively, invariably achieve successful outcomes.

4. Transparency in communications

A consistent finding in the research mentioned above is the degree to which clear, consistent and coherent communication is a factor in meeting the social and emotional needs of children and young people (see Cole *et al.* 1998; Daniels *et al.* 1998). Teachers advocating a range of contrasting approaches all agree that being consistent with behaviour management is integral to successful whole-school approaches. This consistency is best ensured when the school's behaviour policy is clearly set and agreed by both the staff and the children. By developing this consistency across the school, a transparency in communications follows where 'what is said' becomes 'what is meant'. This culture provides clear boundaries for all learners and leads to consistency regarding actions and reactions in any given situation. This, in turn, supports the development of a caring school ethos that meets the needs of pupils with social and emotional difficulties (Visser, Cole and Daniels 2002).

5. Empathy and equity

Empathy is the ability to see the world through the eyes of the child and to understand the world from their perspective. Empathy requires a degree of emotional commitment to the wellbeing of the child, and asks repeatedly, 'Why do I think that this child behaved in this way – and what does this mean for the approaches I should now use?'

Being empathic does not mean excusing inappropriate behaviour or challenging outbursts; rather, it provides an understanding as to why these outbursts have occurred. It also provides the basis upon which equitable and fair decisions can be made and learners can begin to feel valued and understood.

Approaches in the classroom that are devoid of empathy seem to have less effect than those that encourage the development of robust empathy with the children and young people (Visser *et al.* 2002). However, developing empathy in the classroom is not as easy as some would imply. The case histories of most learners with socio-emotional difficulties reveal significant family trauma, poverty in their range of positive experiences, a paucity of expectations, an absence of the emotional capacity to make and sustain relationships and, all too often, the experience of physical, emotional and/or sexual abuse (Fortin and Bigras 1997; Hayden 2007). Though some teachers may have personal experience of one or more of these, few will have experienced them in the depth and range experienced by the children themselves. And yet the capacity to place oneself in the position of a child experiencing SEMH difficulties represents an *eternal verity* when considering approaches that meet emotional needs effectively.

6. Boundaries and challenge

All approaches within the literature speak of the need for structure and, more particularly, the need to provide clear boundaries for learners with SEMH needs. This is hardly surprising, given that it is often the inability to behave and display emotions appropriately and within boundaries that most frequently identifies the learner as being 'difficult to control'. The boundaries need to be set by the teacher and must have a flexibility that bends but never breaks (Cole *et al.* 1998), for approaches that have a rigid structure are unlikely to be effective. As Royer (2001) points out, the inflexible approach fails because it ends up identifying all difficulties as 'nails', because the only tool in the teacher's kit is a hammer! Bentley (1997) saw this *eternal verity* as being vital if learners with socio-emotional problems are to avoid being marginalised within schools yet further, the net result being that they fall behind academically and become even more difficult to manage.

With the clear boundaries should come high, achievable expectations of behaviour and educational achievement (Cole *et al.* 1998; Daniels *et al.* 1998; Ofsted 1999). The therapeutic effect of being set challenging achievable targets, even when initially a great deal of support is required, is noted by Wilson and Evans (1980) and others (Cooper 1996; DCSF 2005; Greenhalgh 1994). Since 1999 Ofsted has reported low expectations in relation to pupils' achievements as a contributory cause in many schools 'causing concern' or with 'serious weaknesses' (Ofsted 1999a).

7. *Building positive relationships*

Bentley (1997) writes that 'social networks are powerful determinants of an individual's life chances', and goes on to indicate that having access to a range of adults as role models is an indispensable resource for children and young people. As a beginning teacher, the relationships that you develop with each individual child will shape the way in which they respond to you, respond to your guidance and respond to their own learning. Daniels (2001) and Ryan (2001) suggest that the ability to develop genuine caring and learning relationships, and knowing where to go to make them, is an important skill for learners to acquire if they are to be integrated members of their community. Children and young people with socio-emotional issues are not good at making and sustaining positive relationships, and they constantly test out the adults they come across (Laslett 1977). They will challenge you, too, and see if you will leave them or reject them as other adults have done in the past. Porter (2000) suggests that successful relationships in the classroom provide emotional safety and protection, personal involvement and trust, plus an acceptance from others. If you can promote this *eternal verity* in your classroom, you will be enhancing the wellbeing of all your learners.

8. *Humour*

As Cole *et al.* (1998), Porter (2000) and Visser (2000) point out, having a sense of humour has been seen as a vital component in any approach to managing behaviour in the classroom. Humour is rarely mentioned in descriptions of strategies and approaches and yet, as one study (Cole *et al.* 1998) found, it is consistently placed as one of the top three characteristics of effective teachers working with pupils with socio-emotional difficulties. Fovet (2009) provides a useful insight into the mechanisms of humour, noting that it is a complex area of human communication rooted in subjective standards, making investigation difficult. He notes from his study that the receptivity of students to humour is dependent upon 'genuine' positive relationships between students and staff. Children are often positive about learning when it is seen as fun, and that does not mean that it lacks rigour. Rather, it is that difficulties and challenges in learning can be overcome by engendering a sense of fun in doing so. Learning doesn't have to be painful!

The range of eternal verities

Teachers now work in an age where there has been an information explosion, and gone are some of the old certainties of testing the veracity of what we are told. The pattern, shape and accessibility of information is radically changing. If schools and teachers are to develop and adapt their abilities to meet the behavioural and learning needs of pupils, then having a set of *eternal verities* may provide a sound base on which to test the information available, rather than just relying on the latest social media quote or website that purports to have the answer!

But are these the only *eternal verities*? Greenhalgh (1994) lists six characteristics he saw as important, while Laslett (1977) gives 17. Ofsted (1999) indicate six features consistently associated with good practice, while the recently published behaviour management report (Bennett 2016) suggests that 'Relationships, Routines and Responses (strategies)' are the key components of managing classroom behaviour effectively. All these accord with the eight listed above, differing in emphasis and range of terminology rather than content. There remains, however, a lack of empirical quantitative evidence to support this qualitative consensus. Cooper *et al.* (2009), completing a meta-analysis of a wide range of reported research, point to a lack of replicable evidence to support approaches deemed to be good practice and delivering positive outcomes.

Final thoughts

Educationalists have long had the task of managing the behaviour of children and young people in schools. The evidence base for the effectiveness of many of the approaches utilised is questionable (Dyson 2001), and there is a need to halt the cycle of 'wheel reinvention' while establishing a set of *eternal verities* that may guide practice across time, allowing the fads to come and go. Recent analysis by Visser (2014) shows an ever-increasing listing of terms to describe children's behaviours, and yet no amount of labelling will negate the need for teachers to use their independent and professional judgements when responding to a child's behaviour (Pirrie 2001). It is to be hoped that the eight *eternal verities* that feature here and that reflect a range of approaches over time may provide the basis upon which the beginning teacher makes a judgement as to the veracity of approaches on offer.

▰ REFLECTION POINTS ▰▰▰▰▰▰

1. Reflecting on the eight *eternal verities*, are there others you would add and any you would disregard?

2. To what extent do you think that the verities described in this chapter contribute to a sense of 'belonging', which is the 'true' meaning of inclusion?

3. In planning a particular lesson, which of these verities plays a part in your planning and which in your 'natural' delivery of the lesson?

4. How do the children and young people you teach know the behaviours that support their learning?

Bibliography

Ayers, H., Clarke, D. and Murray, A. (2000) *Perspectives on Behaviour: A Practical Guide to Effective Interventions for Teachers*. London: David Fulton.

Bentley, T. (1997) *Learning to Belong*. Demos Collection, 12, pp.44–46.

Bennett, T. (2016) *Developing Behaviour Management Content for Initial Teacher Training*. London: Department for Education.

Bowlby, J. (1969) *Attachment and Loss: Vol. 1. Attachment*. New York: Basic Books.

Bowlby, J. (1973) *Attachment and Loss: Vol. 2. Separation, Anxiety and Anger*. New York: Basic Books.

Cole, T., Visser, J. and Upton, G. (1998) *Effective Schooling for Pupils with Emotional and Behavioural Difficulties*. London: David Fulton.

Cooper, P. (1996) 'Giving it a name: The value of descriptive categories in educational approaches to emotional and behavioural difficulties.' *Support for Learning 4*, 146–159.

Cooper, P. (2001) *We Can Work it Out: What Works in Educating Pupils with Social, Emotional and Behavioural Difficulties Outside Mainstream Classrooms*. Barkingside: Barnardo's.

Cooper, P., Jacobs, B. and Martin, M. (2009) *Caring to Make a Difference: Educating Children and Young People with Social, Emotional and Behavioural Difficulties*. Dublin: National Council for Special Education.

Daniels, H. (2001) *Vygotsky and Pedagogy*. London: Routledge.

Daniels, H., Visser, J., Cole, T. and de Reybekill, N. (1998) *Emotional and Behavioural Difficulties in Mainstream Schools*. Research Report RR90. London: Department for Education and Employment.

DCSF (Department for Children, Schools and Families) (2005) *Social and Emotional Aspects of Learning: Improving Behaviour, Improving Learning*. London.

Dyson, A. (2001) 'Special need education as the way to equity: An alternative approach.' *Support for Learning 16*, 3, 99–104.

Elton, Lord (1989) *Discipline in Schools: Report of Committee of Enquiry Chaired by Lord Elton*. London: HMSO.

ERIC (1997) *Common Features of School Wide Behaviour Management*. ERIC Research Papers 1, 1.

Fortin, L. and Bigras, M. (1997) 'Risk factors exposing young children to problems.' *Emotional and Behavioural Difficulties 2*, 1, 3–14.

Fovet, F. (2009) 'The use of humour in classroom interventions with students with social, emotional and behavioural difficulties.' *Emotional and Behavioural Difficulties 14*, 4, 275–289.

Greenhalgh, P. (1994) *Emotional Growth and Learning.* London: Routledge.

Hayden, C. (2007) *Children in Trouble: The Role of Families, Schools and Communities.* Basingstoke: Palgrave/Macmillan.

Kauffman, J. (2001) *Characteristics of Emotional and Behavioural Disorders of Children and Youth* (7th edn). Upper Saddle River, NJ: Merrill Prentice Hall.

Laslett, R. (1977) *The Education of Maladjusted Children.* London: Crosby, Lockwood Staples Publishing.

Laslett, R. (1999) 'Respecting the past: Regarding the present.' *Emotional and Behavioural Difficulties 3*, 1, 5–11.

Laslett, R., Cooper, P., Maras, P. and Rimmer, A. (1998) *Changing Perceptions: Emotional and Behavioural Difficulties Since 1945.* Maidstone: AWCEBD.

Maslow, A.H. (1943) 'A theory of human motivation.' *Psychological Review 50*, 370–396.

Maslow, A.H. (1954) *Motivation and Personality.* New York: Harper & Row.

Ofsted (1999) *Principles into Practice: Effective Education for Pupils with EBD.* London: Ofsted.

Ofsted (1999a) *Lessons Learnt from Special Measures.* London: Ofsted.

Ofsted (2005) *Managing Challenging Behaviour.* London: Ofsted.

Pirrie, A. (2001) 'Evidence-based practice in education: The best medicine.' *British Journal of Educational Studies 49*, 2, 124–136.

Porter, L. (2000) *Behaviour in Schools: Theory and Practice for Teachers.* Buckingham: Open University Press.

Rodway, S. (1993) 'Children's rights: Children's needs. Is there a conflict?' *Therapeutic Care 2*, 2, 375–391.

Royer, E. (2001) 'The Education of Students with EBD: One Size Does Not Fit All.' in J. Visser, H. Daniels and T. Cole (eds) *International Perspectives on Inclusive Education: Emotional and Behavioural Difficulties in Mainstream Schools* (pp.129–142). Amsterdam: JAI.

Ryan, K. (2001) *Strengthening the Safety Net: Home Schools Can Help Youth with Emotional and Behavioural Needs.* Burrington, VT: School Research, University of Vermont.

Steer, A. (2005) *Learning Behaviour. The Report of the Group on School Behaviour and Discipline.* Nottingham: Department for Education and Skills.

Steer, A. (2009) *The Steer Report: Learning Behaviour. Lessons Learnt.* London: Department for Children, Schools and Families.

Visser, J. (2000) *Managing Behaviour in Classrooms.* London: David Fulton.

Visser, J. (2014) *Transforming Troubled Lives.* London: Routledge.

Visser, J., Cole, T. and Daniels, H. (2002) 'Inclusion for the difficult to include.' *Support for Learning 17*, 1, 23–26.

Whelan, R.J. (1998) *Emotional and Behavioural Disorders: A 25-Year Focus.* Denver, CO: Love Publishers.

Wilson, M. and Evans, K. (1980) *Education for Disturbed Pupils.* Schools Council Working Paper 65. London; Methuen.

19

Supporting the Emotional Development of Teenagers

JANICE CAHILL

This is life, a wonderful gift.
Accept it, embrace it.
It starts with a new day, wake up and greet it.

Year 11 student, Pendlebury Centre Pupil Referral Unit

Five consecutive Ofsted inspections (2003, 2007, 2008, 2013, 2017) have recognised the Pendlebury Centre in Stockport, UK, as being an 'Outstanding' Pupil Referral Unit (PRU) for secondary-aged students with social, emotional and mental health (SEMH) needs. Our success in re-engaging students and helping them to return to mainstream school has been identified by Ofsted as a core strength. This chapter discusses the values of the centre, and how every mainstream school and every individual teacher can create a climate for themselves that promotes positive attachment and success.

Despite the bravado that often accompanies their stage of development, adolescents are sensitive and easily influenced by the world and people around them (Steinberg 2008). Their sensitivity activates strong emotions and, as these emotions are not always rationally rooted or rationally expressed, a young person's response can often present as an over-reaction to any given situation. However, to the adolescent who is experiencing rapid physical and emotional change, the world can seem both daunting and hostile – and this 'over-reaction' is symptomatic of this natural confusion, uncertainty and fear.

While most young people experience a degree of emotional instability during their school years, many are resilient enough to cope with these setbacks, using established protective factors that might include family support, peer support and personal factors.

Personal factors that promote resilience in adolescents might include experiencing secure attachment in the home, having an outgoing temperament and/or having a positive attitude (DfE 2014). However, for some teenagers, their life experiences and personal predispositions undermine their resilience and they become disaffected and unable to participate in school life. Their lack of emotional skills and reduced emotional capacity can affect their behaviour, their cognitive development, socialisation skills and their ability to make and sustain friendships.

The Department for Education (DfE) guidance *Mental Health and Behaviour in Schools* (2014) sets out a range of risk factors regarding adolescent mental health, and these factors may be within the child (e.g. communication difficulties, difficult temperament, academic failure, low self-esteem) and/or within the family (e.g. overt parental conflict including domestic violence, family breakdown) including where children are taken into care or adopted.

For many students referred to the Pendlebury Centre, the risks outlined by the DfE (2014) have already been played out, and their attachment to school reflects the poor attachment they have to most adults in their lives. Many of our students have lost any sense of being 'lovable'. They often do not like themselves or 'don't care', and their behaviour is communicating a simple message: 'I am not lovable – so don't try.' They have lost confidence in what the adults say and do because this is what their experience has taught them. Many live in families where the traditional family unit is not present, and they struggle to see where they belong. By the time they get into school they feel that they have little to lose and will therefore systematically destroy relationships by kicking out or withdrawing before they can develop into something positive, for losing a close relationship can be painful (too painful) and this cannot be allowed to be repeated. Why not protect yourself by smashing every attempt by an adult to get close?

This would explain a range of adolescent responses to support from well-meaning professionals. The reality is that for many teenagers, the need to feel in control and to self-protect overwhelms the need for adult guidance and support.

And so how does the Pendlebury Centre begin to build bridges across this socio-emotional divide?

We asked our Year 11 students (aged 15–16) to provide some advice for beginning teachers on what they feel are the qualities needed to be a good teacher. Based on the student responses to three key questions, let us explore the theory and practice of the Pendlebury Centre.

Three key questions
Q1: What makes a good teacher?

Year 11 response:

- A good teacher needs to be patient and firm, but should not shout. The teacher needs to be inspiring and to captivate us so we feel we want to learn, not 'have to'.

- A good teacher knows how to control a class while still maintaining a fun and happy learning atmosphere.

- A good teacher doesn't insult your capabilities.

- A good teacher is someone who is more bothered about your learning than your grades.

To promote the skills of the 'good teacher', the Pendlebury Centre supports the teaching team in developing a range of skills. *Staff resilience* is important, and you need to be confident in yourself as a teacher – and in the organisation of your classroom. Experience will teach you many things but, as a beginning teacher, planning carefully and delivering lessons with pace and passion will maximise your chances of early success.

A sense of humour is essential, and learning not to take things too seriously is central to longevity in the profession. Teaching is a great career, and children are fun. We are privileged to be leading the learning of the young people in our care – so enjoy it.

The good teacher working in the area of SEMH difficulties must ensure *a balance of structure and nurture.* Key adults need to put in boundaries so that everyone is kept safe – for example, not sharing personal phone numbers or responding to crises outside school time. If the family has a crisis, then it is social care and not the teacher who should be providing support late at night. The key adult needs to stay outside the child's crisis and be a fresh, positive and neutral force at 9am each morning.

At Pendlebury, the rule is 'never shout', and staff are required to develop *the ability to remain calm*. Students are far more adept at shouting than you, and once you model their behaviour, they are controlling the 'tennis match'. Game, set and match to them!

In addition, *being a team player* is central to the role. Teachers cannot work in isolation, so be prepared to ask for help when you need it. As a beginning teacher, this will be inevitable and is not a sign of weakness – indeed, quite the contrary. At the same time, you may be in a position to offer support or specific skills to a colleague. Do this willingly and reciprocation will follow.

At the Pendlebury Centre, *a positive sense of self* is valued. Know who you are and be proud of it, but recognise your own failings and how that contributes to the person you are. Be careful, however, as arrogance can be a close relative. With that in mind, do not assume that all advice on your teaching is a criticism. We all need to be able to accept that not everything we do is right, and the aspect of good teaching illustrated here is *the ability to listen to and act on advice*.

It is important to understand the difference between sympathy and empathy, and staff at Pendlebury are encouraged to reflect on this distinction. Sympathy is to feel sorrow or pity for the hardships that a student may have encountered, while empathy is putting yourself 'in the shoes' of that student. *Empathy is different to sympathy*, and this should be made clear.

Sometimes even the best laid lessons go wrong in the classroom. We cannot always anticipate the mood or atmosphere that the students will bring and so, ensure that you have a bag of 'tricks', diversions and quick-fix activities to hand. If needs be, be ready to play a game for 5 minutes before bringing the students back to the learning activity. For the good teacher, *imagination and resourcefulness* are key.

In addition to the skills set out above, *restorative questioning* is used by all staff at the centre and has become a common language at Pendlebury.

Restorative questioning differs from standard practice in that it seeks to establish not only 'what happened' but also explores the thoughts and feelings of those who undertook the act. There are four discrete stages associated with restorative questioning, and these are undertaken in the following order at the centre:

Restorative questioning stage 1. 'What?' Establishing the facts

- Give the young person speaking your full attention – open with a simple question, 'What has happened?' or 'What has been happening?'

- Repeat the conversation back to them, in their own words, as often as possible, to confirm content and accuracy.

- Check/clarify any particular aspects.

Restorative questioning stage 2. 'How?' Focusing on feelings

- Move the discussion on to feelings, e.g. 'How did you feel when…?' 'How did that affect you?' 'It looks like that made you really angry.'

Restorative questioning stage 3. 'Why?'

- Create some links, if necessary, to other similar situations, e.g. 'Why do you think this happened?' 'Has this happened before? Why?'

Restorative questioning stage 4. Repairing the harm

- Move to a solution-based conversation, e.g. 'How might we move forward?' 'Who has been affected?' 'How can the harm be repaired?'

An additional approach employed by staff at the Pendlebury Centre will be to challenge negative interpretations or slumps into hopelessness that students may exhibit. Staff will challenge this in a non-threatening and subtle manner by *reframing* situations or crises, for example:

Student: 'This is hopeless…' 'I can't do it…' 'I'm rubbish…' 'There is nothing I can do…'

Staff: 'I know it seems hopeless to you right now but…' or 'I understand you can't find anything that would fix this easily but…'

As a good teacher at the Pendlebury Centre, it is important to engage in *careful listening* rather than jumping to a reaction. Avoid 'magical cure' and 'quick-fix' thinking, and recognise that you are part of a multi-agency community sending a clear and consistent message to students with SEMH difficulties. The clear message to the students is:

...you have agency, the harm done can be repaired, you can grow and change – you can succeed.

Q2: What is different about the Pendlebury Centre?

Year 11 response:

- People are a lot more understanding.

- We all actually care about each other.

- You don't feel as alone here.

- It's like a massive family!

The values and principles of the Pendlebury Centre are informed by empathy, attunement and attachment theory. The students are accepted for who they are, and there is an acknowledgment of the difficulties they might face, including the sense of self-worth that may have been lost over time. Staff will strive to help the students recover their own sense of self-worth, to live in peace with themselves, and to understand that they are, indeed, 'loveable'.

At Pendlebury, emotional growth and learning is understood to be developmental, following a natural path based on early life experiences (see Figure 19.1). Emotional growth begins with relationships and finishes with relationships. In this sense, quality relationships form the bedrock of positive and healthy child development, and Figure 19.1 illustrates how thinking, literacy, numeracy and complex adaptive behaviours emanate from this foundation.

Attachment theory has been critically evaluated in great detail by the preceding chapters of this book. Suffice to say that most of the young people in society are (more or less) securely attached and have had a relatively positive experience of key relationships in a 'good enough', nurturing home environment. They come into school with the developmental perquisites set out in Figure 19.1 largely in place. School will not necessarily be a perfect experience for them – they will encounter risks, conflict, challenges and the unknown – but they do so with a level of emotional awareness and social skills that enable them to cope. At the end of a difficult or exhilarating day, they can return to 'the nest' for sustenance, approval, warmth and recuperation.

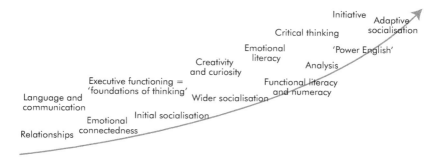

Figure 19.1: 'Learning to Learn' – How it all begins with relationships/attachment

Source: Reproduced with permission from Matt Grant, HumansNotRobots.co.uk (2016)

But there is also a significant minority of young people who are insecurely attached and who have not fully developed the prerequisite skills to face the world outside of the home. For some, they do not have a safe, nurturing base to return to where they can rest, recuperate or experience warmth and positive regard. As a result, they can find themselves caught up in a swirl of low-level conflict that does not cease. From time to time – and sometimes on a daily basis – this unceasing, low-level tension can erupt into open conflict – and we know from our own experiences that such conflicts are inherently draining for all concerned. This drain on energy reduces clear thinking and resilience, and so the cycle perpetuates.

With the young people caught up in this spiral of negative relationships, we have to do something to break this cycle. In a sense, our schools – be they mainstream, specialist or PRUs – have to offer some kind of provision that can replace aspects of the 'nest' or safe base. This does not mean simply trying to be a young person's friend or saviour, but rather offering a place and practice that provides the safe base (including missing aspects of the home) as well as modelling good attachment for the students to witness and experience.

At the Pendlebury Centre, we aim to provide students with a supportive, consistent educational environment that promotes positive mental health alongside academic achievement. The centre seeks to develop social skills, independence, self-motivation and respect for others that will pave the way for student's successful reintegration or transition into an appropriate mainstream educational environment.

The mission statement of the Pendlebury Centre can be summarised by the '5 PCs', set out below.

Positive Contribution

At its most basic level, the expectation in mainstream schools is that the contribution made by students will be to learn and, specifically, to achieve academic results. Running alongside this, there may be a contribution – expressed through the school's behaviour policy, and extra-curricular programme – that the young person makes to the school community. Collectively, these student contributions shape the overall success, reputation and 'feel' of the school.

For many of our students, a cycle of failure has meant that they have developed perceptions and habits that lead them to only ever contribute to school in a negative way. For example, a student who has experienced difficulty with the academic demands in a lesson may begin to try and gain attention and affirmation through more negative means, or may simply try to avoid the academic demands through disruption.

The school behaviour policy may then be applied as they move from one busy lesson to the next, from one busy day to another. They may develop a reputation. Teachers might, very naturally and understandably, become frustrated with them – apprehensive at their arrival to lessons and perhaps also a little too reactive. The student then perceives this and reacts accordingly.

The work of the PRU involves taking the student out of this situation. It does not necessarily involve going over every detail of their past 'transgressions', but it does involve identifying some of the habits the student has adopted, and trying to get 'under their skin' to identify any underlying difficulties and triggers. Our work involves re-modelling positive contributions to the community as a whole, and working intensively to bring about calmness and recovering an enthusiasm for learning.

Positive Communication

Many of the students at the Pendlebury Centre have times when they are feeling anxious and angry. We stress that this is a normal emotional experience, but the key point for development is how we express this. There is work to be done around lessening anxiety and anger as a day-to-day experience, but equally it is about accepting we all feel worried at times, we all feel aggrieved at times – and it is how we explain this to others with a view to moving forward.

Staff themselves are a model of this 'communicative approach' to difficult times – by the very fact we work in a school environment, we operate in the classroom and corridors where there are situations that we find troubling, be that disruption, aggression or non-cooperation. We therefore place emphasis on communicating calmly yet assertively with our students.

Where there have been difficult or complex incidents of conflict, we use more specialist practices such as restorative justice meetings (Hopkins 2003), fierce conversations (Scott 2003) and comic strip conversations (Gray 1994). We try to break the cycle, which sometimes occurs in busy mainstream schools, whereby students – and staff – 'bounce' from conflict to conflict within a reflective dialogue in-between.

To achieve this, there needs to be an excellence in team working and cooperation. There is no such thing as 'ploughing your own furrow' in a PRU, and positive cooperation is just as vital in mainstream school settings.

Positive Cooperation

Good team working is central to our practice, and the recommendations of Nancarrow *et al.* (2013) are adhered to closely at the Pendlebury Centre. These are of great relevance to mainstream settings and include the need for:

- clear leadership, working on the ground with the rest of staff and avoiding 'ivory tower' leadership

- a clear set of values and 'moral purpose' to the work being undertaken, rather than simply a business model, for example

- planned and routinely implemented facilities for all participants within the team to 'answer back' and to question decisions rationally and constructively – rather than just taking orders

- a diverse mix of skills, competencies – and personalities – rather than a one-dimensional 'type' of operative.

The mix of professional backgrounds among staff at the centre includes teachers with mainstream training, teaching assistants with vocational training and therapists with medical backgrounds. Coalescing this diverse mix of skills into an effective team for the students requires positive cooperation from all parties.

Positive Creativity

A diverse team that is drawn from a range of professional backgrounds promotes vibrant and creative thinking. For our students, the very fact they have arrived in a PRU indicates strongly that what has been on offer historically has not worked. For the team, there is an ongoing discussion that asks 'What are we going to do that is different for this student?' 'Are we going to repeat past interventions but simply on a smaller scale?' Or 'Are we going to review and re-shape the planned intervention completely?'

The creative solution must relate directly to the student – their needs, interests and strengths. On this basis, the learning is tailored to meet those needs in a safe and supportive environment.

In *A Kestrel for a Knave* (Hines 1968), we see a fictional example of this approach where a teacher engages with a disaffected teenager through his interest in falconry. The teaching approach is to cognitively relocate to where the student is and not the other way around. The creative process can then develop the learning from this starting point, whether in a PRU or mainstream setting

Positive Confidence

The final of the 'PCs' – confidence or self-esteem – represents the culmination of the previous four processes undertaken over time. We understand that confidence is not a final or complete state and that self-esteem can wax and wane. This is natural and inevitable. However, at the Pendlebury Centre, we draw on the work of Seymour Epstein (1917–2011) to help guide our practice. Epstein broke down the concept of 'confidence' into the following areas:

- Global confidence, that is, how we feel about ourselves in general, in terms of worthiness and competency.

- Specific domains of confidence, that is, how we feel about definable areas of our lives in terms of worthiness and competency such as learning, intimate relationships, relationships with authority, sports driving etc.

- Situational confidence, that is, how we feel about very specific situations that draw on these definable areas in terms of worthiness and competency. This could apply to discussion groups, interviews, sitting an exam etc.

Our aim is to build the confidence and self-esteem of our students at every opportunity, primarily in the situation of the classroom, the corridor, and the school social room. We understand the limitations of our power, but by developing the confidence of our students in specific domains and situations, we believe that we are contributing to the whole – or global – outlook of the young person in question.

At the Pendlebury Centre we aim to promote students' self-esteem by providing opportunities for them to fully engage with their learning and to use their abilities to the utmost in pursuit of something that they themselves value. Reasoner (2010) suggests that:

> Attempts by pro-esteem advocates to encourage self-pride in students solely by reason of their uniqueness as human beings will fail if feelings of well-being are not accompanied by well-doing. It is only when students engage in *personally meaningful endeavours for which they can be justifiably proud* that self-confidence grows, and it is this growing self-assurance that in turn triggers further achievement.

In addition to the focus on 'well-doing', the centre's approach is also informed by Branden (2008) who argues that if a teacher treats students with respect, avoids ridicule and deals with everyone fairly and justly, then that teacher is supporting both self-esteem and the process of learning and mastering challenges. For such a teacher, self-esteem is tied to reality and not to faking reality. Conversely, if a teacher tries to nurture self-esteem through empty praise that bears no relationship to the students' actual accomplishments (i.e. dropping all objective standards, over-simplifying tasks or allowing young people to believe that the only passport to self-esteem is their 'uniqueness'), then self-esteem can be undermined, along with academic achievement.

The '5 PCs' that are set out above focus on positivity, growth and the chance to change. At Pendlebury, students may get a second, third and even a fourth chance to start again. This does not make the centre a 'soft option' but demonstrates the centre's tenacity, for we do not accept excuses. Indeed, our record suggests that we rarely fail, and that most young people and their families come to accept the help and support we offer (in time).

When a baby bird falls out of the nest, the instinct should be to protect and nurture it until it is ready to fly – and that is our approach to meeting the socio-emotional needs of our students.

Q3: What kind of classroom promotes good behaviour and learning?

Year 11 response:

- A teacher needs to understand how you learn.

- A teacher needs to understand how hard it is to be a teenager.

- A teacher needs to show respect for our individual needs.

At Pendlebury, the promotion of good behaviour and learning is central to the aims and ethos of the centre. All staff are encouraged to keep both voices and body language grounded and calm at all times. Students can spot a communication of weakness very quickly, and will pounce equally as quickly. It is important that staff present the student with two or three choices, rather than engaging in control battles in the classroom. Once the options have been offered, do not then negotiate further, but be firm regarding the offer made.

.   In terms of the language used, employ 'Let's…' rather than 'Don't…', and give prior warning and preparation if there are expected changes to the daily routine. Students with autism or who are very anxious will struggle with change, so providing them with as much warning as possible and support during these changes will be important.

Staff will provide supportive scaffolding for tasks requiring organisation. This builds confidence in the students' own abilities and allows staff to see if they are having difficulties. Activities are designed to give opportunities for kinaesthetic learning whenever possible, and are broken down into bite-sized chunks. Concentration can be an issue for many students, and activities that are 'chunked' are often more achievable.

In the Pendlebury classroom, the teacher will check back on student understanding by asking them to repeat instructions back to the staff member. This technique is a two-way process as it confirms that both teacher and student are equally clear on what the expectations are and that no misunderstanding has taken place. Staff try to maintain an atmosphere of mutual respect at all times. The traditional use of 'discipline' and sanctions is discouraged as this may trigger negative memories from the past and be interpreted by the student as a form of rejection.

To meet the needs of students, staff will put problems into perspective for them and offer a form of emotional 'containment' for the anxieties being experienced. Staff are encouraged to remember that they might not *have* the solution and might not *be* the solution. By listening carefully and then asking students questions informed by restorative approaches, staff will seek to empower young people in taking control of outcomes for themselves. This form of 'co-regulation' is a key feature of practice at Pendlebury, and promotes teamwork, collaboration, respect and solution-focused outcomes.

Staff at the Pendlebury Centre understand the importance of mirroring, modelling and keeping students 'in mind'. Students will imitate your behaviours (both good and bad!), and it is incumbent upon staff to set high standards and model ways of responding and managing challenges effectively. Letting students know that you are thinking of them, even though you may be in different parts of the school, maintains the relationship over space and time. This can be vital for some students (and for some, this may be their first experience of being 'held in mind' by someone else).

Staff at the centre are always sensitive to possible emotional triggers within the curriculum content. We cannot always know how emotions and memories might be triggered by the lessons being delivered, but by knowing our students, we will avoid subject content that is difficult for them to hear or difficult for them to reflect upon.

Looking after yourself – professional resilience and the beginning teacher

Everyone has mental health needs, and within the school environment all members of the community should be treated equally. The needs of the school leaders and school staff are as important as that of the students, and to get this balance right is everyone's responsibility. Teaching is a tough job, but it is equally the best job in the world. Just having excellent subject matter is not enough. You have to like children! This may sound obvious, but we have all witnessed teachers who do not like children and who see the post as a simply a job when it is so much more than that. Teaching is a vocation and it can completely take over your life – if you let it. That is why the work–life balance and the self-care of your own emotional and mental wellbeing is also important. Getting the balance can be tricky as there are times in the academic year where deadlines have to be met and home life has to come second. So how can you keep yourself emotionally well and ready for each day?

The team at Pendlebury are asked to consider the following:

1. Remember to leave your personal problems at the school gate. Students expect 100 per cent, and if you feel you cannot deliver, make other arrangements. Being a teacher is like being an actor on a stage and the classroom of students are your audience. They expect and deserve the best performance you can give. If you are in a bad mood, had a heavy night out on the town with friends or an argument with your partner, leave it at the school gate! You have no right to impose that mood on your classes. This is the comment that has stayed with me throughout my career, and one I use to staff at Pendlebury as their headteacher.

2. Keep yourself emotionally and physically strong – use your support mechanisms and always build some free time into your day.

3. Implement an effective work–life balance. Ensure that you pursue a hobby (and protect that evening/time with determination); actively create times where you do not log on to emails or computers, and create protected family or personal time (e.g. Sundays or Sunday afternoons).

4. All staff should receive above and beyond in terms of training around safeguarding and behaviour management – 'Team Teach' and 'Responses to Self-Harm' are two examples.

5. Make use of restorative approaches to resolve conflicts, help build empathetic responses and repair relationships when they have broken down.

6. Develop an understanding of your own emotional state and avoid casting yourself as saviour!

7. Tenacity – never give up!

8. Resilience – build up your responses to student behaviour and attitudes (that can be hurtful at times).

9. Peer-to-peer support – remember you are not the only one to have a bad lesson or day. Build up a support network within the staff team.

10. Sense of humour – essential for survival.

Final thoughts: the impact we have

What impact can we have on the emotional development and attachment of the young people who walk into our classroom every day and look to us for guidance? All staff who work in the Pendlebury Centre are presented with a small card during their induction that contains the following observation made by teacher, psychologist and author, Haim Ginott (1975):

> I have come to a frightening conclusion. I am the decisive element in the classroom.
>
> It is my personal approach that creates the climate. It is my daily mood that makes the weather.
>
> As a teacher I possess tremendous power – to make a child's life miserable or joyous.
>
> I can be a tool of torture – or an instrument of inspiration.
>
> I can humiliate or humour, hurt or heal.
>
> In all situations it is my response that decides
>
> Whether a crisis will be escalated or de-escalated.
>
> And a child humanised or de-humanised.

That is the impact you can have in the classroom – prepare to use that power wisely.

REFLECTION POINTS

1. Imagine you are the headteacher. Choose one piece of advice that you would give to a new teacher and explain why you feel this would make a difference.

2. Make the student know that you are not a robot and have a personality, because students are more likely to comply if you seem friendly and reliable

3. You won't succeed all the time. Teaching young people is not easy, and being trained doesn't mean you will be successful all of the time. Remember why you are a teacher, and what school was like for you.

4. Remember that we are all individuals and we are all different, but we should get an equal say in the things we do.

5. Some of the children can be challenging, so learn to deal with them as calmly and easily as can be done – but don't be a pushover.

6. Be firm and enjoyable, but don't be a pushover and let the students dictate what you do.

Bibliography

Branden, N. (2008) *Six Pillars of Self Esteem*. New York: Bantam.

DfE (Department for Education) (2014) *Mental Health and Behaviour in Schools*. London: DfE.

Ginott, H. (1975) *Teacher and Child: A Book for Parents and Teachers*. New York: Macmillan.

Gray, C. (1994) *Comic Strip Conversations: Illustrated Interactions That Teach Conversation Skills to Students with Autism and Related Disorders*. Michigan, MI: Future Horizons.

Hines, B. (1968) *A Kestrel for a Knave*. London: Penguin.

Hopkins, B. (2003) *Just Schools: A Whole School Approach to Restorative Justice*. London: Jessica Kingsley Publishing.

Nancarrow, S.A., Booth, A., Ariss, S., Smith, T., Enderby, P. and Roots, A. (2013) 'Ten principles of good interdisciplinary team work.' *Human Resources for Health 11*, 19.

Ofsted (2003) *The Pendlebury Centre*. Available at https://reports.ofsted.gov.uk/inspection-reports/find-inspection-report/provider/ELS/106022.

Ofsted (2007) *The Pendlebury Centre*. Available at https://reports.ofsted.gov.uk/inspection-reports/find-inspection-report/provider/ELS/106022.

Ofsted (2008) *The Pendlebury Centre*. Available at https://reports.ofsted.gov.uk/inspection-reports/find-inspection-report/provider/ELS/106022.

Ofsted (2013) *The Pendlebury Centre*. Available at https://reports.ofsted.gov.uk/inspection-reports/find-inspection-report/provider/ELS/106022.

Ofsted (2017) *The Pendlebury Centre*. Available at https://reports.ofsted.gov.uk/inspection-reports/find-inspection-report/provider/ELS/106022.

Reasoner, R.W. (2010) *Review of Self-esteem Research*. Fulton, MD: Fulton Books Publishing.

Scott, S. (2003) *Fierce Conversations: Achieving Success in Work and in Life, One Conversation at a Time*. London: Piatkus.

Steinberg, L. (2008) 'A social neuroscience perspective on adolescent risk-taking.' *Developmental Review 28*, 1, 78–106. doi:10.1016/j.dr.2007.08.002.

20

Conclusion: Drawing Together the Threads

DAVID COLLEY AND PAUL COOPER

Understanding the emotional development and attachment needs of the children and young people that we work with in the classroom is central to our work as teachers. For this reason, the Department for Education (DfE) (2016) is recommending that all providers of Initial Teacher Training (ITT) ensure that trainee teachers are well versed in key aspects of child development and the impact of unmet attachment needs in the classroom.

To second-guess why a learner is behaving in the way they are is to miss the point. This may be due to inattentive care in the early years but equally it may not – and this is something that we cannot really know. What we can know (and develop as a series of professional skills) is how we respond to the presentation of social, emotional and attachment difficulties in the classroom, whatever its basis. For this reason, it is important that you learn about how attachment works, and how this knowledge can inform relationship building and the promotion of emotional security in the classroom.

For the majority of children and young people, their journey towards emotional maturity will be closely allied to their cognitive, social and physical development. From birth to adulthood, this journey will feature periods of rapid growth and also periods of gentle consolidation. Experiences of success and failure, understanding and confusion, elation and despair will all be close companions as children move through the natural and inevitable stages of human development. For these children, the attentive care and support that they receive from their carer(s) will be 'good enough' to get by and to develop in a wholesome way. As the celebrated child psychiatrist Donald Winnicott (1965) points out, most of us get by being 'good enough' parents, just as we got by being the children of 'good enough' parents.

But for some children, a combination of life experiences can impair emotional development and threaten their sense of worth. Instead of a carefree childhood there sits a dull ache and an all-pervading doubt about whether they are wanted and whether they belong.

Your classroom may contain a number of learners who are so preoccupied with this nagging self-doubt that the lesson you have prepared so meticulously will not engage them. Their worries and anxieties are deep-seated and unconscious. These feelings are hard to unearth and hard to articulate, but they are there and are driving a range of observable behaviours that communicate this anxiety, if we choose to see it. Work avoidance, teacher avoidance, daydreaming, aggression, disruption, fleeing the classroom, fleeing the school, bullying, attention seeking and verbal abuse may all be communicating a single, latent primary emotion: fear.

Assuaging the unconscious emotion of fear that may reside deep within the child or young person will take skill and commitment – but it begins with a recognition that it exists. From this starting point, a range of interventions can then be offered to reassure and support learners with social-emotional difficulties, to fire new neural pathways and create a sense of belonging and connectedness in school.

For some students this might require the development of whole-school, systemic practices that place attachment awareness at its very core, and where the academic attainment, behaviour, emotional regulation and wellbeing of all learners are actively valued and promoted (Chapter 4). For other students, a more specific attachment relationship may be required in school, and this may be provided by you personally or by an attachment advisory teacher (Chapter 14), a mentoring team member (Chapter 8) or the staff leading the school's nurture group (Chapter 7).

Where specific social-emotional skills need to be taught, the chapters on Emotion Coaching (Chapter 5), mentalising techniques (Chapter 6) or broader whole-school approaches (Chapter 16) might be employed to generate a classroom climate that is structured, empathic and compassionate.

Several chapters make reference to the way that beginning teachers might approach their work, to maximise the quality of relationships in the classroom and the learning that will then follow (see Chapters 17, 18 and 19). The common features of these approaches include the belief that positive relationships are at the heart of effective practice in the classroom. Establishing these relationships with learners who display avoidant, ambivalent or disorganised attachment styles can be challenging at times, but in Chapter 2 a range of attachment specific approaches to relationship building has been set out.

A belief that change can occur represents a further message from the chapters of this book. Authors go to great lengths to confirm that disengaged, poorly attached students can re-engage and make positive contribution to both your classroom and your school. Indeed, the neuroscientific research set out in Chapter 3 supports this assumption with an emphasis on the 'plasticity' of the brain and its ability to change and forge new neural pathways based on positive, nurturing experiences.

Empathy and equity are additional features recommended to the beginning teacher who is seeking to attune with the emotional needs of the learners in his or her class. Empathy should not be confused with sympathy. Where sympathy might be associated with a form of sorrow and pity for the circumstances of the child, empathy is about imagining how it might feel to be in those circumstances, and offering an understanding around this. This does not preclude the instigation of sanctions for inappropriate behaviour, but it does provide a basis for understanding why the behaviours have occurred. The equity that follows is based on an honest interpretation of events that is then translated into fair decisions that affect the learner. In this way the learner is encouraged to feel valued, understood and included in the decision-making process.

The emotionally attuned professional will communicate clearly with students and colleagues alike, and will think creatively about approaches and interventions. The needs and interests of the learners will be central to the learning experience, and there will be an emphasis on prevention over intervention. That is to say, providing a learning environment that is emotionally attuned to the wellbeing of every learner is preferable to the introduction of an intervention that seeks to restore wellbeing that has been eroded or undermined.

In the course of this book, attachment theory (Bowlby 1969, 1973, 1980) has offered one understanding of how emotional development can be supported or impaired in the children and young people we teach, depending on the quality of relationships experienced with the 'significant other'. The securely attached child will have experienced 'good enough', attentive, nurturing care, and will have an internal working model of both themselves and others as positive, helpful and worthy of trust. Where the relationship with the significant other has been inattentive, inconsistent or frightening, attachment theory suggests that three insecure attachment types might emerge, with specific attachment behaviours and styles:

- insecure-avoidant – the pupil who avoids relating to the teacher

- insecure-ambivalent – the 'attention-seeking' pupil

- insecure-disorganised – the unpredictable, anxious and behaviourally challenging pupil.

The assumptions set out by the psychodynamic approach and attachment theory pervade this book and inform a range of practical interventions for schools that include the Attachment Aware Schools (AAS)project(seewww.bathspa.ac.uk/education/research/attachment-aware-schools), Emotion Coaching (www.emotioncoachinguk.com) and nurture group intervention (www.nurturegroups.org). But alternative models of social, emotional development have also been included, and the approaches of behaviourism, humanism, cognitive behaviourism, systemic theory and a biopsychosocial framework offer invaluable insights into how children and young people develop emotionally. Every model has something to offer, and as a beginning teacher, you may choose from a range of approaches to find 'what works for you'.

The final thread that draws the book to a close concerns your own wellbeing and resilience. As a beginning teacher, entering a fascinating and valued role, you will be tested and challenged as your career progresses. The children and young people you work with will be fun, caring, thought-provoking, challenging, interesting, interested, surprising and bemusing. What they will need is committed and caring staff who are passionate about their learning and willing to go that extra mile to make the learning work. Supporting learners with social, emotional and attachment needs can be taxing and emotionally draining for staff, and in order that staff are retained and supported, professional staff supervision is required in schools at all levels. This process recognises the emotional impact on staff working alongside all children, but especially those who experience social, emotional and attachment difficulties. Through the use of supervision, we argue that staff can become more attuned and ultimately more able to meet the wide range of needs of the children in their classrooms.

A key message of this book is that, regardless of early life experiences, there is a great deal that schools and teachers can do for children and young people who exhibit social, emotional and attachment difficulties. We can make schools places where learners feel secure and cared for, and if we are successful in achieving this, then we are providing the foundations for successful social-emotional development – as well as for academic success. We can contribute to this process when we become aware of how our behaviour influences the thoughts and feelings of the students in our classroom.

The thing we must be very careful of is to avoid making judgements about how 'good or bad' a job a child's carers are doing or have done in their parenting. While it is true that sometimes carers do fall short of the 'good enough' standard described by Winnicott (1965), it is rarely of any value for us as teachers to dwell on or blame those who fall into this category. We are far better occupied with examining our own behaviour towards our students, and doing our best to make their time in school as nurturing as we can. Obviously, Child Protection principles and procedures have an important role to play in meeting children's needs, but these need to be applied with sensitivity and insight, and always with the best interests of the child as the main priority.

Enjoy your teaching and enjoy the children. You cannot affect the experiences that they have had in the past – but you can affect the experiences to come. Promote the emotionally attuned classroom and be ready to teach the skills that have been missed. Try to place behaviour in context and understand that all behaviour is a form of communication. While you set firm boundaries in a well-ordered classroom, you can then seek to meet the emotional and attachment needs of the learners in your care.

REFLECTION POINTS

1. How would you summarise the key messages of this book?

2. How has your thinking changed given the key messages of this book?

3. How will this affect your approach to classroom management?

4. What steps will you take to ascertain which of your children are currently 'in care'?

5. How emotionally competent are *you* with regard to emotional self-awareness, self-regulation, empathy, relationship management and responsible decision-making?

6. How do you plan to promote these competencies on a range of levels within your classroom?

7. How will you ensure that you have the opportunity to share your reflections and experiences through professional supervision?

Bibliography

Bowlby, J. (1969) *Attachment and Loss. Volume 1: Attachment*. London: Hogarth Press and The Institute of Psychoanalysis.

Bowlby, J. (1973) *Attachment and Loss. Volume 2: Separation: Anxiety and Anger*. London: Hogarth Press and The Institute of Psychoanalysis.

Bowlby, J. (1980) *Attachment and Loss. Volume 3: Loss: Sadness and Depression*. London: Hogarth Press and The Institute of Psychoanalysis.

DfE (Department for Education) (2016) *A Framework of Core Content for Initial Teacher Training (ITT)*. Available at www.gov.uk/government/uploads/system/uploads/attachment_data/file/536890/Framework_Report_11_July_2016_Final.pdf, accessed on 23 March 2017.

Winnicott, D.W. (1965) *The Maturational Processes and the Facilitating Environment*. London: Karnac Books.

Author Biographies

Michael Bettencourt has worked with looked-after children since 2002, and has been Head of the Virtual School for Looked-After Children in South Tyneside since 2010. He has responsibility for promoting the attendance, attainment and progress of approximately 300 school-age children. Michael is also a Research Associate with the Institute of Education at University College London where he has been working with colleagues on PALAC, a knowledge exchange programme that seeks to support practice in schools to improve the educational outcomes of children in care.

Contact: michael.bettencourt@southtyneside.gov.uk

Dr **Emma Black** is an Educational Psychologist, chartered with the British Psychological Society and registered with the Health and Care Professions Council (HCPC). Prior to being awarded a Doctorate in Applied Educational Psychology, Emma worked as a Primary School Teacher, a Nurture Group Teacher and a Montessori Teacher. During this time she worked as a manager and front line practitioner. These roles have provided Emma with a useful first-hand experience of some of the many challenges schools, teachers, families and children are faced with on a daily basis. Emma is the director of Illuminate Psychology, a solution-focused educational psychology service empowering schools, families and young people to bring about positive change. Emma works across a wide range of settings including early years settings, primary schools, secondary schools, colleges and universities.

Contact: emma@illuminatepsychology.co.uk

Janice Cahill has been headteacher of the Pendlebury Centre Pupil Referral Unit (PRU) for 22 years, which has received five consecutive judgements of 'Outstanding' by Ofsted. The Centre has developed a range of services for children and young people who present with a range of complex social, emotional and behavioural/mental health difficulties. The centre provides a Key Stage 3 and 4 therapeutic and assessment provision for those at risk of exclusion, and an accredited mental health training programme has been developed. Janice is a National Leader of Education, and Pendlebury PRU is a National Support School.

Contact: headteacher@pendlebury.stockport.sch.uk

Claire Cameron is Professor of Social Pedagogy at the Thomas Coram Research Unit, UCL Institute of Education, University College London. She has conducted many studies of the children's workforce, including comparative studies, and is a leading figure in the development of the continental European discipline of social pedagogy for care and education of looked-after children and young people in the UK. She coordinated the first major EU-funded study of the further and higher education pathways of looked-after children, which resulted in two books, *Improving Access to Further and Higher Education for Young People in Public Care*, and *Educating Children and Young People in Care: Learning Placements and Caring Schools*, both co-authored with Sonia Jackson. Since 2014, she has supported the PALAC programme, working with schools to run knowledge exchange projects to improve the educational attainment and wellbeing of children in care in school and in 2017, a book documenting the project, *Taking Action for Looked After Children in School*, was published.

Contact: c.cameron@ucl.ac.uk

Professor **Barry Carpenter**, CBE, OBE, PhD, is a Visiting Professor at universities in the UK, Ireland, Germany and Australia. He has been a Fellow of the University of Oxford and is the author of over 150 articles and texts on a range of learning disability/special needs topics. In the last 12 months, his work has been translated into German, French, Dutch, Norwegian and Russian. His most recent book publications (with Carolyn Blackburn and Jo Egerton) focus on foetal alcohol spectrum disorders (FASD) and on children with complex needs, with particular reference to their mental health. He is the co-founder of the National Forum for Neuroscience in Special Education and, on behalf of the Mental Health Foundation, he chaired the National Inquiry into the Mental Health of Young People with Learning Disabilities. He is currently chairing a working group looking at the needs of girls on the autism spectrum, which will be the focus of his next book.

Contact: carpenterbarry@mac.com

Tony Clifford is Head of the Virtual School for Children in Care and Care Leavers in Stoke-on-Trent, with responsibility for the education, training and employment pathways for young people aged 0–25. He was previously a headteacher and deputy head in mainstream and special education for children with social, emotional and mental health needs. Tony has contributed to national policy and practice development including Edward Timpson's expert group on the education of looked-after children (2014); the Parliamentary sub-committee on the mental health of children in care (2015); as an education representative on the NICE guideline on attachment (2015); and the Social Care Institute for Excellence (SCIE) expert group on the mental health of children in care (2016). Tony is also Chair of the Attachment Research Community (ARC) (https://the-arc.org.uk).

Contact: Tony.Clifford@stoke.gov.uk

David Colley, PhD, is a Senior Lecturer in SEN/Inclusion at Oxford Brookes University and Chair of SEBDA (Social, Emotional and Behavioural Difficulties Association) (www.sebda.org). Having trained as a primary school teacher, he has spent over 25 years working with children and families experiencing a range of learning difficulties in both primary and secondary settings. David has undertaken research into the development of nurture groups in secondary schools, and currently leads the National Award for SEN Coordination in Oxfordshire and Buckinghamshire.

Contact: dcolley@brookes.ac.uk

Paul Cooper, PhD, CPsychol, FBPsS, is Emeritus Professor of Social-Emotional Learning and Inclusion at Brunel University London, and Visiting Professor at the European Centre for Resilience & Socio-Emotional Health at the University of Malta. His expertise is in the field of social, emotional difficulties, mental health and social-emotional learning. A former school teacher, since 1988 Paul has held academic posts at universities in England (Birmingham, Oxford, Cambridge and Leicester) and Hong Kong (formerly, the Hong Kong Institute of Education). He was editor of *Emotional and Behavioural Difficulties* for 14 years, and is now honorary editor of this journal. He is founding co-editor of the *International Journal of Emotional Education*, and founding co-chair of the European Network for Social-Emotional Competence in Children (ENSEC). In 2011 he was made Honorary Lifelong Vice President of the Social Emotional and Behavioural Difficulties Association (SEBDA). Paul has led numerous research projects, has over 200 publications to his name, and has (to date) supervised 34 doctoral students to successful completion. Paul is a past winner of the National Association for Special Educational Needs/Times Educational Supplement book award, and was runner up for this award on several other occasions.

Contact: paul.cooper@brunel.ac.uk

Betsy de Thierry qualified as a teacher and psychotherapist over 20 years ago and founded the Trauma Recovery Centre (TRC) (www.trc-uk.org) in 2011, which has therapy centres and alternative education centres in four cities across the UK. She has authored *Teaching the Child on the Trauma Continuum* (Grosvenor 2015) and also *The Simple Guide To Child Trauma* published by Jessica Kingsley Publishers. She also founded the Therapeutic Mentoring Rooms that are within schools across the UK. She delivers training across the

UK and is a consultant to many organisations, schools, Pupil Referral Units (PRUs), virtual schools and therapy centres about the impact of trauma on a child (see www.betsytraininguk.co.uk).

Contact: betsytraininguk@gmail.com

Dr **Kathy Evans** was a teacher and manager for 15 years in both mainstream and specialist settings. Her doctorate was a cross-national study of the educational inclusion of pupils with social, emotional and behavioural difficulties. Since 2010 she has been a Senior Lecturer at the University of South Wales where she runs the Master's in Child and Adolescent Mental Health.

Contact: kathy.evans@southwales.ac.uk

Heather Geddes, PhD, is author of the influential book *Attachment in the Classroom: The Links Between Children's Early Experience, Emotional Well-being and Performance in School* (Worth Publishing Ltd 2006). She has worked as a teacher and educational psychotherapist in a range of settings including schools, social services and CAMHS (Child and Adolescent Mental Health Services) teams. Her work is primarily concerned with pupils presenting with challenging behaviours, and her particular interest is the way in which social, emotional and behaviour difficulties inhibit learning and adversely affect equality of opportunity.

Contact: heathergeddes@ripeworsley.co.uk

Louise Gilbert worked in health and education before becoming a university Senior Lecturer in Child Wellbeing. With Janet Rose, she designed and delivered the UK's first community and education-based Emotion Coaching project, and is currently writing her doctoral thesis on the research findings. She was also involved in the creation and delivery of the Attachment Aware Schools and Setting project. Louise is a published writer promoting early years education with a focus on sustainable health and wellbeing, and has co-authored *Health and Well-being in Early Childhood* (Sage 2015).

Contact: louisegilbert.ec@outlook.com

Licette Gus is an educational psychologist, chartered with the British Psychological Society and registered with the Health and Care Professions Council (HCPC). She has over 20 years' experience working for local authorities and the private sector; Licette is currently working across the West Midlands and the Home Counties. She is a co-founder of Emotion Coaching UK, which aims to promote Emotion Coaching as a way of supporting and sustaining children and young people's emotional and behavioural wellbeing.

Licette has co-authored a paper on Emotion Coaching in the peer-reviewed journal *Educational and Child Psychology* with Janet Rose and Louise Gilbert, and is actively engaged in training and research applying Emotion Coaching in educational and community settings.

Contact: licette.gus@gmail.com

Dr **Anne-Marie McBlain** originally worked as a science teacher in a mainstream secondary school before working in a Pupil Referral Unit (PRU), a mental health charity and the Prison Service. With this experience she then undertook training as an educational psychologist. Anne-Marie currently works as a senior educational psychologist for Stoke Virtual School supporting children and young people in care. This involves complex case work carried out within a multi-agency context, leading the delivery of nationally respected 'attachment aware' training for all educational settings in the authority, and supporting these settings to conduct action research to develop cutting-edge practice both within the authority and nationally.

Contact: Anne-Marie.McBlain@stoke.gov.uk

Poppy Nash, PhD, is a Lecturer in Education in the Department of Education, Psychology in the Education Research Centre, University of York. Poppy's research projects have largely focused on the development, implementation, evaluation and dissemination of intervention programmes for promoting psychological resilience in vulnerable learners. She is currently looking at the mental wellbeing of students in their transition from sixth form education and on to university.

Contact: poppy.nash@york.ac.uk

Erica Pavord worked as an English teacher in secondary education for 15 years and then as a school counsellor for six years. She is now a Lecturer/Practitioner in Child and Adolescent Mental Health at the University of Worcester, and works as a systemic counsellor with families in Monmouthshire. She has co-written two books: *An Introduction to Child and Adolescent Mental Health* with Briony Williams, Erica Pavord and Maddie Burton, and *Communication and Interpersonal Skills* with Erica Pavord and Elaine Donnelly.

Contact: epavord@worc.ac.uk

Jon Reid, MSc Oxon, PCTHE, PGDES, PGCE, BA (Hons), MBPsS, FHEA, joined Oxford Brookes University as Senior Lecturer in SEN/Inclusion following a teaching career in both primary and secondary education. During his mainstream educational experiences, Jon developed an interest in supporting pupils with additional learning needs. Subsequently, he spent time teaching in a therapeutic residential school catering for pupils who had experienced severe emotional trauma due to the accumulation of adverse experiences in infancy and early childhood. He later became the deputy headteacher of an independent secondary SEMH (social, emotional and mental health) school that specialised in supporting pupils with complex educational needs, communication difficulties and challenging behaviours.

Contact: j.reid@brookes.ac.uk

Dave Roberts, MA, BA, Dip SW, AA SW, is Head of the Mulberry Bush Outreach Service, a part of the Mulberry Bush Organisation, a national charity working therapeutically with children and families who have experienced trauma. He has worked in the residential childcare sector for over 25 years with both primary and secondary-age children. His work primarily involves training, supervision and consultation to schools and children's homes across Southern England. He has led the Mulberry Bush to two National Training Awards in 2007 and 2012 and is currently completing a PhD looking at the benefits of therapeutic settings for children who have experienced trauma.

Contact: droberts@mulberrybush.org.uk

Janet Rose, MA, PhD, FHEA, is a former Reader in Education and Programme Leader at Bath Spa University. Whilst at Bath Spa, she led and developed a project entitled 'Attachment Aware Schools and Settings', a comprehensive training programme for children affected by early attachment difficulties, trauma and neglect. In addition to her academic career, Janet has worked as a specialist teacher with children and young people at risk, as well as a consultant for various local authorities developing training programmes for supporting children and young people. She is the author of numerous publications, including the co-authored *Health and Well-being in Early Childhood (Sage 2015)*. She is a co-founder of Emotion Coaching UK and a trustee of the Attachment Research Community (ARC). Janet is now Principal of Norland College, Bath.

Contact: janet.rose@norland.co.uk

Maisie Satchwell-Hirst graduated from the University of Oxford in 2016 with a degree in Psychology and Linguistics, and is a team member of the University's neuroscience-based Research into Emotional Development and Disorders (REDD) laboratory. Maisie has an ongoing interest in the emotional and psychological issues affecting children and young people from the perspective of the latest neuroscientific research and evidence.

Contact: maisie.satchwell-hirst@oxon.org

Dr **Mike Solomon** is a consultant clinical psychologist at the Tavistock and Portman NHS Foundation Trust. He has worked for many years in specialist education provisions for children with social, emotional and mental health difficulties. He provides training and consultancy for education professionals and school staff teams around children's mental health and related organisational issues. He has a particular interest in multi-agency working in this area, as shown in his publications and presentations at national and international conferences.

Contact: MSolomon@tavi-port.nhs.uk

Maggie Swarbrick was, until April 2017, Team Leader and Advisory Teacher for Treatment Foster Care Oregon (TFCO-UK) in Oxfordshire, UK. She continues to work with Oxfordshire's vulnerable, young, looked-after children, leading the newly formed Oxfordshire County Council programme, 'Oxfordshire Treatment Foster Care (OTFC)'. This offers an intensive treatment intervention for children in foster care between the ages of 3–11. Based on attachment and social learning theory, the programme delivers intensive support to the child, foster carer, school and birth family.

Contact: maggie.swarbrick@oxfordshire.gov.uk

Professor **John Visser** is the Visiting Professor in Inclusive and Special Education at the University of Northampton, having retired as Professor of Social Emotional and Behavioural Difficulties (SEBD) at the University of Birmingham. John is much published including seminal books such as *Transforming Troubled Lives* (Emerald 2012). Previous research has included work in practice, policy and provision for the broad group of children and young people labelled as having social emotional and behavioural difficulties.

Contact: John.Visser@northampton.ac.uk

Peter Wilson, BA, Dip Applied Soc Std, MACP, MBPF, is a consultant child and adolescent psychotherapist. He trained at the Anna Freud Centre and practised as a child psychotherapist for many years in the NHS and in the voluntary sector. He has held a variety of senior posts during the last 40 years, including Senior Clinical Tutor, Institute of Psychiatry; Consultant Psychotherapist, Peper Harow Therapeutic Community; and Director of the Brandon Centre. Peter was the co-founder and Director of YoungMinds and the Clinical Adviser of Place2Be. He is the author of *Young Minds in Our Schools* (YoungMinds 2004).

Contact: peterjbwilson@btinternet.com

Felicia Wood, MSc, PGCE, BA Hons, has been a teacher for 15 years, mainly within secondary education where she was Head of Year for five years. After completing the pilot Emotion Coaching research project with Janet Rose, she worked within the primary sector to experience educating children of younger ages. Felicia is currently Training Director for Kate Cairns Associates (KCA). KCA focus on providing information and training on attachment, trauma and resilience for those working with vulnerable children and their families.

Contact: fwoodresearch@gmail.com

Biddy Youell trained as a child psychotherapist and has worked in generic CAMHS (Child and Adolescent Mental Health Services) clinics and in specialist teams in the Tavistock and Portman NHS Foundation Trust. Between 2003 and 2008 she was Head of Training at the Northern School of Child and Adolescent Psychotherapy (NSCAP). Whilst being committed to child and adolescent psychotherapy as a model of treatment, Biddy has always been particularly interested in the application of psychoanalytic thinking to work in non-clinical settings, and many of her publications reflect this.

Contact: BYouell@tavi-port.nhs.uk

Subject Index

Author Index

Visser, J. 282, 284–7
Vrouva, I. 101–2, 107
Vygotsky, L. 123–4, 132

Wang, S.C. 49–50
Ward, J. 87
Watkins, H.H. 139
Watkins, J.G. 139
Watson, J.B. 28
Watzlawick, P. 86
Weare, K. 84, 252, 257
Weissman, M.M. 58
Welford, M. 259–60
Westergaard, J. 238
Wetz, J. 211–12
Whelan, R.J. 279–80
Whitebread, D. 14, 66, 122–3, 130
Whiting, B.A. 158
WHO 101–2, 249
Williams, G. 111, 113

Williams, L.M. 53
Willis, T.J. 199
Wilson, M. 285
Wilson, P. 161
Winnicott, D.W. 307, 311
Wittig, B.A. 40, 41–2
Wittling, W. 53
Wolke, D. 8
Wolpert, M. 178
Wonnacott, J. 244
Wood, F. 85
Woods, R. 253

York, A. 216
Youell, B. 111, 113, 167
Young Minds 11

Zautra, A.J. 102